Women in Panchayats

(A Study of Role Conflict)

Women in Panchayats

(A Study of Role Conflict)

U.B. Singh

SERIALS PUBLICATIONS
NEW DELHI (INDIA)

First Published – 2011

ISBN: 978-81-8387-307-9

Published by

SERIALS PUBLICATIONS
4830/24, 1st Floor, Ansari Road
Darya Ganj, New Delhi-110002 (India)
Phone : 23245225. Fax : 91-11-23272135
E-mail: serials@satyam.net.in

CONTENTS

FOREWORD

Uttar Pradesh is not only the most populous state in the country but also has the largest network of rural local government. The state has a long history of Panchayat Raj and it is probably the first state in the country to provide 30 per cent reservation to women some two decades ago. In pursuance of Seventy Third Amendment to the Constitution, the state restructured its Panchayat Raj system and three tier system - Zila (District) Panchayat, Kshetra (Block) Panchayat and Gram (Village) Panchayat was introduced. Uttar Pradesh is the only state having regular elections to Panchayati Raj Institutions. So far three elections have been held under the new dispensation. As a result of the last elections more than 40 per cent women belonging to different vulnerable classes of the society have been brought into political mainstream.

We are grateful to the National Commission for Women, New Delhi for sponsoring the research study for studying the Role Conflict among Women Representatives in Panchayati Raj Institutions in U.P. This shows the keen interest of the Commission in empowerment process of women, in general and, rural women, in particular.

I am thankful to Dr. U.B. Singh, Joint Director of the centre and his team of researchers for undertaking the study satisfactorily.

I am confident this volume would be of immense help to the policy makers, administrators and academics in appreciating the problems of woman representatives at the grassroots level administration in the country.

May, 2009

Prof. Nishith Rai
Director, RCUES,
Lucknow University,
Lucknow

PREFACE

The 73rd and 74th Amendments to the Indian Constitution provide representation to the tune of not less than one-third of the seats for women belonging to different social groups. As such a large number of women per force have been imposed the political role at the grass root level governance. Thus Indian women now have to perform multidimensional roles. As a house-wife and daughter-in-law, she is responsible for household activities and, as people's representative, she has to perform for the fulfillment of people's aspirations and expectations. Therefore these women have to perform two sets of roles i.e. traditional or prescribed, as a woman and, an achieved or ascribed, by acquiring political role and status. As such, a woman, as a role occupant finds now lesser time for family. Her role is now divided over two sets of roles, for family and, for society. This leads to a constant and continuous phenomenon of role conflict. A woman representative has therefore to make a balance between the two roles for a harmonious and peaceful family life and effective role in decision making at local governance level.

Uttar Pradesh, the most populous state in the country, enjoys the privilege of having largest network of rural local bodies. There are 70 Zila Panchayats, 820 Kshetra Panchayats and 52,000 Gram Panchayats. The third elections to Panchayati Raj Institutions were held in 2005 and as a result in all 12,48,402 elected representatives including women belonging to different segments of society were got elected. It consists of about 45 per cent of women. As such, a large number of women, mainly housewives, are associated with decision making at grassroot level. This may lead to increase in their work load. They have now to devote time for both the roles.

In this backdrop, the present study was conceived and undertaken under the sponsorship by the National Commission for Women. For the purpose, Panchayati Raj Institutions from all the geographical regions of Uttar Pradesh were selected. These included 12 Zila Panchayats, 36 Kshetra Panchayats and 108 Gram Panchayats. In all, 1003 elected women representatives belonging to these local government units were contacted and personally interviewed. These local units consisted of Panchayats with female chairpersons as well as male chairpersons. For having a holistic view, officials and family members were also interviewed.

This volume is the culmination of the revised and updated version of the study undertaken in 2007. The book is divided into six chapters. *Prologue* covers the status of women in Indian society and their role in political arena, including identification of conflict areas. The research methodology also forms part of this chapter. Chapter II is devoted to introducing the universe and discussing the socio-economic profile of the women representatives covered under the study.

Chapter III attempts to analyse the conflicts and adjustments as arisen in political role of women. Chapter IV deals with conflicts and adjustments in family role. Chapter V is devoted to discussions on status of women representatives in wider society and their person. *Epilogue* summarizes the study. The major findings are discussed at length. Conflict areas have been identified and the measures to reduce or minimize the conflicts have also been discussed. The chapter incorporates major recommendations as well.

Lucknow **U.B. Singh**
Budha Purnima, 2009

ACKNOWLEDGEMENTS

At the outset, I express my sincere gratitude to the National Commission for Women, New Delhi for sponsoring this academic exercise and extending financial assistance.

I am grateful to Professor Nishith Rai, Director, Regional Centre for Urban and Environmental Studies, Lucknow University, Lucknow for entrusting the study to me.

My research team of three young members did a tremendous job of undertaking field work, tabulation and analysis of data in a record time. They, although part of the exercise, deserve all the thanks.

In this endeavour I received cooperation from all the women representatives, their family members and officials of Panchayats. I am grateful for their valuable contribution.

I would be failing in my duty for not expressing my sincere gratitude to the scholars on the subject whose previous works in this field helped me a lot and whom I have quoted frequently. It would not be inappropriate to place on record that a study sponsored by the Indian Council of Social Science Research, New Delhi created interest in me to study the subject more.

The suggestions of my colleague Dr. A. K. Singh enriched the work to a great extent. I am thankful to him as well.

I wish to express my thanks to Dr. R.K. Trivedi, our librarian, for providing good literature. I am thankful to Sri Amit K. Singh and Sri D.C. Pant for all the computer works and giving it a proper shape.

Last but not the least, I am thankful to M/s Serials Publications, New Delhi for publishing the book in a record time.

U.B. Singh

1
PROLOGUE

Women who constitute nearly half of the human population can certainly play a key role in influencing the cause of history as well as shaping the destiny of mankind. The future of development and society lies in future of women, equally with men. One more stark reality is that women not only form a major section of the society but also hold greater responsibilities than men towards many facets of life. However, since time immemorial women are being treated as inferior human and their position is looked down as general subordination to men irrespective of the position they hold in and out side their family. Generally in almost all the societies, women play most important roles towards family starting from childhood, through motherhood till the late stage of life. From generation to generation they help not only in propagation and continuing hereditary lineage but also provide a conscience factor for social structure and an adhesive for family semblance. Irrespective of their contribution to family and society, they were looked down upon through ages.

The status of women in India has fluctuated from time to time during the different phases of her history. The position of women in a society is usually regarded as a fair index of the excellence of its culture and the character of its civilization. Indian tradition has generally respected womanhood. Even God is regarded as a half man, half woman, 'Ardhanarishwar'. In the Vedic Age, women enjoyed equal opportunities for education and work. The general picture of women in the hymns of Rig Veda was one of dignity and importance and she enjoyed peace, happiness and prosperity as a rule.

In the 2500 years that intervened between the Rig Vedic Age and the close of the ancient period at about 1200 AD, several far-reaching changes had taken place in Indian society. This position of very low status of women continued throughout the Muslim period and did not improve till the introduction of Western ideas ushered in a new era in the latter half of the 19th century. The socio-religious movements in the last quarter of the 19th century, marked by the rise and growth of Brahmo Samaj and Arya Samaj which had an impetus to the process of emancipation of women.

Among the great changes that have taken place in recent times in India, the most important one has been the growing status of women. The recent years have brought great change in the life of women all over the world, influencing their attitudes, values, aspirations, ways of feeling and acting for effective participation in all walks of life. Many factors have combined to free women from the shackles of unknown traditions, prejudice and ignorance. An important aspect of this public awakening has been the truer appraisal of women's place, both within and outside the home.

One of the main enduring consequences of the recent social evaluation for women has been their emancipation from their traditional bond ethos, both legally and politically, by the virtue of various acts and statutes.

Over the last few decades, women's rights supporters have made their voices heard in every arena. Now women have expanded the role of housewife into dominant, mature feminine role. Urbanisation, education and employment, which were the contributors of social evaluation, have provided them with new avenues to express and assert themselves. The changed social milieu along with new wave of modernization has altered their roles and relationships drastically. Indian urban women have come out of the four walls of their homes in search of economic gain as well as fulfillment of their personal hopes and desires. By coming out of their homes in gainful employment and social participation they have added new roles to their old roles of mother and wife.

Being subjected to the dual demands of home and work, which are often antagonistic in nature, the working mother is liable to experience role conflict. In addition to the biological function she has to perform the culturally defined role in which she has to act, she is confronted with responsibilities and duties connected with her role outside home. The dual responsibilities not only overload her but also may be so incompatible that they cannot be performed properly. Due to the limited time and a greater degree of incongruous demands of the dual role, the working women (in any role) experience more and more role conflict.

While analyzing the roles of women it is important to focus on the general status of Indian women. The social status of women in India is comparatively lower than many other countries of the world. Though Constitution of India guarantees 'Equality of Status' to women, they do not enjoy full equality in the society. The vast majority of women are illiterate, underpaid, exploited and disadvantaged. They have been suppressed to inferior positions in society, completely dominated by men. But in urban areas with the spread of education and increase in the number of working women outside their homes, the situation is gradually changing. Women have risen above socio-cultural traditions and well-defined roles of housewife, and gradually evolved into dual and more fulfilling roles of working woman and a housewife. The major contributing factors for such a change are better education, changing socio-cultural values and need for supplementary income due to inflation. But despite these changes Indian society remains 'male dominated'.

WOMEN IN INDIA: A STATUS

The plight of women in India is no better than that of women in other developing countries. Despite the honour and reverence accorded to them as deities, the general reality speaks otherwise. In a patriarchal society like India, the unfounded belief that only man is the bread winner, the male child gets the best of the limited facilities and resources within the family and the girl child runs the risk of being aborted.

SEX RATIO

The sex ratio is an important social indicator to measure the extent of prevailing equity between males and females in a society at any given point of time. The clearest indicator of discrimination against Indian women is the skewed sex ratio. According to Census of India 2001, the sex ratio stands at 933 for country as a whole, a little more than 1991 Census that recorded 927 (World average 990) females per 1000 males. It is a welcome improvement. Yet cause for concern remains. The sex ratio of the 0-6 age group has declined during the decade. The table below (Table 1) indicates the sex ratio of total population in all the states and Union Territories in the country.

Table 1
Sex Ratio (1991-2001)

	Sex Ratio (Females per 1000 males)	
State	*1991*	*2001*
India	*927*	*933*
Kerala	1,036	1,058
Pondicherry (Puducherry)	979	1,001
Chhattisgarh	985	989
Tamil Nadu	974	987
Manipur	958	978
Andhra Pradesh	972	978
Meghalaya	955	972
Orissa	971	972
Himachal Pradesh	976	968
Karnataka	960	965
Uttaranchal (Uttarakhand)	937	962
Goa	967	961
Tripura	945	948
Lakshadweep	943	948
Jharkhand	922	941
Mizoram	921	935
Assam	923	935
West Bengal	917	934

Contd.

	Sex Ratio (Females per 1000 males)	
State	*1991*	*2001*
Maharashtra	934	922
Rajasthan	910	921
Gujarat	934	920
Bihar	907	919
Madhya Pradesh	912	919
Nagaland	886	900
Uttar Pradesh	876	898
Arunachal Pradesh	859	893
Jammu & Kashmir	NA	892
Punjab	882	876
Sikkim	878	875
Haryana	865	861
Andman & Nicobar Islands	818	846
Delhi	827	821
Dadra & Nagar Haveli	952	812
Chandigarh	790	777
Daman & Diu	969	710

Source: Primary Census Abstract, Census of India 2001, Series 1, Statement 4

EDUCATION

The status of women's education in not merely as issue for academic discussions but a sociological problem. Parallel universe exists for men and women. The women and men still live in different worlds with different access, opportunities, incentives, rewards and legal protection. Experiences around the world shows that educating women and empowering them with a stronger rule enhances the quality of not merely their own but also contributes to economic growth, child survival, etc. Hence investing in women's education is critical to sustainable development whereby the returns cause enormous, generation after generation. With regard to literacy rate, the population of literates for country as a whole, in 1951, shortly after Independence, the Census recorded that only 25 percent of women were literate. By the 1991 Census, female literacy rose to 39.3 percent, which according to 2001 Census, increased to 53.7 per cent. The corresponding figures for males are 64.1 per cent and 75.3 per cent respectively, thus showing male and female literacy gap rate of 21.69 per cent. The table below (No. 2) shows the latest literacy rate in the states and Union Territories in the country.

Table 2
Literacy Rate (sex-wise) (1991-2001)

(Percent)

	Persons		*Males*		*Females*	
States	*1991*	*2001*	*1991*	*2001*	*1991*	*2001*
India	*52.2*	*64.8*	*64.1*	*75.3*	*39.3*	*53.7*
Kerala	89.8	90.9	93.6	94.2	86.2	87.7
Mizoram	82.3	88.8	85.6	90.7	78.6	86.7
Lakshadweep	81.8	86.7	90.2	92.5	72.9	80.5
Goa	75.5	82.0	83.6	88.4	67.1	75.4
Chandigarh	77.8	81.9	82.0	86.1	72.3	76.5
Delhi	75.3	81. 7	82.0	87.3	67.0	74.7
Andaman and Nicobar Islands	73.0	81.3	79.0	86.3	65.5	75.2
Puducherry	74.7	81.2	83.7	88.6	65.6	73.9
Daman and Diu	71.2	78.2	82.7	86.8	59.4	65.6
Maharashtra	64.9	76.9	76.6	86.0	52.3	67.0
Himachal Pradesh	63.9	76.5	75.4	85.3	52.1	67.4
Tamil Nadu	62.7	73.5	73.7	82.4	51.3	64.4
Tripura	60.4	73.2	70.6	81.0	49.6	64.9
Uttarakhand	57.8	71.6	72.9	83.3	41.7	59.6
Manipur	59.9	70.5	71.6	80.3	47.6	60.5
Punjab	58.5	69.7	65.7	75.2	50.4	63.4
Gujarat	61.3	69.1	73.1	79.7	48.6	57.8
Sikkim	56.9	68.8	65.7	76.0	46.8	60.4
West Bengal	57.7	68.6	67.8	77.0	46.6	59.6
Haryana	55.8	67.9	69.1	78.5	40.5	55.7
Nagaland	61.6	66.6	67.6	71.2	54.7	61.5
Karnataka	56.0	66.6	67.3	76.1	44.3	56.9
Chhatisgarh	42.9	64.7	58.1	77.4	27.5	51.9
Madhya Pradesh	44.7	63.7	58.5	76.1	29.4	50.3
Assam	52.9	63.3	61.9	71.3	43.0	54.6
Orissa	49.1	63.1	63.1	75.3	34.7	50.5
Meghalaya	49.1	62.6	53.1	65.4	44.9	59.6
Andhra Pradesh	44.1	60.5	55.1	70.3	32.7	50.4
Rajasthan	38.6	60.4	55.0	75.7	20.4	43.9
Dadra & Nagar Haveli	40.7	57.6	53.6	71.2	27.0	40.2
Uttar Pradesh	40.7	56.3	54.8	68.8	24.4	42.2
Jammu & Kashmir	N.A.	55.5	N.A.	66.6	N.A.	43.0
Arunachal Pradesh	41.6	54.3	51.5	63.8	29.7	43.5
Jharkhand	41.4	53.6	55.8	67.3	25.5	38.9
Bihar	37.5	47.0	51.4	59.7	22.0	33.1

Source: Primary Census Abstract, Census of India 2001

EMPLOYMENT

Despite the fact that women are massively involved in almost all sectors of economy their activities as producers are not reflected in National Income Statistics, thus making their contribution unrecognized and invisible. As per UNDP estimates, $ 11 trillion of unpaid or invisible economic activity is performed by women world wide. In fact they contribute more than half of the wealth of nations, yet they are denied economic, social and even political and legal rights and privileges that such a contribution is entitled to.

Most of the works that women do goes unrecorded in the census. Women and girls who work on family land are not recorded as workers. Women constitute about 90 percent of the total marginal workers of the country. Rural women in agriculture form 78 percent of all women in regular work.

CONSTITUTIONAL AND LEGAL RIGHTS OF INDIAN WOMEN

In India, both pre and post Independence, various enactments have been passed for protection and upliftment of women. The framers of the Indian Constitution realized the unequal status of women and assured that women get equal rights. The preamble itself secures to all Indian citizens 'Justice' - social, economic and political; 'Liberty' - of thought and expression; and 'Equality' of status and opportunity.

It further resolves to promote among all citizens 'Fraternity' assuring the dignity of the individual.

The Constitution in Articles 14, 15 and 16 guarantees the principle of equality as fundamental rights:

- Art. 14 – Equality before law
- Art. 15 – Prohibition of discrimination on grounds of religion, race, caste, sex or place of birth
- Art. 16 – Equality of opportunity in matters of public employment

Apart from various Constitutional rights, several other enactments have been legislated for protection and upliftment of women. Some of the major social enactments relating to women are:

- The Immoral Traffic (Prevention) Act, 1956
- The Dowry Prohibition Act, 1961
- The Indecent Representation of Women (Prohibition) Act, 1986
- The Commission of Sati (Prevention) Act, 1987
- The Guardians and Wards Act, 1860
- Indian Penal Code, 1860
- The Christian Marriage Act, 1872
- The Indian Evidence Act, 1872
- The Married Women's Property Act, 1874
- The Workmen's Compensation Act, 1923
- The Legal Practitioners (Women) Act, 1923
- The Indian Succession Act, 1925
- The Child Marriage Restraint Act, 1929
- The Payment of Wages Act, 1936
- The Muslim Personal Law (Shariat) Application Act, 1937
- The Factories Act, 1948
- The Minimum Wages Act, 1948
- The Employees State Insurance Act, 1948
- The Plantation Labour Act, 1951
- The Cinematography Act, 1952
- The Special Marriage Act, 1954
- The Hindu Adoptions & Maintenance Act, 1956
- The Hindu Minority & Guardianship Act, 1956
- The Hindu Succession Act, 1956
- The Maternity Benefit Act, 1961
- The Beedi & Cigar Workers (Conditions of Employment) Act, 1966
- The Foreign Marriage Act, 1969
- The Indian Divorce Act, 1969

- The Medical Termination of Pregnancy Act, 1971
- Code of Criminal Procedure, 1973
- The Bonded Labour System (Abolition) Act, 1976
- The Equal Remuneration Act, 1976
- The Contract Labour (Regulation & Abolition) Act, 1979
- The Inter-State Migrant Workmen (Regulation of Employment and Conditions of Service) Act, 1979
- The Family Courts Act, 1984
- Juvenile Justice Act, 1986
- The Child Labour (Prohibition & Regulation) Act, 1986
- National Commission for Women Act, 1990
- The Infant Milk Substitutes, Feeding Bottles and Infant Foods (Regulation of Production, Supply and Distribution) Act, 1992
- The Pre-Natal Diagnostic Technique (Regulation and Prevention of Misuse) Act, 1994

Thus the country has a plethora of laws to protect the rights of women. However, the government, many a times, fails to enforce these laws effectively in rural areas where traditions are deeply rooted. The obstacles are extremely controversial subjects of reform. Examining them often directly challenges the traditional roles of women in society and may prove particularly uncomfortable for those who benefit from women's subordination.

In addition to the Constitutional provisions and other legal enactments, the Five Year Plans have also focused on women development, which has contributed greatly on the upliftment, development and empowerment of women in all sectors.

In the earlier phase of Indian planning, women's development concerns had a low profile. There were however some significant beginnings to promote and assist voluntary organizations in the field of women welfare. Some legislative measures were also undertaken to protect the interests of women. The Third and Fourth Plans accorded high priority to education of women. The Fifth Plan supported economic development, employment and training for women as the principal focus for their socio-economic development. The main approach in these Plans was generally to view women as the beneficiaries of social services rather than contributors to development. The decade of seventies brought women to the forefront of development concerns with the publication of the Report of the Committee on Status of Women in India, the observance of the International Women's Year in 1975 and the preparation of a National Plan of Action for Women. To this effect, the Approach of the Tenth Plan was to create an enabling environment where women could freely exercise their rights, both within and outside home, as equal partners along with men. The Eleventh Plan focuses on empowering the women.

According to the indicators published by the UNDP, the socio-economic status of women in India is very low in comparison to other developing countries. While such indicators obviously cannot fully describe the true conditions in any society, such a poor performance in the case of India must be considered a cause for concern. India is obliged to ensure that women participate equally in the formulation and implementation of government policy and perform all public functions at all levels of government.

WOMEN IN POLITICS

Although Indian women played a major role in the freedom movement, it did not continue participation in public life in post Independence era. On the contrary they withdrew in their homes, secure in the belief that they had ushered in a democracy in which the dreams and aspirations of the mass of people would be achieved.

Political rights of women are right to vote, to contest elections, to hold political office and to vote in legislature. Equal participation of women in political life plays a pivotal role in the process of their advancement, development and empowerment and also strengthening the role of governance and decision making structures at all levels.

Historically, women have played a very significant role in the growth and development of parliamentary democracy in India. They have held important positions both in the legislature and government. Their contribution to the growth and development of parliamentary procedures and practices are in no sense less significant than their male counterparts.

A study of Indian literature indicates that women of royal families besides being expert in knowledge of science and arts, used to learn politics and warfare. They were housewives as well secretary of their husbands.

Kautilya has mentioned in 20th chapter of 'Arthshastra' that women were main part of Mauryan courts. Manu has not found any difference between men and women in administration.

Since olden times women have been providing active assistance to their husbands in politics. But common women had no entry in the administrative setup, only women of royal families used to participate.

Indian women's involvement in politics in the modern era started in the late 18th and 19th centuries. Although British imperialism profoundly influenced the political engagement of both elite and non-elite women, its impact on the character and the purpose of their engagement was very different.

During the freedom movement, many women leaders actively participated and strongly advocated the protection of women's interest and their rights. Prior to 1926, women could not become the members of any assembly. From 1926 only nominated women could become member of legislative assemblies but they had no voting rights.

In 1935 when new Government of India Act was framed, women also started demanding privileges on par with men, but their demand was given a deaf ear.

In 1937 elections, women contested from reserved seats. Only 41 seats were reserved for them in whole of India. Smt. R.B. Subharayan became the members of state council and Smt. Renuka Ray became member of central legislative council. But overall women in pre-Independence era had no political privileges.

In Independent India, the Constitution, after guaranteeing equality to women in all spheres, left their political representation to their own willingness, opportunity and support. Several committees on local self-government advocated reservation for women representation. Balwantrai Mehta Committee (1957) also suggested a token co-option of two women members in rural local bodies. The Committee on Status of Women in India was setup in 1971 to look into all aspects of women's status in India with a special focus on their political participation. The committee recommended separate women panchayats at the village level. To make women's political right more functional and to give them more opportunities to participate in the formal political places, the Committee recommended that political parties fix a quota for women candidates. It also proposed allotting a block of seats to women in municipal councils. The committee recommended the setting up of permanent independent commission on women at both state and national levels.

The National Perspective Plan for Women was drawn up as a long-term action blueprint for 1988-2000 but women's group pointed out several shortcomings in its approach, coverage and methodology. National Commission for Women set up in 1992 has initiated planning process involving women and protecting their interests. The 73rd and 74th Amendments to the Constitution became the watershed for women's political empowerment at the grassroots level institutions and providing for not less than one-third of seats reserved for women in rural and urban local bodies in the country.

REPRESENTATION OF WOMEN IN LEGISLATURE

The Constitution of India has granted women equal rights but in practice these rights have no meaning due to their poor representation in legislative bodies. Even after more than five decades of democracy women's participation and role in political life has been low.

During 1952 to 1996, representation of women in Lok Sabha shows their per seat candidature as low as 0.30 per cent. The ratio of women candidates has been computed as 3.2 per cent.

During 1952-1999, in Lok Sabha, on an average, there were 31 women members in the House of 528, constituting 5.95 per cent. In 2009 general elections, first time women reached to ten percent. Women representation from U.P. was recorded highest (9 members) in 1996, 1998 and 1999. In general elections major political parties put women candidates in less numbers.

Table 3
Women's Representation in Lok Sabha

Year	*Total Seats*	*No. of Women's Members*	*Percentage*
1952-57	499	22	4.4
1957-62	500	27	5.4
1962-67	503	34	6.8
1967-71	523	31	6.0
1971-77	521	22	4.2
1977-80	544	19	3.5
1980-84*	544	28	7.9
1984-89	544	44	8.1
1989-91**	517	27	5.3
1991	544	39	7.2
1996	543	39	7.2
1998	543	43	7.9
1999	543	49	9.0
2004	539	44	8.2
2009	543	59	10.8

Source: Election Commission of India/India Country Report.

* Elections were not held in 12 constituencies in Assam and in Meghalaya

** Elections were not held in J & K and Punjab; figures include women elected from Punjab during by elections in 1992

*** Two seats vacant

Women's representation in Rajya Sabha during 1952 to 1996 demonstrates that women members comprised 9.51 per cent only. The table below shows that even in Rajya Sabha where there is indirect election and nomination there has been low representation of women.

According to a UNDP report, of 116 countries, India is ranked 101 on 'women's participation', behind Sri Lanka & Bangladesh, which ranked 79 & 88 respectively.

Table 4
Women's Representation in Rajya Sabha

Year	*Total Seats*	*No. of Women Members*	*Percentage*
1952	219	16	7.3
1957	237	18	7.6
1962	238	18	7.6
1967	240	20	8.3
1971	243	17	7.0
1977	244	25	10.2
1980	244	24	9.8
1985	244	28	11.4
1990	245	24	9.7
1991	245	38	15.5
1992	245	17	6.9
1994	245	20	8.1
1996	245	18	7.3
1997	245	18	7.3
1998	245	18	7.3
2006	240	24	10.0

Source: Election Commission of India & India Country Report

Table 5
Women Members in XV Lok Sabha

States	*No. of Women*	*Percent*
Andhra Pradesh	5	8.5
Assam	2	3.4
Bihar	4	6.8
Chattisgarh	2	3.4
Delhi	1	1.7
Gujarat	4	6.8
Haryana	2	3.4
Karnataka	1	1.7
Madhya Pradesh	6	10.2
Maharashtra	3	5.1
Meghalaya	1	1.7
Punjab	4	6.8
Rajasthan	3	5.1
Tamil Nadu	1	1.7
Uttar Pradesh	13	22.0
West Bengal	7	11.7

Source: Lok Sabha web site

The status of representation of women in state legislatures has also not been upto the mark. During 1952 to 1997 average representation of women in state legislatures was recorded just 4.0 per cent. In the state of Uttar Pradesh the average number of women members during 1946-47 to 1996 has been computed as 15 members constituting 3.80 per cent of the House. In the U.P. State Assembly elections 2002, 341 women contested out of which only 26 got elected. Thus the success rate has been quite low.

The status of representation of women from different states in XV Lok Sabha is quite revealing.

WOMEN IN RURAL LOCAL GOVERNMENT

The 73rd and 74th Amendments to the Constitution have provided one-third reservation of seats for women in grassroots governance. The participation of women in local self-institutions is considered essential not only for ensuring political participation in the governance but also for realizing the developmental goals of development. Participation of women in these local bodies involves:

- (i) women as voters
- (ii) women as member of political parties
- (iii) women as candidates
- (iv) women as making planning, implementation, monitoring and evaluation of programmes
- (v) women as member of various committees, core groups, associations, task force etc. The emergence of women power structure into grassroots level institutions is a milestone in achieving socio-economic development from different quarters.

The 73rd Constitution Amendment Act 1992 has served as a major break through towards ensuring women's equal access and increased participation in rural local government. This Act aims at providing Constitutional guarantees to safeguard the interest of rural local self-governments to enable them to function as effective democratic and self-governing institutions at the grassroots level. This Amendment provides for reservation of one-third elected seats for women at the level of local government in rural areas. There is also an identical reservation for women at the post of chairpersons of these local government units.

As a consequence, a very active role for women in local governance is envisaged as compared to governance at the state and national levels in India. These provisions have provided great opportunities and challenges to women in India, particularly in the field of local government. This is of great significance, since this grass-root level participation has considerably broadened the base of women's participation in politics at local level.

The interest in women and local governance has recently developed at global, national and local levels and providing some statistics on women's representation in politics worldwide to help put people's concerns into perspective. It is seen that development of women's movement at local level, operating through the process of civil society where women have worked individually and collectively in autonomous women's group to further their cause and raise awareness of women's continuing disadvantaged position has not yielded desired results.

The number of women in politics at local level prior to 1993 has been very small and their influence negligible. The insignificant presence of women at these levels was an important indicator of two basic facts: one that women who were planted at the top often lacked the kind of training required for effective participation, secondly, the society was unable to accept women in politics, particularly at the grass-root level. Due to their secondary status and low esteem, most of them were denied entry in political decision-making.

The 73rd Constitution Amendment Act has ushered a new era in the democratic process of the country, by not only providing constitutional status to the Panchayati Raj Institutions, but has also provided an enabling environment for women to directly participate in local self government and has brought women to the forefront and centre of local development. Involvement of women in the political arena and in decision making roles are an important tool for empowerment as well as monitoring standards of political performance at local level.

The reservation of seats for women in Panchayati Raj Institutions has shown that it has tremendous implications not merely in terms of number of women entering the public arena and holding public office, but also in terms of social, economic and political impact that these reservations have had on the total system.

Women in local government need to develop their capabilities to play their rightful roles in the development process. The role of political representatives at local level is demanding, needs time to gain experience and to understand the rules, regulations and procedures governing the administrative bureaucracy with which they now have to work-often quite closely in service delivery system.

II

SCOPE FOR ROLE CONFLICT

Role is the functional aspect of structural concept status. The position that a person occupies in a society through traditions, customs or achievement is called 'status', a symbol for recognition. As a result of this status, one is expected to discharge certain functions called 'roles'. Role has two elements, one is expectation from society as a whole and other is from the individual for fellow members. Role is a dynamic aspect of status and changes according to change in status. One person may have several status, as a son, as a husband, as a father etc. Every status has role associated with it. One has to discharge several roles according to one's status. There are many factors such as sex, age, kinship, wealth, education, power, courage, occupation, business, and intellectual abilities etc., which determine status. Status and role influence, directly as well as indirectly, the emotions, sentiments, feelings, and thoughts etc. of individual and in turn of society.

The term 'role conflict' is generally used by sociologists and social psychologists to denote the problem situation which arises due to simultaneous occupancy of two positions by an actor, i.e. problem that arises due to role incompatibilities. Role conflict is a state of incompatibility which occurs when there is a mismatch between thought and action, acceptance or rejection of mutually exclusive events of equal importance, simultaneous requirement of presence in two opposing situations, expectations of interacting actors, conceived notion and fact about any event, object or person and when potential antagonism leads to cognitive personalization.

Degree of conflict depends on personality, dispositions, beliefs, attitudes, characteristics, life style, moods and positions in social ladder. When two or more roles are to be fulfilled simultaneously which are contradictory or of mutually exclusive expectations the role conflict becomes even more pronounced. That is what happens when a woman has to perform simultaneously roles of a housewife and a politician.

The differential role of women over the history has been mainly based on role conflict. The level of role conflict has been a major determinant of status of women in Indian society. The revolutionary measure in the form of 73rd Amendment to the supreme law of land is a harbinger in setting the role of women in different sectors-social, political, administrative, ethical, aesthetic, environmental etc.

The women representatives in Panchayati Raj Institutions have multi-dimensional roles to perform. As a housewife, she holds the traditional status of a mother, wife, sister, daughter and daughter-in-law and; as people's representatives, she has to perform for the fulfillment of people's aspirations and expectations. Therefore as compared to their male counterparts in society, these women representatives have to perform two sets of roles i.e. traditional or prescribed, as a woman in a male dominated traditional Indian society and; an achieved or ascribed, by acquiring political status. As such a woman as a role occupant finds now lesser time for family. Her role is now divided into two sets of role for family and for society.

This leads to a constant and continuous phenomenon of role conflict. In case of any biasness, the effectiveness of constitutional provisions may be prejudiced. A woman representative has therefore to make a balance between the two roles for a harmonious and peaceful life and effective role in decision making. There is a need to judiciously distribute time to strike a balance in those conflicting roles. The factors causing conflicts are numerous. The level of education, family background, social traditions and customs, prevailing environment, level of mutual understanding, economic status of family, women empowerment movement and programmes, healthy competition are some of the major determinants influencing role conflicts among women representatives. The influence of these factors and their impact is the major concern.

REVIEW OF LITERATURE

A number of studies, surveys and research have been carried out by social scientists, development experts and academicians. These studies and research focus on various dimensions and aspects of women's empowerment, upliftment, development and welfare. There is scarcity of literature on role conflict among women representatives in local bodies and political institutions. Though plenty of pertinent literature on women's role conflict is available which focuses more on working women in urban settings. The women's liberation movement, particularly constitutional and legal provisions (enactments) followed by conferences and conventions has created interest of many educated elite on the issue of proper roles of men and women in India. Role Conflict is considered as single phenomenon having both psychological consequences. But attention is strictly focused on one type of consequence that is behavioural conflict resulting from the prevalent inconsistent norms within the role system.

Kapur (1960, 1984) dealing with a number of working housewives highlights the issue like role conflict and adjustment. She further presents multidimensional problems of working women in various professions.

Kundu (1999) finds that role conflict varies according to levels of education, economic earnings and social position. Similarly Hemlatha and Suryanarayan (1983) state that working women's problems are greatly influenced by factors such as age and socio-economic status, husband's treatment, children's age and their numbers, family size and type, nature of work etc. They experience that positive attitude of family members towards women's employment help them a great deal to carry on both the roles successfully.

The working mother's role is widely regarded as a classic conflict situation. Potentially, conflict has been suggested from a variety of sources. The diffused nature of role and overload of work are two known sources. Such sources are dealt by eminent scholars like Chakravarty (1978), Rama Kapoor (1969), Kalarani (1976), Orden and Bradburn (1968) and many others. Arora et.al. (1963) observe that strains are felt by all the working women since their husband do not help in house-keeping. The attitude of family members and their nature of co-operation are crucial for the role adjustment of a working wife. This has been discussed in details by Powell (1963), Kalarani (1976) and Hoffman (1963).

These and many other studies no doubt focus on role conflict among working housewives, however no study is directly related to role conflict among working women representatives in unit of democratic governance and decentralized planning. The study undertaken by the author (2004), probably the maiden endeavour studying role conflict among elected women representatives in urban settings, highlights the apathy on part of women representatives to play any active role in governance. By virtue of constitutional guarantees they are there but their political roles are performed by their male counterparts.

III

THE PRESENT STUDY

A number of studies have been undertaken to study the role conflict among women in employment sector but very few have touched the political aspect. So in the present study an attempt has been made to understand the problem of role conflict among women representatives in Panchayati Raj Institutions in the most populated state in the country.

OBJECTIVES OF STUDY

It is basically considered that education is a channel to awareness, which creates role dynamism and facilitates change in role perception. How a woman judiciously and elegantly performs a set of roles under conflicting demand and work stress has to be studied thoroughly. The way for striking a balance in picking roles on priority basis and their order of performance has to be dissected minutely. Hence this study concentrates and attempts to examine various issues related to role conflict among the elected women representatives in Panchayati Raj Institutions in U.P.. The main objectives of the study are:

(i) to trace the background of women entering into this new political role,

(ii) to highlight the change that occurs in status and position of women representatives,

(iii) to measure the degree of change in status and the extent to employment of new roles to the existing traditional ones,

(iv) to identify the determinants of role's selection and performance in order of merit,

(v) to focus the stabilizing and destabilizing forces responsible for affecting the status achieved,

(vi) to assess the long run consequences on family and children,

(vii) to highlight the conflict oriented abnormalities and consequences on adjustments within and without family and self,

(viii) to measure the social benefits in terms of service to society,

(ix) to analyse the family and social variables to determine role status and role conflict.

HYPOTHESES

Political activeness integrates on with a higher status, greater role for society and disintegration from family by curtailing role towards it with increase in role conflict and status factor. Higher the level, higher the status and independence, higher the conflict and lesser degree of association with family and feministic role and vice-versa.

The present study is designed to verify the following:

(i) Higher the level of interest of women representatives in governance, higher respect in political circle and more in role multiplicity;

(ii) Higher the level of interest, higher the freedom and independence and more the decision making power in the family;

(iii) Higher the level of interest, higher the freedom, more the conflict, more the egalitarian relationship and more the ego clash;

(iv) Higher the interest, greater the role performance towards society and more the social work;

(v) Higher the level of interest, more the freedom, lesser the attachment to tradition and more the empowerment with increase in modernity.

SOURCES OF DATA COLLECTION

Both primary and secondary sources were used for data collection under the study. The primary data were collected through personal interview with the help of a structured questionnaire, while secondary data were collected through books, reports, journals etc.

For collecting primary data, following types of questionnaires/interview schedules were developed and used:

(i) Questionnaire for Women Representatives

(ii) Questionnaire for Officials

(iii) Questionnaire for Family Members

Thus, an attempt was made to substantiate the responses of elected representatives with the views from officials as well as from their family members.

METHODOLOGY

In the present study questionnaires/interview schedules were used for collection of data. For fetching primary data a comprehensive questionnaire covering various aspects of roles of women representatives was developed. All the women representatives were personally contacted and interviewed to get a better insight into the various aspects of the study.

LIMITATIONS

The study is mainly based on the responses received through personal interviews, observations and discussions with women representatives, with their family members and with the officials. The views collected through primary sources were supplemented by data reproduced from secondary sources including books, reports etc. The findings have been derived on these counts.

REFERENCES

Sinha, Pushpa (1982), Role Conflict Among the Working Women, Shanti Prakashan for Anmole Publications, New Delhi

Singh, S.K., (2006), Women Empowerment in Urban Local Administration in U.P., in U.B. Singh (ed); Empowerment of Women in Urban Administration in India (Experiences & Strategies), Serials, New Delhi

Singh, U.B., (2006), Empowerment of Women in Urban Administration: In Search of Right Perspectives, in U.B. Singh (ed), Empowerment of Women in Urban Administration in India (Experiences & Stratgies), Serials, New Delhi

Jena, S.K., (1993), Working Women and Modernisation, Ashish, New Delhi

Singh, S. and Srivastava, S.P. (eds) (2001), Gender Equality Through Women's Empowerment (Strategies and Approaches), Bharat Book, Lucknow

Acharya, Itishree Padhi, 1998,Working Mothers (Role Conflict and Adjustments), Reliance, New Delhi

Mishra, P. and Mohapatra, U., (2003), Women Administrators and Professionals (A Global Perspective), Kalinga, Delhi

Kundu, S.K., (1995), Role Conflict Among Employed Women: A Case Study of Bhubaneshwar City, Ph.D. Thesis, (unpublished) RML Avadh University, Faizabad,

Sundaram V., A tireless Fighter for Hindu Women Liberation-I, News Today

Women Rights– Law Speak- http://www. khojhyderabad.com/ women/decore home.htm Info chainge women

Batta, Jaya, Women Empowerment: A Study of Political Status of Women in India, Ph.D. thesis, (unpublished), Jamia Millia Islamia, New Delhi

Singh, U.B., (2006), Role Conflict Among Women Representatives in Urban Local Government (A Case Study of Uttar Pradesh), in U.B. Singh (ed), Leaders in Making, Kalpaz, New Delhi

Singh, U.B., (2004), Role Conflict among elected Women Representatives in Urban Local Government (A Case Study of Uttar Pradesh), Report of the Study sponsored by the Indian Council of Social Science Research, New Delhi.

2

PROFILE OF THE UNIVERSE (RESPONDENTS)

PANCHAYAT RAJ SYSTEM IN UTTAR PRADESH

The modern Panchayat Raj owes its origin to the United Provinces Panchayat Raj Adhiniyam, 1947, which was assented by the Governor-General on 7th December 1947. In pursuance, 35,000 Panchayats were established on 15th August 1949. About 8,000 Panchayat Adalats (courts) were also set up. In 1951-52, the number of Gram Sahbas increased from 35,000 to 35,943 and that of Panchayat Adalats from 8414 to 8492. Since 1952 these panchayats initiated the role of village construction in a planned way. For the successful launch of First Five Year Plan the members of development committees were nominated at the Panchayat Adalat level. After the abolition of Zamindari in 1952-53, Gram Samaj was set up and powers of Gram Sabha were increased.

After the second general elections of panchayats in 1955, the prediction of Gram Sabha as Gram Samaj was made similar. It was decided to constitute Gram Sabha in every village having a population of 250 or more, and therefore the numbers of Gram Panchayat was increased to 72425. With the change in jurisdiction of panchayats in 1957-58, the number of panchayats reduced from 72425 to 72409. In 1955, the Panchayat Adalats were rechristened as Nyaya Panchayat. The U.P. Panchayat Raj Adhiniyam, 1947 was amended in 1960-61 and the election of Pradhan (Head) of Gram Sabha was made by ballot.

In commensurate to the Balwantray Mehta Committee Report a new law entitled Uttar Pradesh Kshetra Samiti and Zila Parishad Adhiniyam was enacted in 1961. The three-tier system in the form of Gram Sabha, Kshetra Samiti and Zila Parishad was introduced in the State. After the third general elections, the numbers of Gaon (village) Panchayats became 72233 and that of Nyaya Panchayats as 8594.

During the fourth general elections in 1972-73, the numbers of Gaon Panchayats and Nyaya Panchayats became 72,834 and 8792 respectivily. The fifth general election was held for 72000 Gaon Panchayats.

The sixth general elections were held in 1988. A great step in this election was to introduce 30 percent reservation for women for the members of Gaon (village) Panchayats. It was also enunciated to ensure representation of at least one woman from Scheduled Castes. The number of Gaon (village) Panchayats was 73,927 and that of Nyaya Panchayats was 8814. First time women were elected in large number as Pradhan (930) and members (1, 50,577), including 65937 women belonging to Scheduled Castes.

In pursuance of the Seventy third Amendment to the Constitution, both the enactments pertaining to Panchayat Raj System in the State (U.P. Panchayat Raj Adhiniyam, 1947 and U.P. Kshetra and Zila Parishad Adhiniyam, 1961) were amended and the latter enactment was rechristened as Kshetra and Zila Panchayat Adhiniyam, 1961. Accordingly, three types of Panchayat Raj Institutions–Gram Panchayat, Kshetra Panchayat and Zila Panchayat–were created in the State.

The new Act provides for constitution of Gram Panchayat in a village or a group of villages with a population of 1000. Accordingly, 58,620 Gram Panchayats (including 6495 in Uttarakhand) were created. The posts of Pradhan were reserved as: 12,526 for Scheduled Castes, 15,863 for Backward Classes and 19,522 for women. The first elections under new dispensation were held in 1995.

The second elections under new system were held in 2000 for 52010 Gram Panchayats, 818 Kshetra Panchayats and 70 Zila Panchayats. Last elections for 52000 Gram Panchayats, 820 Kshetra Panchayats to 70 Zila Panchayats were held in 2005-06. The representations of women as a result of the last elections are quite encouraging.

A comparative study of representation of women in Panchayati Raj Institutions over last three elections after The 73rd Constitution Amendment Act, in this most populated state is quite encouraging:

Table 1
Representation of Women in PRIs

Unit		*Year*		
		1995	*2000*	*2005*
Gram Panchayat	Pradhan	33.00	35.32	50.22
	Member	33.32	37.95	38.40
Kshetra Panchayat	Pramukh	33.29	36.71	51.83
	Member	33.32	35.82	38.23
Zila Panchayat	Adhyaksha	34.96	53.62	75.41
	Member	32.96	37.06	40.22

Source: U.P. State Election Commission

This depicts the increasing representation of women after every election. The number of women has been recorded more than one-third as mandated in the Constitution. Their number is extremely high against the posts where indirect elections are held.

Thus women in rural areas are coming forward in an enthusiastic way to play their role in governance at grassroots level in Uttar Pradesh.

PANCHAYATS STUDIED

With a broader aim in view, while selecting the units of rural local bodies, it was attempted that all the geographical regions in the state are represented. In addition rural local bodies being headed by male chairpersons were also selected and views of elected representatives belonging to those panchayats were also taken into cognizance. It was felt necessary for bringing a balance in study, to collect views of women in different situations. The elected women representatives in female-headed panchayats may not have the similar circumstances to face than that of in the panchayats being headed by a male. Although the study centers on the elected women representatives, it was thought proper to fetch the views of their family members and officials as well, just to collaborate their views.

Accordingly, the state of Uttar Pradesh, for the purpose of this study, was divided into four regions-Central, Eastern, Western and Bundelkhand. From each region three Zila (District) Panchayats-two headed by women Adhyaksha, and one by male Adhyaksha, were purposely selected. While selecting the districts representative character of the region was the main concern. From every district three Kshetra Panchayats(two headed by female Pramukh, and one by male Pramukh)were selected on random basis. From each kshetra (block) three Gram Panchayats (two headed by female Pradhan, and one by male Pradhan) were taken up for in-depth study.

On this basis, 12 Zila Panchayats, 36 Kshetra Panchayats and 108 Gram Panchayats from all over the state were selected. These included four Zila Panchayats, 12 Kshetra Panchayats and 36 Gram Panchayats with male as head. All other rural local government units were headed by female. As regards women representatives, in all 1003 elected representatives from different types of rural local government units were covered under study. It consisted of 12 chairpersons (Adhyaksha) of Zila Panchayats, 36 chairpersons (Pramukh) of Kshetra Panchayats, and 108 chairpersons (Pradhan) of Gram Panchayats and members of these grass-root institutions.

In addition to woman representatives, about 100 officers from all the levels were also interviewed just to substantiate the views expressed by the women representatives. Besides, family members of elected women were also contacted.

The details of Panchayats covered under the study are furnished in Appendix I.

SOCIO-ECONOMIC PROFILE OF WOMEN REPRESENTATIVES

The socio-economic environment of an individual greatly influences the attitudes, values, socialization, participation, efficacy, status and position. Different roles of women in various differing situations are the major cause of role conflict. The socio-economic profile of women like age, marital status, number of children, family type, education, parents'/spouses' background etc. plays a very important role in the performance of their roles and related problems. Hence, in order to study role conflict among women representatives in grass-roots level rural local government, it is important to analyze the socio-economic profile of women representatives covered under the study, which has an impact on their role performance, and the problem of role conflict.

Age

In dealing with the problems of women representatives the factor of age plays a very important role. The roles and responsibilities of women vary significantly in different periods of their life. The young representatives in child rearing age have to devote more time for their children in infancy, whereas, the situation of middle aged women is quite different. The data relating to age of the respondents are analysed in Tables 2, 3, 4.

The analysis reveals that highest number (84.8 percent) of women representatives in Zila Panchayats in the state belong to age group between 30-50 years, followed by(79.76 percent) age group of 30-50 years and by about half (50.64 percent) between 21 and 35 years of age. Amongst regions, Central region tops the list by sending 90 percent of women falling in age–group between 25 and 45 years, followed by Eastern region which elects slightly less (87.50 percent) women to this age group.

Almost same trend is registered at the Kshetra Panchayat level as well. More than 8 out of 10 women elected to Kshetra Panchayats belong to age–group of 25-45 years, while a little less than half falls under 21-35 age category. Majority of the

Table 2
Age of Respondents
Zila Panchayat

(Percentage Distribution)

Region	*District/ Age (yrs.)*	*21-25*	*25-30*	*30-35*	*35-40*	*40-45*	*45-50*	*50-55*	*55-60*	*60>*	*Total*
Eastern	Varanasi				50.00	50.00					100.00
	Gorakhpur		16.66	16.66	16.66	33.36	16.66				100.00
	Ballia		25.00	25.00		37.50	12.50				100.00
Total		16.66	16.66	16.66	37.52	12.50					100.00
Central	Lucknow		14.20	57.40	14.20		14.20				100.00
	Balrampur		20.00	40.00		40.00					100.00
	Sitapur	12.50		37.50	50.00						100.00
Total		5.00	10.00	45.00	25.00	10.00	5.00				100.00
Western	Bagpat		16.66	66.68						16.66	100.00
	Mathura				50.00		25.00	25.00			100.00
	Moradabad		50.00	25.00			25.00				100.00
Total		27.77	33.36	11.11		16.66	5.55			5.55	100.00
Bundel-khand	Banda		16.66	33.36	16.66		33.32				100.00
	Hamirpur			80.00		20.00					100.00
	Jhansi		16.66	16.66	33.36	33.32					100.00
Total		11.76	41.20	17.64	17.64	11.76					100.00
Grand Total		1.26	16.45	32.94	17.72	17.72	11.39	1.26		1.26	100.00

Table 3
Age of Respondents
Kshetra Panchayat

(Percentage Distribution)

Region	*District/ Age (yrs.)*	*21-25*	*25-30*	*30-35*	*35-40*	*40-45*	*45-50*	*50-55*	*55-60*	*60>*	*Total*
Eastern	Varanasi	12.50	12.50	25.00		12.50		37.50			100.00
	Gorakhpur		13.33	20.00	26.67	40.00					100.00
	Ballia		18.18	27.28	18.18	18.18		9.09	9.09		100.00
Total		2.94	14.70	23.55	17.64	26.47		11.76	2.94		100.00
Central	Lucknow	11.11	16.66	5.58	27.77	27.77	11.11				100.00
	Balrampur	7.69	30.79	15.38	15.38	30.76					100.00
	Sitapur		14.28	28.59	28.57	14.28	14.28				100.00
Total		6.66	20.00	15.58	24.44	24.44	8.88				100.00
Western	Bagpat		20.00	40.00	20.00	10.00	10.00				100.00
	Mathura		12.50	50.00	25.00	12.50					100.00
	Moradabad		16.66	25.00	33.35		8.33	16.66			100.00
Total		16.66	36.70	26.66	6.66	6.66	6.66				100.00
Bundel-khand	Banda	8.33	25.00	41.67	25.00						100.00
	Hamirpur		20.00	10.00	50.00	20.00					100.00
	Jhansi		7.69	30.76	23.10	30.76	7.69				100.00
Total		2.85	17.14	28.60	31.42	17.14	2.85				100.00
Grand Total		3.41	17.36	25.00	25.00	19.52	4.86	4.16	0.69		100.00

Table 4
Age of Respondents
Gram Panchayat

(Percentage Distribution)

Region	*District/ Age (yrs.)*	*21-25*	*25-30*	*30-35*	*35-40*	*40-45*	*45-50*	*50-55*	*55-60*	*60>*	*Total*
Eastern	Varanasi	5.88	11.76	11.76	23.54	23.54	5.88	11.76		5.88	100.00
	Gorakhpur		28.57	23.80	38.11	4.76	4.76				100.00
	Ballia	8.33	12.50	16.66	20.85	25.00		8.33	8.33		100.00
Total		4.83	17.74	17.74	27.45	17.74	3.22	6.45	3.22	1.61	100.00
Central	Lucknow	5.71	17.14	20.00	28.60	17.14	5.71	2.85	2.85		100.00
	Balrampur	11.11	22.22	22.22	22.22	11.11	5.56	5.56			100.00
	Sitapur	7.16	7.14	14.28	28.57	28.57	14.28				100.00
Total		7.40	14.81	18.51	27.20	19.75	8.64	2.46	1.23		100.00
Western	Bagpat	11.11	16.66	22.22	22.22	27.79					100.00
	Mathura		10.52	26.31	5.26	31.60	21.05	5.26			100.00
	Moradabad	9.09	13.63	13.63	22.74	22.74	4.54	9.09		4.54	100.00
Total		6.77	13.55	20.33	16.94	27.17	8.47	5.08		1.69	100.00
Bundel-khand	Banda	3.84	23.10	19.23	15.38	15.38	7.69	7.69	7.69		100.00
	Hamirpur	9.09	27.27	31.83	18.18	13.63					100.00
	Jhansi		13.04	26.08	26.08	13.04	13.04	8.72			100.00
Total		4.22	21.12	25.39	19.71	14.08	7.04	5.63	2.81		100.00
Grand Total		5.86	16.84	20.51	23.11	19.41	6.95	4.76	1.83	0.73	100.00

women representatives from all the four regions are in the age group of 30-50 years.

Interestingly, the identical story is written at the Gram (Village) Panchayat level also. Majority of the women (about 8 out of 10) belong to age-group of 25-45 years, followed by about 7 out of 10 falling in 30-50 years group. Even all the regions follow the same trend.

The analysis brings out that women belonging to matured age-group have been elected by the rural community to play their active role in decision making in Panchayati Raj Institutions in Uttar Pradesh. Among the women representatives interviewed the maximum women respondents were found to be between the age group of 25 to 40 years. It is because of this age factor that they are active, dynamic, enterprising, hard-working and sincere.

Marital Status

An important factor that affects the status of women is the institution of marriage. Marriage is universal in India and there has been a tradition of early marriages particularly for females (especially in rural areas) which proves disastrous for their mental, physical, social and economic status. The analysis depicts that women representatives at all the levels are married. A good number (about 15 per cent) of them are leading widow life, while none is found unmarried.

Since most of the women representatives are in the younger age group and are married, they have a major responsibility towards family and home and are likely to have more workload. Managing both family and official, (political) responsibility becomes really tedious for them as both roles are quite incompatible in nature and this may be the major reason for role conflict.

But in case of women representatives who are middle aged or above, they have lesser problems because by this age most of them become free from their basic familial responsibilities and are quite stable in their married as well as family life, hence they face lesser work related conflict and may be able to devote more time to their new role.

Table 5
Marital Status
Zila Panchayat

(Percentage Distribution)

Region	*District*	*Married*	*Unmarried*	*Widow*	*Divorcee*	*Total*
Eastern	Varanasi	100.00				100.00
	Gorakhpur	100.00				100.00
	Ballia	100.00				100.00
Total		100.00				100.00
Central	Lucknow	100.00				100.00
	Balrampur	100.00				100.00
	Sitapur	100.00				100.00
Total		100.00				100.00
Western	Bagpat	83.34		16.66		100.00
	Mathura	100.00				100.00
	Moradabad	100.00				100.00
Total		94.45		5.55		100.00
Bundelkhand	Banda	100.00				100.00
	Hamirpur	80.00		20.00		100.00
	Jhansi	100.00				100.00
Total		94.12		5.88		100.00
Grand Total		97.47		2.53		100.00

Table 6
Marital Status
Kshetra Panchayat

(Percentage Distribution)

Region	*District*	*Married*	*Unmarried*	*Widow*	*Divorcee*	*Total*
Eastern	Varanasi	87.50		12.50		100.00
	Gorakhpur	100.00				100.00
	Ballia	100.00				100.00
Total		97.06		2.94		100.00
Central	Lucknow	100.00				100.00
	Balrampur	100.00				100.00
	Sitapur	100.00				100.00
Total		100.00				100.00
Western	Bagpat	100.00				100.00
	Mathura	100.00				100.00
	Moradabad	100.00				100.00
Total		100.00				100.00
Bundel-khand	Banda	100.00				100.00
	Hamirpur	100.00				100.00
	Jhansi	100.00				100.00
Total		100.00				100.00
Grand Total		99.31		0.69		100.00

Table 7
Marital Status
Gram Panchayat

(Percentage Distribution)

Region	*District*	*Married*	*Unmarried*	*Widow*	*Divorcee*	*Total*
Eastern	Varanasi	100.00				100.00
	Gorakhpur	100.00				100.00
	Ballia	95.84		4.16		100.00
Total		98.39		1.61		100.00
Central	Lucknow	94.29		5.71		100.00
	Balrampur	94.45		5.55		100.00
	Sitapur	100.00				100.00
Total		96.30		3.70		100.00
Western	Bagpat	100.00				100.00
	Mathura	94.74		5.26		100.00
	Moradabad	100.00				100.00
Total		98.31		1.69		100.00
Bundel-khand	Banda	100.00				100.00
	Hamirpur	100.00				100.00
	Jhansi	100.00				100.00
Total		100.00				100.00
Grand Total		98.17		1.83		100.00

Family Structure

The family is the social context in which girls are socialised in there roles of dependency which they will later carry out after they are married and have a family. The structure and size of family influence the behaviour of girls which affects their life style, including way of functioning etc. later on.

The data reveal that more than half (53.18 per cent) women respondents at Zila Panchayats level live in joint family, while about one third come from nuclear family. The trend is however reversed in other levels.At Kshetra Panchayat level, a little less than half of women belong to nuclear family, while more than one third live in joint family. Many women representatives at different tiers are found living in extended family as well.

Those living in nuclear family have lesser obligations to fulfill while in joint families more adjustments are required as there are greater demands and expectations. One positive aspect found with regard to joint family is that women representatives get help from other family members both in household as well as in performing official functions. But women representatives having smaller families are found to be more satisfied and are able to manage both roles effectively. Further women living with in-laws have many more social complexities than the women living in nuclear families with their husband and children.

Table 8
Type of Family
Zila Panchayat

(Percentage Distribution)

Region	*District Family*	*Nuclear Family*	*Joint Family*	*Extended*	*Total*
Eastern	Varanasi		100.00		100.00
	Gorakhpur	41.67	33.33	25.00	100.00
	Ballia	62.50	25.00	12.50	100.00
Total		41.67	41.67	16.66	100.00
Central	Lucknow	14.28	57.15	28.57	100.00
	Balrampur	20.00	80.00		100.00
	Sitapur	50.00	37.50	12.50	100.00
Total		30.00	55.00	15.00	100.00
Western	Bagpat	33.34	50.00	16.66	100.00
	Mathura		100.00		100.00
	Moradabad	25.00	50.00	25.00	100.00
Total		22.22	61.12	16.66	100.00
Bundel-khand	Banda	33.33	66.67		100.00
	Hamirpur	20.00	80.00		100.00
	Jhansi	66.67	33.33		100.00
Total		41.17	58.83		100.00
Grand Total		34.17	53.18	12.65	100.00

Table 9
Type of Family
Kshetra Panchayat

(Percentage Distribution)

Region	*District Family*	*Nuclear Family*	*Joint Family*	*Extended*	*Total*
Eastern	Varanasi	37.50	62.50		100.00
	Gorakhpur	80.00	13.34	6.66	100.00
	Ballia	54.55	27.27	18.18	100.00
Total		61.77	29.41	8.82	100.00
Central	Lucknow	27.78	50.00	22.22	100.00

Contd.

Region	*District Family*	*Nuclear Family*	*Joint Family*	*Extended*	*Total*
	Balrampur	53.85	38.46	7.69	100.00
	Sitapur	14.28	71.44	14.28	100.00
Total		31.11	53.34	15.55	100.00
Western	Bagpat	30.00	50.00	20.00	100.00
	Mathura	62.50	25.00	12.50	100.00
	Moradabad	50.00	33.34	16.66	100.00
Total		46.68	36.66	16.66	100.00
Bundelkhand	Banda	33.33	41.67	25.00	100.00
	Hamirpur	40.00	40.00	20.00	100.00
	Jhansi	76.93	23.07		100.00
Total		51.44	34.28	14.28	100.00
Grand Total		46.54	39.58	13.88	100.00

Table 10
Type of Family
GramPanchayat

(Percentage Distribution)

Region	*District Family*	*Nuclear Family*	*Joint Family*	*Extended*	*Total*
Eastern	Varanasi	23.52	70.60	5.88	100.00
	Gorakhpur	47.63	38.09	14.28	100.00
	Ballia	62.50	16.66	20.84	100.00
Total		46.79	38.70	14.51	100.00
Central	Lucknow	57.15	20.00	22.85	100.00
	Balrampur	50.00	38.89	11.11	100.00
	Sitapur	42.86	50.00	7.14	100.00
Total		50.63	34.56	14.81	100.00
Western	Bagpat	38.88	44.46	16.66	100.00
	Mathura	52.64	36.84	10.52	100.00
	Moradabad	31.81	54.56	13.63	100.00
Total		40.67	45.78	13.55	100.00
Bundelkhand	Banda	38.46	46.16	15.38	100.00
	Hamirpur	36.36	40.92	22.72	100.00
	Jhansi	39.14	34.78	26.08	100.00
Total		38.02	40.86	21.12	100.00
Grand Total		44.33	39.56	16.11	100.00

Children

Children are major responsibility for a married woman and also the major cause of concern and worry for those who work outside. Age of children is one of the important factors that may encourage or discourage a mother's involvement in roles other than a mother.

It is observed that less than one fifth women representatives at Zila Panchayat level have grown up children, as against more than one-fifth having only minor children. More than half of the women have minor as well as major children. At the Kshetra Panchayats level, majority of women (62.50 per cent) have minor and major children, whereas every fifth woman has only minor children.The similar situation exists in Gram Panchayats as well.

Table 11
No. of Children
Zila Panchayat

(Percentage Distribution)

Region	*District Family*	*Nuclear Family*	*Joint Family*	*Extended*	*Total*
Eastern	Varanasi	25.00	25.00	50.00	100.00
	Gorakhpur	25.00	16.67	58.33	100.00
	Ballia	12.50	25.00	62.50	100.00
Total		20.83	20.83	58.34	100.00
Central	Lucknow	28.57	28.57	42.86	100.00
	Balrampur	20.00		80.00	100.00
	Sitapur	25.00	37.50	37.50	100.00
Total		25.00	25.00	50.00	100.00
Western	Bagpat	16.67	16.67	66.66	100.00
	Mathura		25.00	75.00	100.00
	Moradabad	25.00	25.00	50.00	100.00
Total		16.67	22.22	61.11	100.00
Bundelkhand	Banda	16.67	16.67	66.66	100.00
	Hamirpur		20.00	80.00	100.00
	Jhansi	16.67	33.33	50.00	100.00
Total		11.76	23.53	64.71	100.00
Grand Total		18.98	22.78	58.24	100.00

Because of prevalence of traditional outlook regarding division of labour within the family, it is the mother who remains in charge of young children even if she is involved in any other profession.

It is observed that women representatives having minor and more number of children experience maximum role conflict because they have a major responsibility and have to devote more time and attention towards managing their children. It is experienced that women representatives who have grown up (major) and lesser number of children experience lesser role conflict.

Table 12
No. of Children
Kshetra Panchayat

(Percentage Distribution)

Region	*District Family*	*Nuclear Family*	*Joint Family*	*Extended*	*Total*
Eastern	Varanasi	25.00		75.00	100.00
	Gorakhpur	20.00	20.00	60.00	100.00
	Ballia	18.18	18.18	63.64	100.00
Total		20.59	14.71	64.70	100.00
Central	Lucknow	11.11	16.67	72.22	100.00
	Balrampur	15.38	30.76	53.86	100.00
	Sitapur	14.29	21.42	64.29	100.00
Total		13.33	22.22	64.45	100.00
Western	Bagpat	20.00	10.00	70.00	100.00
	Mathura	12.50	25.00	62.50	100.00
	Moradabad	16.67	25.00	58.33	100.00
Total		16.67	20.00	63.33	100.00
Bundelkhand	Banda	16.67	41.67	41.66	100.00
	Hamirpur	10.00	30.00	60.00	100.00
	Jhansi	15.38	15.38	69.24	100.00
Total		14.29	28.57	57.14	100.00
Grand Total		15.97	21.53	62.50	100.00

Table 13
No. of Children
Gram Panchayat

(Percentage Distribution)

Region	*District Family*	*Nuclear Family*	*Joint Family*	*Extended*	*Total*
Eastern	Varanasi	17.64	23.53	58.83	100.00
	Gorakhpur	19.05	14.29	66.66	100.00
	Ballia	25.00	12.50	62.50	100.00
Total		20.97	16.13	62.90	100.00
Central	Lucknow	11.43	20.00	68.57	100.00
	Balrampur	11.11	16.67	72.22	100.00
	Sitapur	14.29	14.29	71.42	100.00
Total		12.35	17.28	70.37	100.00
Western	Bagpat	16.67	27.78	55.55	100.00
	Mathura	21.05	11.58	67.37	100.00
	Moradabad	11.81	27.27	60.92	100.00
Total		23.73	28.81	47.46	100.00
Bundelkhand	Banda	15.38	19.23	65.39	100.00
	Hamirpur	13.63	9.09	77.28	100.00
	Jhansi	26.09	21.74	52.17	100.00
Total		18.31	16.90	64.79	100.00
Grand Total		18.31	19.41	62.28	100.00

Religious Affiliation

Another important factor which affects women's self-perception and maintains traditional images in spite of social and economic change, is religion. Women and religion is a different matter of deep study, however it cannot be denied that wherever the ascetic ideal has been too prominent in religion, women were denigrated. Today although women have reached a critical stage of self reflection and a new status in the contemporary world, religions itself are undergoing a crisis at present. No religion can after an adequate model for contemporary women's self understanding. The newness of the situation has to be matched by a corresponding new creative effort and the part of religious leaders and thinkers, male and female alike.

Table 14
Religious Affiliation
Zila Panchayat

(Percentage Distribution)

Religion	*District*	*Hindu*	*Muslim*	*Chris-tian*	*Sikh*	*Other (Specific)*	*Total*
Eastern	Varanasi	100.00					100.00
	Gorakhpur	100.00					100.00
	Ballia	100.00					100.00
Total		100.00					100.00
Central	Lucknow	71.43	28.57				100.00
	Balrampur	20.00	80.00				100.00
	Sitapur	100.00					100.00
Total		70.00	30.00				100.00
Western	Bagpat	83.34	16.66				100.00
	Mathura	100.00					100.00
	Moradabad	50.00	50.00				100.00
Total		72.23	27.77				100.00
Bundel-khand	Banda	100.00					100.00
	Hamirpur	100.00					100.00
	Jhansi	100.00					100.00
Total		100.00					100.00
Grand Total		86.08	13.92				100.00

With regard to religion of respondents, an absolute number (86.08 percent) of women at Zila Panchayats are Hindu, while more than one tenth (13.92 per cent) are Muslims. Surprisingly, at Kshetra Panchayat level the number of women following the Muslim religion has increased to a little less than one fifth (18.75 percent). Interestingly, Central and Western regions have elected more than one fourth women belonging to Muslim religion for Zila and Kshetra Panchayats. Unfortunately, not a single woman at any tier comes from any other religions.

Table 15
Religious Affiliation
Kshetra Panchayat

(Percentage Distribution)

Religion	*District*	*Hindu*	*Muslim*	*Chris-tian*	*Sikh*	*Other (Specific)*	*Total*
Eastern	Varanasi	75.00	25.00				100.00
	Gorakhpur	86.67	13.33				100.00
	Ballia	63.64	36.36				100.00
Total		76.48	23.52				100.00
Central	Lucknow	94.45	5.55				100.00
	Balrampur	30.76	69.24				100.00
	Sitapur	100.00					100.00
Total		77.78	22.22				100.00
Western	Bagpat	90.00	10.00				100.00
	Mathura	62.50	37.50				100.00
	Moradabad	58.34	41.66				100.00
Total		70.00	30.00				100.00
Bundel-khand	Banda	100.00					100.00
	Hamirpur	100.00					100.00
	Jhansi	100.00					100.00
Total		100.00					100.00
Grand Total		81.25	18.75				100.00

Table 16
Religious Affiliation
Gram Panchayat

(Percentage Distribution)

Religion	*District*	*Hindu*	*Muslim*	*Chris-tian*	*Sikh*	*Other (Specific)*	*Total*
Eastern	Varanasi	94.12	5.88				100.00
	Gorakhpur	90.48	9.52				100.00
	Ballia	75.00	25.00				100.00

Contd.

Religion	District	Hindu	Muslim	Chris-tian	Sikh	Other (Specific)	Total
Total		85.49	14.51				100.00
Central	Lucknow	85.72	14.28				100.00
	Balrampur	83.34	16.66				100.00
	Sitapur	100.00					100.00
Total		90.13	9.87				100.00
Western	Bagpat	94.45	5.55				100.00
	Mathura	89.48	10.52				100.00
	Moradabad	63.64	36.36				100.00
Total		81.36	18.64				100.00
Bundel-khand	Banda	100.00					100.00
	Hamirpur	95.46	4.54				100.00
	Jhansi	100.00					100.00
Total		98.60	1.40				100.00
Grand Total		89.54	10.46				100.00

Class of Society

It is found that Other Backward Classes(OBC) have dominated in the Panchayat elections held recently. Majority (6 out of 10) of the women representatives at Zila Panchayat level belong to OBC, while one fifth each belong to General and Scheduled Castes. At Kshetra Panchayat level, majority of women comes from OBC category and one third belong to the Scheduled Castes and little more than one tenth comes from General category. The similar trend is seen at Gram Panchayats level as well, where more than half of the women representatives belong to OBCs, and about two fifth's come from Scheduled Castes and less than one tenth fall under General category. A meager number of women are found from Scheduled Tribes. Balrampur (Central region) is the only district having sent women belonging to Scheduled Tribes to Gram Panchayats.

The observations indicate that representation of women in Panchayati Raj Institutions in this most populated state is coming from all castes and sections, which is a positive sign of equal representation and participation by all segments of the society.

Table 17
Class of Society
Zila Panchayat

(Percentage Distribution)

Region	*District*	*General*	*Backward*	*S.C.*	*S.T.*	*Total*
Eastern	Varanasi	25.00	75.00			100.00
	Gorakhpur		50.00	50.00		100.00
	Ballia	25.00	50.00	25.00		100.00
Total		12.50	54.17	33.33		100.00
Central	Lucknow	14.28	71.44	14.28		100.00
	Balrampur	20.00	80.00			100.00
	Sitapur	25.00	25.00	50.00		100.00
Total		20.00	55.00	25.00		100.00
Western	Bagpat	16.66	83.34			100.00
	Mathura	25.00	75.00			100.00
	Moradabad	37.50	37.50	25.00		100.00
Total		27.77	61.12	11.11		100.00
Bundel-khand	Banda	66.67	33.33			100.00
	Hamirpur a	20.00	60.00	20.00		100.00
	Jhansi		83.34	16.66		100.00
Total		29.41	58.83	11.76		100.00
Grand Total		21.51	59.98	21.51		100.00

Table 18
Class of Society
Kshetra Panchayat

(Percentage Distribution)

Region	*District*	*General*	*Backward*	*S.C.*	*S.T.*	*Total*
Eastern	Varanasi	12.50	50.00	37.50		100.00
	Gorakhpur		66.67	33.33		100.00
	Ballia	36.36	45.46	18.18		100.00
Total		14.70	55.89	29.41		100.00
Central	Lucknow	16.66	50.00	33.34		100.00
	Balrampur		61.54	38.46		100.00
	Sitapur		28.57	71.43		100.00
Total		6.68	46.66	46.66		100.00
Western	Bagpat	10.00	90.00			100.00
	Mathura	12.50	75.00	12.50		100.00
	Moradabad	16.66	50.00	33.34		100.00
Total		13.33	70.00	16.67		100.00
Bundelkhand	Banda	16.66	41.68	41.66		100.00
	Hamirpur a	30.00	40.00	30.00		100.00
	Jhansi	7.69	61.55	30.76		100.00
Total		17.14	48.58	34.28		100.00
Grand Total		12.50	54.17	33.33		100.00

Table 19
Class of Society
Gram Panchayat

(Percentage Distribution)

Region	*District*	*General*	*Backward*	*S.C.*	*S.T.*	*Total*
Eastern	Varanasi	11.76	47.07	41.17		100.00
	Gorakhpur	4.76	71.44	23.80		100.00
	Ballia	4.16	54.18	41.66		100.00
Total		6.45	58.07	35.48		100.00
Central	Lucknow	8.57	40.00	51.43		100.00
	Balrampur	22.22	33.35	27.77	16.66	100.00
	Sitapur		50.00	50.00		100.00
Total		8.64	41.97	45.69	3.70	100.00
Western	Bagpat	27.78	50.00	22.22		100.00
	Mathura	10.52	68.43	21.05		100.00
	Moradabad		63.64	36.36		100.00
Total		11.86	61.03	27.11		100.00
Bundelkhand	Banda	7.70	50.00	42.30		100.00
	Hamirpur a		40.90	59.10		100.00
	Jhansi	4.34	52.19	43.47		100.00
Total		4.24	47.88	47.88		100.00
Grand Total		7.69	51.30	39.92	1.09	100.00

Education Level

Education plays a very important role in building up the mind, personality and perception of an individual, which has an impact on the performance of his/her roles. Even in the political role it is observed that those having good education level are able to participate, socialize and perform better than those who are less educated or illiterate.

The high incidence of illiteracy among female constitutes are of the greatest barriers to their development. It limits their scope of employment training, utilization of health facilities and exercise of legal and constitutional rights.

The analysis highlights that little more than one-fourth of elected women at Zila Panchayats are illiterate and little less than them are just literate. They can read and write and have no formal educational qualifications. Where every sixth woman possesses a certificate of High School and every tenth woman has studied up to Intermediate level, more than one-tenth of elected women have obtained graduate degree and a meagre

Table 20
Education Level
Zila Panchayat

(Percentage Distribution)

Region	*District/ Age (yrs.)*	*21-25*	*25-30*	*30-35*	*35-40*	*40-45*	*45-50*	*50-55*	*55-60*	*60>*	*Total*
Eastern	Varanasi		50.00	25.00			25.00				100.00
	Gorakhpur	33.34	33.34	16.66	16.66						100.00
	Ballia	25.00		25.00	50.00						100.00
Total		25.00	25.00	20.84	25.00		4.16				100.00
Central	Lucknow		14.20		14.20	28.70	28.70		14.20		100.00
	Balrampur	80.00	20.00								100.00
	Sitapur		25.00			25.00	50.00				100.00
Total		20.00	20.00		5.00	20.00	30.00		5.00		100.00
Western	Bagpat	33.34	50.00					16.66			100.00
	Mathura		50.00	25.00				25.00			100.00
	Moradabad	62.50			37.50						100.00
Total		38.88	27.80	5.55	16.66			11.11			100.00
Bundelkhand	Banda	33.33	33.33			33.34					100.00
	Hamirpur		40.00		20.00	20.00	20.00				100.00
	Jahnsi	33.34			33.34	16.66	16.66				100.00
Total		23.69	23.69		17.34	23.52	11.76				100.00
Grand Total		26.61	24.05	7.59	16.45	10.12	11.39	2.53	1.26		100.00

Table 21
Education Level
Kshetra Panchayat

(Percentage Distribution)

Region	*District/ Age (yrs.)*	*21-25*	*25-30*	*30-35*	*35-40*	*40-45*	*45-50*	*50-55*	*55-60*	*60>*	*Total*
Eastern	Varanasi	37.50	37.50			25.00					100.00
	Gorakhpur	33.34	60.00		6.66						100.00
	Ballia		36.37	27.27	9.09	27.27					100.00
Total		23.55	47.05	8.82	5.88	14.70					100.00
Central	Lucknow	61.12	22.22	11.11	5.55						100.00
	Balrampur	92.31	7.69								100.00
	Sitapur	14.28	71.44	14.28							100.00
Total		55.57	33.33	8.88	2.22						100.00
Western	Bagpat	20.00	50.00	10.00	20.00						100.00
	Mathura	12.50	62.50	25.00							100.00
	Moradabad	41.67	50.00		8.33						100.00
Total		26.66	53.34	10.00	10.00						100.00
Bundelkhand	Banda	8.33	41.67	33.34	16.66						100.00
	Hamirpur	20.00	50.00	20.00	10.00						100.00
	Jahnsi	53.84	30.78	15.38							100.00
Total		28.60	40.00	22.83	8.57						100.00
Grand Total		35.41	42.37	12.50	6.25	3.47					100.00

Table 22
Education Level
Gram Panchayat

(Percentage Distribution)

Region	*District/ Age (yrs.)*	*21-25*	*25-30*	*30-35*	*35-40*	*40-45*	*45-50*	*50-55*	*55-60*	*60>*	*Total*
Eastern	Varanasi	41.18	41.18		5.88	11.76					100.00
	Gorakhpur	52.36	23.84	14.28	9.52						100.00
	Ballia	66.68	29.16				4.16				100.00
Total		54.87	30.64	4.83	4.83	3.22	1.61				100.00
Central	Lucknow	62.84	28.60	5.71			2.85				100.00
	Balrampur	50.00	50.00								100.00
	Sitapur		92.86	7.14							100.00
Total		38.27	55.57	4.93			1.23				100.00
Western	Bagpat	33.33	55.56	11.11							100.00
	Mathura	36.84	52.64	10.52							100.00
	Moradabad	27.27	54.55	18.18							100.00
Total		32.20	54.25	13.55							100.00
Bundelkhand	Banda	42.31	50.00		7.69						100.00
	Hamirpur	72.73	27.27								100.00
	Jahnsi	43.47	47.81	8.72							100.00
Total		52.11	42.27	2.81	2.81						100.00
Grand Total		44.32	46.17	6.22	1.83	0.73	0.73				100.00

number has either post-graduate or any other higher degree at this level.

At the Kshetra Panchayat level, the situation is totally different. More than one third of women representatives at this tier are illiterate, and about two-fifths are just literate, and another one-tenth have studied up to middle(8th)class. A meager number have earned certificates of High School and Intermediate. Surprisingly, none of the respondents was found graduate or possessing any other higher degree at this level.

The scenario in Gram Panchayats is even more pathetic. A little less than half women representatives at this level are just literate, while little less than that are totally illiterate.

Among districts, Ballia (Eastern region) and Lucknow (Central region) are the districts having elected women even with graduate degree to Gram Panchayats. It is the Eastern region of the state which has sent women with Intermediate certificate to Kshetra Panchayats. Sitapur (Central region) has sent half of the women with graduate degree to Zila Panchayat.

This shows that bloods of educationally qualified women are entering, slowly but steadily, into local political arena. Those who were probably illiterate initially made an effort to learn at least to read and write and they are now literate. Such a situation reflects that educational level of elected women in Panchayati Raj Institutions in Uttar Pradesh, which is at lower pedestal of female literacy in the country, is quite good.

It is a clear evidence of women with good and high education entering into their new avatar as people's representatives. Such educated women representatives would be able to perform better and participate actively in decision making at local level.

It is observed that those women representatives who are just literate and have low education level are found to be unclear about their roles and responsibilities as people's representatives and so are more dependent on their husband and other male family members for helping in discharging their official functions. Low education and ignorance about their roles and responsibilities and also that of the Panchayats create low self-esteem and lack of confidence among women representatives.

Place of Birth

It was further aimed to know the place of birth of the women representatives. It was in tune to assess the awareness level among rural folks about their new constitutional mandates. The analysis was also made to establish the relationship of place of birth with their thanking pattern.

Table 23
Place of Birth
Zila Panchayat

(Percentage Distribution)

Region	*District*	*Rural*	*Semi Urban*	*Urban*	*Total*
Eastern	Varanasi	50.00	25.00	25.00	100.00
	Gorakhpur	50.00	50.00		100.00
	Ballia	25.00	50.00	25.00	100.00
Total		41.66	45.84	12.50	100.00
Central	Lucknow	28.57	42.86	28.57	100.00
	Balrampur	80.00	20.00		100.00
	Sitapur	25.00	50.00	25.00	100.00
Total		40.00	40.00	20.00	100.00
Western	Bagpat	50.00	33.34	16.66	100.00
	Mathura		75.00	25.00	100.00
	Moradabad	37.50	50.00	12.50	100.00
Total		33.34	50.00	16.66	100.00
Bundelkhand	Banda	66.67	33.33		100.00
	Hamirpur	20.00	60.00	20.00	100.00
	Jhansi	33.34	16.66	50.00	100.00
Total		41.19	35.29	23.52	100.00
Grand Total		39.24	43.04	17.72	100.00

It is a well-established fact that level of literacy is directly related to place of birth or stay. The women having born and brought up in urban or semi-urban areas are found educationally higher than those born in rural areas. It is also observed that more than one third (39.24 percent) women representatives at Zila Panchayats have their root in villages, against the majority having been born in semi-urban or urban areas. It is understandable at Zila Panchayat level as district headquarters are mostly urban centres.In Kshetra Panchayats seven out of ten women were reported born in rural areas and about one-fourth of them in semi-urban areas. Surprisingly, one tenth of women representing in Gram Panchayats were born in semi-urban areas.

Eastern region tops the list in sending women with their roots in semi-urban areas. Gorakhpur (Eastern region) is the district which elects more than one third women born in semi-urban areas, followed by Ballia (Eastern region) and Mathura(Western region) districts.

Table 24
Place of Birth
Kshetra Panchayat

(Percentage Distribution)

Region	*District*	*Rural*	*Semi Urban*	*Urban*	*Total*
Eastern	Varanasi	100.00			100.00
	Gorakhpur	60.00	40.00		100.00
	Ballia	54.55	45.45		100.00
Total		67.55	32.35		100.00
Central	Lucknow	77.79	16.66	5.55	100.00
	Balrampur	100.00			100.00
	Sitapur	100.00			100.00
Total		91.12	6.66	2.22	100.00
Western	Bagpat	40.00	60.00		100.00
	Mathura	50.00	50.00		100.00
	Moradabad	83.34	16.66		100.00
Total		60.00	40.00		100.00
Bundelkhand	Banda	41.66	58.34		100.00
	Hamirpur	90.00	10.00		100.00
	Jhansi	76.93	23.07		100.00
Total		68.58	31.42		100.00
Grand Total		73.62	25.69	0.69	100.00

Table 25
Place of Birth
Gram Panchayat

(Percentage Distribution)

Region	*District*	*Rural*	*Semi Urban*	*Urban*	*Total*
Eastern	Varanasi	82.36	17.64		100.00
	Gorakhpur	61.90	38.10		100.00
	Ballia	79.17	20.83		100.00
Total		74.20	25.80		100.00
Central	Lucknow	91.43	8.57		100.00
	Balrampur	88.89	11.11		100.00

Contd.

Region	*District*	*Rural*	*Semi Urban*	*Urban*	*Total*
	Sitapur	100.00			100.00
Total		93.83	6.17		100.00
Western	Bagpat	88.89	11.11		100.00
	Mathura	84.22	15.78		100.00
	Moradabad	100.00			100.00
Total		91.53	8.47		100.00
Bundelkhand	Banda	92.31	7.69		100.00
	Hamirpur		100.00		100.00
	Jhansi		100.00		100.00
Total		97.19	2.81		100.00
Grand Total		89.75	10.25		100.00

This needs further probing, as it provides more scope for proxy representation. Eastern region with comparatively low literacy may be the victim of male representing women who are residing in semi-urban areas with their family.

Employment

The 73rd Constitution Amendment Act makes provision for reservation of seats for women belonging to vulnerable sections of society as well. It is seen that poor women are invariably involved in economic activities, but they are invisible workers. Rural women in general may be put in three main groups of women as self employed, wage earners or impound family helpers. The women's personal contribution gets merged with the family and becomes invisible.

In this context the elected women respondents were asked to reveal their employment pattern. The employed and professionals were further asked to divulge the nature of their employment. The responses (Table-29, 30, 31) are quite revealing. Almost all women members of Zila Panchayats are housewives. Lucknow (Central region) and Hamirpur (Bundelkhand), however, present a pleasant surprise. In Lucknow more than two-fifths of Zila Panchayat women representatives claim to be full time politicians, whereas in Hamirpur every fifth woman claims so.

At the Kshetra Panchayat level more or less same trend is seen. In Lucknow and Balrampur (both Central region) only, some full time politicians among women are found elected.

Table 26
Employment Pattern of Women Representatives
Zila Panchayat

(Percentage Distribution)

Region	*District*	*Self Emp-loyed*	*Profe-ssional*	*Indus-trialists*	*Full Time Politician*	*House Wife*	*Agri-culture*	*Labour*	*Total*
Eastern	Varanasi					100.00			100.00
	Gorakhpur					100.00			100.00
	Ballia					100.00			100.00
Total						100.00			100.00
Central	Lucknow				42.85	57.15			100.00
	Balrampur					100.00			100.00
	Sitapur					100.00			100.00
Total					15.00	85.00			100.00
Western	Bagpat					100.00			100.00
	Mathura					100.00			100.00
	Moradabad					100.00			100.00
Total						100.00			100.00
Bundelkhand	Banda					100.00			100.00
	Hamirpur				20.00	80.00			100.00
	Jhansi					100.00			100.00
Total					5.88	94.12			100.00
Grand Total					5.06	94.94			100.00

Table 27
Employment Pattern of Women Representatives
Kshetra Panchayat

(Percentage Distribution)

Region	*District*	*Self Emp-loyed*	*Profe-ssional*	*Indus-trialists*	*Full Time Politician*	*House Wife*	*Agri-culture*	*Labour*	*Total*
Eastern	Varanasi	12.50				87.50			100.00
	Gorakhpur					100.00			100.00
	Ballia					100.00			100.00
Total		2.94				97.06			100.00
Central	Lucknow			5.55		94.45			100.00
	Balrampur			7.69		92.31			100.00
	Sitapur					100.00			100.00
Total				4.44		95.56			100.00
Western	Bagpat					100.00			100.00
	Mathura					100.00			100.00
	Moradabad					100.00			100.00
Total						100.00			100.00
Bundelkhand	Banda					100.00			100.00
	Hamirpur					80.00	20.00		100.00
	Jhansi					92.31	7.69		100.00
Total						91.43	8.57		100.00
Grand Total		0.69		1.38		95.85	2.08		100.00

Varanasi is the only district which has sent about one–eighth self-employed women. Bundelkhand region has the distinction of sending some women involved in agriculture. Hamirpur in the region has contributed one fifth women agriculturists.

In respect of Gram Panchayats, the number of full time politician women is meager. Besides women associated with agricultural activities, a few labour women have also joined the mainstream. Banda (Bundelkhand) and Gorakhpur (Eastern) districts have sent good number of women involved in farming. Hamirpur (13.63 per cent), Ballia (8.33 per cent) and Jhansi (4.34 per cent) have witnessed labour women having been elected to Gram Panchayats.

The analysis reflects that the highest number of women representatives are found to be housewives, followed by a good number of them as full time politicians. None of the women respondents is employed professionally. Self-employment probably means the male counterparts (husband) performing business activities in the name of women or these women help their husbands in doing business activities.

The elected women practicing as full time politician are those on whose behalf the male counterparts are doing politics. This reflects the inherent tendency of educated women to have an independent and individual social personality.

At this juncture it was thought imperative to get more information about husbands of elected women. The data reflect that husbands of about one- fourth of elected women representatives at Zila Panchayat level are self-employed. Equal number of women (31.64 per cent each) at this tier have their husbands doing some business or involved in agriculture. Very few women have employed or industrialist husbands.

Interestingly, at Kshetra Panchayat level,the trend is towards attracting women from the families depending on agriculture or allied activities. More than half of the women at this level of Panchayats have farmer husbands. The husbands of good number of women (7.63 per cent) are working even as labour. Balrampur (30.76 per cent) is found at the top in sending labour women, followed by Gorakhpur and Hamirpur (each subscribing one-fifth of women representatives). A good

Table 28
Employment Pattern of Women Representatives
Gram Panchayat

(Percentage Distribution)

Region	*District*	*Self Emp-loyed*	*Profe-ssional*	*Indus-trialists*	*Full Time Politician*	*House Wife*	*Agri-culture*	*Labour*	*Total*
Eastern	Varanasi				5.88	94.12			100.00
	Gorakhpur					85.72	14.28		100.00
	Ballia				4.16	83.35	4.16	8.33	100.00
Total					3.22	87.11	6.45	3.22	100.00
Central	Lucknow					100.00			100.00
	Balrampur				5.55	94.45			100.00
	Sitapur					100.00			100.00
Total					1.23	98.77			100.00
Western	Bagpat					100.00			100.00
	Mathura				10.52	89.48			100.00
	Moradabad					100.00			100.00
Total					3.38	96.62			100.00
Bundelkhand	Banda					76.93	23.07		100.00
	Hamirpur					81.83	4.54	13.63	100.00
	Jhansi					91.32	4.34	4.34	100.00
Total						83.11	11.26	5.63	100.00
Grand Total					1.83	91.59	4.39	2.19	100.00

number of women are found having husbands employed professionally. Mathura and Lucknow contribute such women in substantial number.

The scenario in Gram Panchayats is quite revealing. About three-fourths of women representatives at this level are purely from rural background. Their husbands are earning their livelihoods by farming or doing labour. Sitapur and Moradabad districts have sent absolute number of women whose husbands are agriculturists, followed by Mathura, Bagpat, Lucknow and Ballia districts. About one-seventh of women representatives have self–employed husbands.

It clearly signifies that the elected women belonging to families categorized either as self employed or doing some petty business, in real sense, do not have their own independent business but term the employment of their husband as their own. In the circumstances, women representatives might not feel illegal to allow their male counterparts to perform their new role as politician as well. They seem to feel their (wife-husband) role interchangeable.

Income Level

As regards income level, majority of the women representatives belong to middle class family. Varanasi and Balrampur are the only districts which have sent middle and upper middle class of women to their Zila Panchayats. At this level of Panchayats, the women respondents are almost equally divided between income-group of less than Rs. 5000 per month (48.10 per cent) and between Rs. 5000 to Rs. 10,000 (45.56 per cent). The respective figures at Kshetra Panchayats level are 87.50 per cent and 11.80 per cent, as against 91.57 per cent and 6.22 per cent at Gram Panchayat level.

It has been that in case of husband being the head of the family, he dominates in all matter and all family decisions are taken by him though claimed to be in consultation with his wife.

Since status of the family is determined by the occupation and income of the head of the family, it is seen that maximum women representatives belong to families having good or high status but most of them do not have political background.

Table 29
Husband's Employment Pattern
Zila Panchayat

(Percentage Distribution)

Region	*District*	*Self Employed*	*Professional*	*Businessman*	*Industria-*	*Agriculturelist*	*Labour*	*Not-Applicable (Respondent Widow)*	*Total*
Eastern	Varanasi	100.00							100.00
	Gorakhpur	16.66		16.66		66.68			100.00
	Ballia			50.00		50.00			100.00
Total		25.00		25.00		50.00			100.00
Central	Lucknow		28.56	14.28	28.58	28.58			100.00
	Balrampur	40.00		40.00		20.00			100.00
	Sitapur	75.00				25.00			100.00
Total		40.00	10.00	15.00	10.00	25.00			100.00
Western	Bagpat	16.66		50.00		16.66		16.68	100.00
	Mathura	50.00	25.00	25.00					100.00
	Moradabad	12.50		62.50		25.00			100.00
Total		22.22	5.55	50.00		16.66		5.57	100.00
Bundelkhand	Banda	16.66		50.00		33.34			100.00
	Hamirpur	20.00		40.00		20.00		20.00	100.00
	Jhansi	16.66	16.66	33.34		33.34			100.00
Total		17.64	5.88	41.17		29.41		5.90	100.00
Grand Total		26.58	5.06	31.64	2.53	31.64		2.55	100.00

Table 30
Husband's Employment Pattern
Kshetra Panchayat

(Percentage Distribution)

Region	*District*	*Self Employed*	*Professional*	*Businessman*	*Industria-*	*Agriculturelist*	*Labour*	*Not-Applicable (Respondent Widow)*	*Total*
Eastern	Varanasi	37.50				50.00		12.50	100.00
	Gorakhpur	20.00		13.33		46.67	20.00		100.00
	Ballia	18.18		18.18		54.55	9.09		100.00
Total		23.52		11.76		50.00	11.76	2.96	100.00
Central	Lucknow		22.22	27.78		50.00			100.00
	Balrampur	15.38	7.69	7.69		38.48	30.76		100.00
	Sitapur	14.28				85.72			100.00
Total		8.88	11.11	13.33		57.80	8.88		100.00
Western	Bagpat	50.00				50.00			100.00
	Mathura	50.00	25.00			25.00			100.00
	Moradabad	25.00		8.33		66.67			100.00
Total		40.00	6.67	3.33		50.00			100.00
Bundelkhand	Banda	33.37		16.66		50.00			100.00
	Hamirpur			30.00		50.00	20.00		100.00
	Jhansi	7.69		7.69		76.93	7.69		100.00
Total		14.28		17.15		60.00	8.57		100.00
Grand Total		20.13	4.86	11.88		54.86	7.63	0.64	100.00

Table 31
Husband's Employment Pattern
Gram Panchayat

(Percentage Distribution)

Region	*District*	*Self Emp-loyed*	*Profe-ssional*	*Busine-ssman*	*Indus-tria-*	*Agri-culture list*	*Labour*	*Not-Applicable (Respondent Widow)*	*Total*
Eastern	Varanasi	23.52		11.76		58.84	5.88		100.00
	Gorakhpur	14.29		28.57		28.57	28.57		100.00
	Ballia	12.50		8.33		62.50	12.50	4.16	100.00
Total		16.12		16.12		50.00	16.12	1.64	100.00
Central	Lucknow	14.28		11.42		68.57		5.73	100.00
	Balrampur	22.22				38.88	33.33	5.57	100.00
	Sitapur	14.28				85.72			100.00
Total		16.04		4.93		67.90	7.40	3.73	100.00
Western	Bagpat	27.77				66.68	5.55		100.00
	Mathura	21.05				73.68		5.27	100.00
	Moradabad	9.09		4.54		81.83	4.54		100.00
Total		18.64		1.69		74.57	3.38	1.72	100.00
Bundelkhand	Banda	23.07				53.86	23.07		100.00
	Hamirpur	22.72				31.81	45.47		100.00
	Jhansi	13.04				56.53	30.43		100.00
Total		19.71				47.90	32.39		100.00
Grand Total		17.58		5.49		60.07	15.01	1.85	100.00

Table 32
Family Income
Zila Panchayat

(Percentage Distribution)

Region	*District*	*< 5000*	*5000-10000*	*10000-15000*	*>15000*	*No Response*	*Total*
Eastern	Varanasi		50.00		50.00		100.00
	Gorakhpur	66.67	33.33				100.00
	Ballia		75.00	25.00			100.00
Total		58.34	33.33		8.33		100.00
Central	Lucknow	28.57	71.43				100.00
	Balarampur	20.00	60.00	20.00			100.00
	Sitapur	50.00	50.00				100.00
Total		35.00	60.00	5.00			100.00
Western	Bagpat	50.00	33.33			16.67	100.00
	Mathura	25.00	75.00				100.00
	Moradabad	62.50	37.50				100.00
Total		50.00	44.44			5.56	100.00
Bundel-khand	Banda	83.34	16.66				100.00
	Hamirpur	20.00	60.00			20.00	100.00
	Jhansi	33.33	66.67				100.00
Total		47.05	47.05			5.90	100.00
Grand Total		48.10	45.56	1.26	2.53	2.55	100.00

Table 33
Family Income
Kshetra Panchayat

(Percentage Distribution)

Region	*District*	*< 5000*	*5000-10000*	*10000-15000*	*>15000*	*No Response*	*Total*
Eastern	Varanasi	87.50				12.50	100.00
	Gorakhpur	100.00					100.00
	Ballia	100.00					100.00
Total		97.05				2.95	100.00
Central	Lucknow	83.34	16.66				100.00
	Balarampur	92.31	7.69				100.00
	Sitapur	100.00					100.00
Total		91.12	8.88				100.00
Western	Bagpat	90.00	10.00				100.00
	Mathura	62.50	37.50				100.00
	Moradabad	83.34	16.66				100.00
Total		80.00	20.00				100.00

Contd.

Region	*District*	*< 5000*	*5000-10000*	*10000-15000*	*>15000*	*No Response*	*Total*
Bundel-khand	Banda	100.00					100.00
	Hamirpur	70.00	30.00				100.00
	Jhansi	69.24	30.76				100.00
Total		80.00	20.00				100.00
Grand Total		87.50	11.80			0.70	100.00

Table 34
Family Income
Gram Panchayat

(Percentage Distribution)

Region	*District*	*< 5000*	*5000-10000*	*10000-15000*	*>15000*	*No Response*	*Total*
Eastern	Varanasi	76.48	17.64	5.88			100.00
	Gorakhpur	90.48	9.52				100.00
	Ballia	91.66	4.16			4.18	100.00
Total		87.10	9.67	1.61		1.62	100.00
Central	Lucknow	88.57	5.71			5.72	100.00
	Balarampur	88.88	5.55			5.57	100.00
	Sitapur	100.00					100.00
Total		92.59	3.70			3.71	100.00
Western	Bagpat	83.34	16.66				100.00
	Mathura	78.94	15.78			5.28	100.00
	Moradabad	95.46	4.54				100.00
Total		86.44	11.86			1.70	100.00
Bundel-khand	Banda	100.00					100.00
	Hamirpur	100.00					100.00
	Jhansi	95.66	4.34				100.00
Total		98.60	1.40				100.00
Grand Total		91.57	6.22	0.36		1.85	100.00

Head of the Family

As regards head of the family, the traditional system of male dominance prevails even after women earning independent income and performing political role. It is observed that majority of the families of women representatives are headed by their husbands. Surprisingly, lower the tier of Panchayats, more the cases of husbands playing the dominance. Quite good number of households is found headed by in-laws. A reverse trend is seen in this case. Lower the tier, lower the number of families headed by in-laws.

Significantly, very few number of women are found heading their families. Hamirpur (20.00 per cent) and Bagpat (16.66 per cent) at Zila Panchayat level; and Varanasi (5.88 per cent), Lucknow (5.71 per cent), Balrampur (5.55 per cent) and Mathura (5.26 per cent) at Gram Panchayats level, have sent women heading their families.

It is of some significance to witness the trend of woman representatives herself heading their families, but this includes mostly those women who have lost their husband and in-laws and are widows.

Table 35
Head of the Family
Zila Panchayat

(Percentage Distribution)

Region	*District*	*Self*	*Husband*	*Father/ Mother/ In-laws*	*Total*
Eastern	Varanasi		100.00		100.00
	Gorakhpur		83.34	16.66	100.00
	Ballia		75.00	25.00	100.00
Total			83.34	16.66	100.00
Central	Lucknow		42.85	57.15	100.00
	Balrampur		60.00	40.00	100.00
	Sitapur		75.00	25.00	100.00
Total		60.00	40.00	100.00	
Western	Bagpat	16.66	50.00	33.34	100.00
	Mathura		100.00		100.00
	Moradabad		50.00	50.00	100.00
Total		5.55	61.12	33.33	100.00
Bundelkhand	Banda		66.67	33.33	100.00
	Hamirpur	20.00	80.00		100.00
	Jhansi		66.67	33.33	100.00
Total		5.88	70.60	23.52	100.00
Grand Total		2.53	69.63	27.84	100.00

The income of the family is also an important determinant of the status of the family as well as extent of conflicts in role performance by women representatives. It is observed that where family income is good, the problems are less and there are less chances of conflict between husband and wife in relation to financial matters and this affects their role performance as well.

Table 36
Head of the Family
Kshetra Panchayat

(Percentage Distribution)

Region	*District*	*Self*	*Husband*	*Father/ Mother/ In-laws*	*Total*
Eastern	Varanasi		87.50	12.50	100.00
	Gorakhpur		100.00		100.00
	Ballia		81.82	18.18	100.00
Total			91.18	8.82	100.00
Central	Lucknow		72.23	27.77	100.00
	Balrampur		69.24	30.76	100.00
	Sitapur		100.00		100.00
Total			80.00	20.00	100.00
Western	Bagpat		40.00	60.00	100.00
	Mathura		100.00		100.00
	Moradabad		66.67	33.33	100.00
Total			66.67	33.33	100.00
Bundelkhand	Banda		66.67	33.33	100.00
	Hamirpur		80.00	20.00	100.00
	Jhansi		92.31	7.69	100.00
Total			80.00	20.00	100.00
Grand Total			79.87	20.13	100.00

Table 37
Head of the Family
Gram Panchayat

(Percentage Distribution)

Region	*District*	*Self*	*Husband*	*Father/ Mother/ In-laws*	*Total*
Eastern	Varanasi	5.88	76.48	17.64	100.00
	Gorakhpur		61.91	38.09	100.00
	Ballia	4.16	87.51	8.33	100.00
Total		3.22	75.82	20.96	100.00
Central	Lucknow	5.71	60.00	34.29	100.00
	Balrampur	5.55	72.23	22.22	100.00
	Sitapur		92.86	7.14	100.00

Contd.

Region	*District*	*Self*	*Husband*	*Father/ Mother/ In-laws*	*Total*
Total		3.70	74.08	22.22	100.00
Western	Bagpat		77.78	4.72	100.00
	Mathura	5.26	78.96	15.78	100.00
	Moradabad		95.46	4.54	100.00
Total		1.69	84.76	13.55	100.00
Bundelkhand	Banda		69.24	30.76	100.00
	Hamirpur		86.37	13.63	100.00
	Jhansi		82.61	17.39	100.00
Total			78.88	21.12	100.00
Grand Total		2.19	78.03	19.78	100.00

In sum, the respondents of the study belong to different strata of society. The representative character of respondents assimilates various facets of society, numerous familial characteristics and personal traits.

APPENDIX

Panchayats-wise Coverage

Region	*District*	*Zila Panchayat*	*Kshetra Panchayat*	*Gram Panchayat*	*Total*
Eastern	Varanasi	10	36	34	80
	Gorakhpur	20	30	42	92
	Ballia	18	22	40	80
Total		48	88	116	252
Central	Lucknow	10	36	40	86
	Balrampur	10	26	36	72
	Sitapur	20	28	42	90
Total		40	90	118	248
Western	Bagpat	7	31	36	74
	Mathura	10	26	38	74
	Moradabad	18	34	44	96
Total		35	91	118	244
Bundelkhand	Banda	12	44	52	108
	Hamirpur	10	25	40	75
	Jhansi	7	27	42	76
Total		29	96	134	259
Grand Total		152	365	486	1003

3

CONFLICTS AND ADJUSTMENTS IN POLITICAL ROLE

Following Ratter's (1970) expectancy theory we can assume that working women develop certain expectations from job and family. These expectations from job/profession may be of economic or personal gain. Similarly, while playing different roles of wife or mother, a woman may develop expectancies that her husband as an equal or true partner may treat her or she may be given full respect and protection. When the fulfillments of her expectancies are not to the amount of ideal-self, she feels frustration. In other words the extent of discrepancy between the two i.e. the amount of expectancy and the amount of the fulfillment of expectancy may be an index of psychological deficit which may lead to role conflict. The above facts have been supported by Hall & Gordon (1974) and Kapur (1974). Kapur (1974) found a vast gap between what privileges as an earning member of the family a woman expected and the privileges she in reality enjoyed–the gap affected the family and emotional adjustment of the workingwoman.

Role conflict situations may arise from a variety of circumstances and the contents in which the role is performed will be an important determinant.

Whatever may be the nature of conflict the consequence is always unhappiness and suffering. Conflict keeps people far from each other and everyone loses other's help and assistance without which it is not possible to run a smooth life. It is not that only the focal person suffers. Everyone directly or indirectly associated with the focal person is affected with the conflict, the consequence of which is always harmful. But conflict can be resolved through a number of ways. By adopting any one or more measures depending upon the situation, conflict can be resolved in order to make proper adjustment in every sphere of life.

The situation on role conflict and role strain tends support to the fact that tolerance level of the strain might bear some relationship with personality of the role players (Sinha, 1973). If the conflict is deeply felt, it may reflect in lack of adjustment either in family, in social and emotional life (Burchard 1954, Cousia, 1951) or in job setting (Kahn, 1964). The adjustment process also by its inherent nature involves active coping with internal and external stressful conflicts, frustration, etc. The individual has to respond in such a way that he becomes more adequately and more effectively related to self and environment (Phadke & Kulkarni, 1977). Investigations suggest that working wives are less adjusted than housewives. Chakraborty (1977) and Kapur (1969) find that highest number of working mothers experience role conflict because of their limited physical capacity and energy and stigma.

ENTERING INTO ROLE

On being asked to divulge the reasons for joining the politics, about two-fifths of women representatives feel that they had no choice of their own, and political role was imposed upon them by their family members. Since 73rd Amendment to the Indian Constitution provides for not less than one-third of seats reserved for women, those local leaders, old politicians and influential persons interested in politics are forced to place women candidates. In such cases women are found to be mostly disinterested and ignorant about their political role as a representative and the male members handle the entire official works. But about one-tenth of women joined politics because they wanted a career in politics. These women representatives were found to be quite active in their political

Table 1
Reasons for Joining Politics
Zila Panchayat

(Percentage Distribution)

Region	*District*	*For Financial Help*	*For Independence*	*For Good Status*	*For a Career in Politics*	*To Utilize Education*	*Imposed by Male/ Family Members*	*Others (specify) To Maintain Family Tradition*	*Total*
Eastern	Varanasi			50.00			50.00		100.00
	Gorakhpur			33.33			66.67		100.00
	Ballia			50.00			50.00		100.00
Total				41.66			58.34		100.00
Central	Lucknow			14.28	28.57		14.28	42.87	100.00
	Balrampur			40.00			40.00	20.00	100.00
	Sitapur						62.50	37.50	100.00
Total				15.00	10.00		40.00	35.00	100.00
Western	Bagpat			16.66	16.66		33.34	33.34	100.00
	Mathura			25.00	75.00				100.00
	Moradabad			25.00	25.00		12.50	37.50	100.00
Total				22.22	33.35		16.66	27.77	100.00
Bundelkhand	Banda			33.34			16.66	50.00	100.00
	Hamirpur			40.00	20.00		20.00	20.00	100.00
	Jhansi			16.66	50.02		16.66	16.66	100.00
Total				29.43	23.52		17.64	29.41	100.00
Grand Total				27.84	15.18		35.47	21.51	100.00

Table 2
Reasons for Joining Politics
Kshetra Panchayat

(Percentage Distribution)

Region	*District*	*For Financial Help*	*For Independence*	*For Good Status*	*For a Career in Politics*	*To Utilize Education*	*Imposed by Male/ Family Members*	*Others (specify) To Maintain Family Tradition*	*Total*
Eastern	Varanasi			25.00	12.50		62.50		100.00
	Gorakhpur			26.66			73.34		100.00
	Ballia			54.55			18.18	27.27	100.00
Total				35.29	2.91		52.98	8.82	100.00
Central	Lucknow	5.55		27.77	5.55		27.77	33.36	100.00
	Balrampur			46.16			38.46	15.38	100.00
	Sitapur						78.58	21.42	100.00
Total		2.22		24.44	2.22		46.68	24.44	100.00
Western	Bagpat			20.00			30.00	50.00	100.00
	Mathura				12.50	50.00	25.00	12.50	100.00
	Moradabad			16.66	16.66		25.00	41.68	100.00
Total				16.66	20.00		26.66	36.68	100.00
Bundelkhand	Banda			50.02	16.66		16.66	16.66	100.00
	Hamirpur						70.00	30.00	100.00
	Jhansi	7.69		7.69	30.76		15.38	38.48	100.00
Total		2.85		20.00	17.14		31.44	28.57	100.00
Grand Total		1.38		24.30	9.72		40.30	24.30	100.00

Table 3
Reasons for Joining Politics
Gram Panchayat

(Percentage Distribution)

Region	District	For Financial Help	For Independence	For Good Status	For a Career in Politics	To Utilize Education	Imposed by Male/ Family Members	Others (specify) To Maintain Family Tradition	Total
Eastern	Varanasi			23.52			64.72	11.76	100.00
	Gorakhpur	28.57		14.29			28.57	28.57	100.00
	Ballia	16.66			8.33		41.68	33.33	100.00
Total		16.12		11.29	3.22		43.57	25.80	100.00
Central	Lucknow	8.57		28.57	8.57	2.85	34.30	17.14	100.00
	Balrampur			44.46			38.88	16.66	100.00
	Sitapur			17.85			60.73	21.42	100.00
Total		3.70		28.39	3.70	1.23	44.47	18.51	100.00
Western	Bagpat			38.89	11.11		38.89	11.11	100.00
	Mathura			5.26	47.38		26.31	21.05	100.00
	Moradabad			13.63	9.09		31.81	45.47	100.00
Total				18.64	22.03		32.22	27.11	100.00
Bundelkhand	Banda			23.07	7.69		38.48	30.76	100.00
	Hamirpur			22.72			54.56	22.72	100.00
	Jhansi			17.39	21.73		39.15	21.73	100.00
Total				21.12	9.85		43.68	25.35	100.00
Grand Total		4.76		20.51	9.15	0.36	41.42	23.80	100.00

role. There are women in significant number who entered in this arena for gaining social status and, a negligible number of women wanted to utilize their education. Pleasantly, every seventh woman representative is there for rendering social services. (Tables 1, 2, 3)

As regards their having been in politics, eight out of ten women representatives have first time entered into politics. There are about one tenth of respondents who have been in politics for one to five years. These women representatives are found more active and confident than fellow women who are first timers. Those who are new to this role experience more conflict because they are not yet adapted to their new role.

Table 4
Experience in Politics
Zila Panchayat

(Percentage Distribution)

Region	*District*	*I[st] Time*	*1 – 5 Years*	*5 – 10 Years*	*10 – 15 Years*	*Total*
Eastern	Varanasi	100.00				100.00
	Gorakhpur	83.34	16.66			100.00
	Ballia	100.00				100.00
Total		91.67	8.33			100.00
Central	Lucknow	71.44	14.28		14.28	100.00
	Balrampur	40.00	60.00			100.00
	Sitapur	75.00		25.00		100.00
Total		65.00	20.00	10.00	5.00	100.00
Western	Bagpat	83.34	16.66			100.00
	Mathura	75.00	25.00			100.00
	Moradabad	100.00				100.00
Total		88.89	11.11			100.00
Bundelkhand	Banda	83.84	16.66			100.00
	Hamirpur	60.00	40.00			100.00
	Jhansi	100.00				100.00
Total		82.36	17.64			100.00
Grand Total		82.29	13.92	2.53	1.26	100.00

Women having been in politics were further asked to divulge the capacity in which they had earned political experience. At the Zila Panchayats level none of the women was Adhyaksha of Zila Panchayat but a few were Pramukh of Kshetra Panchayat and one fifth were Pradhan of Gram

Panchayats, the majority were members of either Panchayats. Lucknow is the only district having elevated half of the past Pramukhs, while Balrampur (one-third) and Sitapur (half) have promoted their Pradhans to this level. Majority of the past members in many districts got re-elected.

Table 5
Experience in Politics
Kshetra Panchayat

(Percentage Distribution)

Region	*District*	*Ist Time*	*1 – 5 Years*	*5 – 10 Years*	*10 – 15 Years*	*Total*
Eastern	Varanasi	37.50	62.50			100.00
	Gorakhpur	80.00	20.00			100.00
	Ballia	81.82	18.18			100.00
Total		70.59	29.41			100.00
Central	Lucknow	83.34	16.66			100.00
	Balrampur	76.93	23.07			100.00
	Sitapur	100.00	–			100.00
Total		86.67	13.33			100.00
Western	Bagpat	90.00	10.00			100.00
	Mathura	100.00	–			100.00
	Moradabad	66.67	33.33			100.00
Total		83.34	16.66			100.00
Bundelkhand	Banda	75.00	25.00			100.00
	Hamirpur	80.00	20.00			100.00
	Jhansi	69.24	30.76			100.00
Total		74.29	25.71			100.00
Grand Total		79.17	20.83			100.00

Table 6
Experience in Politics
Gram Panchayat

(Percentage Distribution)

Region	*District*	*Ist Time*	*1 – 5 Years*	*5 – 10 Years*	*10 – 15 Years*	*Total*
Eastern	Varanasi	47.05	52.95			100.00
	Gorakhpur	95.24	4.76			100.00
	Ballia	80.00	20.00			100.00
Total		77.42	22.58			100.00
Central	Lucknow	65.72	34.28			100.00
	Balrampur	72.23	27.77			100.00
	Sitapur	100.00	–			100.00

Contd.

Region	*District*	*Ist Time*	*1 – 5 Years*	*5 – 10 Years*	*10 – 15 Years*	*Total*
Total		79.02	20.98			100.00
Western	Bagpat	77.78	22.22			100.00
	Mathura	100.00	–			100.00
	Moradabad	90.91	9.09			100.00
Total		89.84	10.16			100.00
Bundelkhand	Banda	84.62	15.38			100.00
	Hamirpur	81.82	18.18			100.00
	Jhansi	86.96	13.04			100.00
Total		84.51	15.49			100.00
Grand Total		82.42	17.58			100.00

At other tiers also majority of the women got re-elected. Hamirpur re-elected half of its Past Pramukhs, while Bagpat returned half of its old Pradhans.

Table 7
Earlier Political Post
Zila Panchayat

(Percentage Distribution)

Region	*District*	*Pradhan*	*Pramukh*	*Adhyaksha*	*Member*	*Nominated Member*	*Total*
Eastern	Varanasi						
	Gorakhpur				100.00		100.00
	Ballia						–
Total					100.00		100.00
Central	Lucknow			50.00	50.00		100.00
	Balrampur		66.67		33.33		100.00
	Sitapur		50.00		50.00		100.00
Total			42.87	14.28	42.85		100.00
Western	Bagpat				100.00		100.00
	Mathura				100.00		100.00
	Moradabad						–
Total					100.00		100.00
Bundelkhand	Banda				100.00		100.00
	Hamirpur				100.00		100.00
	Jhansi						–
Total					100.00		100.00
Grand Total			21.42	7.14	71.44		100.00

Table 8
Earlier Political Post
Kshetra Panchayat

(Percentage Distribution)

Region	*District*	*Pradhan*	*Pramukh*	*Adhyaksha*	*Member*	*Nominated Member*	*Total*
Eastern	Varanasi				100.00		100.00
	Gorakhpur				100.00		100.00
	Ballia				100.00		100.00
Total					100.00		100.00
Central	Lucknow				100.00		100.00
	Balrampur				100.00		100.00
	Sitapur						–
Total					100.00		100.00
Western	Bagpat				100.00		100.00
	Mathura						–
	Moradabad				100.00		100.00
Total					100.00		100.00
Bundelkhand	Banda				100.00		100.00
	Hamirpur		50.00		50.00		100.00
	Jhansi				100.00		100.00
Total			11.11		88.89		100.00
Grand Total			3.33		96.67		100.00

Table 9
Earlier Political Post
Gram Panchayat

(Percentage Distribution)

Region	*District*	*Pradhan*	*Pramukh*	*Adhyaksha*	*Member*	*Nominated Member*	*Total*
Eastern	Varanasi	11.11			88.89		100.00
	Gorakhpur				100.00		100.00
	Ballia				100.00		100.00
Total		7.14			92.86		100.00
Central	Lucknow				100.00		100.00
	Balrampur	20.00			80.00		100.00
	Sitapur						–
Total		5.88			94.12		100.00
Western	Bagpat	50.00			50.00		100.00
	Mathura						–
	Moradabad				100.00		100.00

Contd.

Region	*District*	*Pradhan*	*Pramukh*	*Adhyaksha*	*Member*	*Nominated Member*	*Total*
Total		33.33			66.67		100.00
Bundelkhand	Banda				100.00		100.00
	Hamirpur				100.00		100.00
	Jhansi				100.00		100.00
Total					100.00		100.00
Grand Total		8.33			91.67		100.00

Commanding Respect

As regards commanding respects in their Panchayats, the responses varied at every level. In Zila Panchayats a little less than one-third of women feel to be liked by all, the number of such women is about one tenth at Kshetra Panchayats level and further less at Gram Panchayat level. Significantly, every four out of ten women representatives in Gram Panchayats feel isolated. Surprisingly, data reflect that higher the tier of Panchayats, more the respect to elected women representatives. This illustrates the biasness towards women in rural areas, may be because of low literacy of rural Indian traditions.

Table 10
Respect in Panchayats
Zila Panchayat

(Percentage Distribution)

Region	*District*	*All Like*	*Most Like*	*Some Like*	*Indifferent*	*Total*
Eastern	Varanasi	100.00				100.00
	Gorakhpur	16.66	16.67	50.00	16.67	100.00
	Ballia	25.00		50.00	25.00	100.00
Total		33.33	8.33	41.68	16.66	100.00
Central	Lucknow	57.15	14.28	28.57		100.00
	Balrampur			80.00	20.00	100.00
	Sitapur		25.00	75.00		100.00
Total		20.00	15.00	60.00	5.00	100.00
Western	Bagpat	33.33	16.67	50.00		100.00
	Mathura	25.00	75.00			100.00
	Moradabad	25.00	25.00	37.50	12.50	100.00
Total		27.79	33.33	33.33	5.55	100.00

Contd.

Region	*District*	*All Like*	*Most Like*	*Some Like*	*Indiff-erent*	*Total*
BundelKhand	Banda	33.33		66.67		100.00
	Hamirpur	80.00		20.00		100.00
	Jhansi	16.67	50.00	33.33		100.00
Total		41.18	17.64	41.18		100.00
Grand Total		30.37	17.72	44.32	7.59	100.00

Table 11
Respect in Panchayats
Kshetra Panchayat

(Percentage Distribution)

Region	*District*	*All Like*	*Most Like*	*Some Like*	*Indiff-erent*	*Total*
Eastern	Varanasi	37.50	12.50	25.00	25.00	100.00
	Gorakhpur		33.33	6.67	60.00	100.00
	Ballia		36.36	45.46	18.18	100.00
Total		8.82	29.41	23.52	38.25	100.00
Central	Lucknow	11.11	16.66	55.57	16.66	100.00
	Balrampur	7.69	7.69	46.15	38.47	100.00
	Sitapur			85.72	14.28	100.00
Total		6.66	8.88	62.24	22.22	100.00
Western	Bagpat		10.00	50.00	40.00	100.00
	Mathura			37.50	62.50	100.00
	Moradabad		33.33	41.67	25.00	100.00
Total			16.67	43.33	40.00	100.00
BundelKhand	Banda	33.33	33.33	33.34		100.00
	Hamirpur	30.00	10.00	30.00	30.00	100.00
	Jhansi	7.69	23.07	38.48	30.76	100.00
Total		22.85	22.85	34.30	20.00	100.00
Grand Total		9.72	18.75	42.37	29.16	100.00

The officials pay full respect to women representatives because in their views. Women representatives are found to be sincere and sensitive towards the needs and problems of the citizens in their area. They are sobre, soft and gentle. Their behavior with officials, most of the times, is congenial, friendly and cooperative.

Table 12
Respect in Panchayats
Gram Panchayat

(Percentage Distribution)

Region	*District*	*All Like*	*Most Like*	*Some Like*	*Indiff-erent*	*Total*
Eastern	Varanasi	11.76	17.64	47.08	23.52	100.00
	Gorakhpur		38.10	38.10	23.80	100.00
	Ballia		29.16	33.33	37.51	100.00
Total		3.22	29.03	38.72	29.03	100.00
Central	Lucknow	5.71	5.71	45.73	42.85	100.00
	Balrampur	27.77	22.22	33.33	16.68	100.00
	Sitapur		14.28	28.58	57.14	100.00
Total		8.64	12.34	37.03	41.99	100.00
Western	Bagpat	11.11	16.67	50.00	22.22	100.00
	Mathura	5.26	10.52	42.11	42.11	100.00
	Moradabad		9.09	31.81	59.10	100.00
Total		5.08	11.86	40.69	42.37	100.00
Bundelkhand	Banda	11.53	19.23	38.48	30.76	100.00
	Hamirpur	9.09	13.63	45.47	31.81	100.00
	Jhansi	4.34	13.04	43.49	39.13	100.00
Total		8.45	15.49	42.26	33.80	100.00
Grand Total		6.59	16.84	39.58	36.99	100.00

Getting the Work Done

Responses in this regard are an eye opener. By nature women representatives are not authoritative and they try to get their work done by persuasion and through personal touch. But in the Zila Panchayats, majority of the women representatives get their work done by asserting authority, whereas at the Kshetra Panchayats level the number of such women representatives is reduced to about one-third. The number further goes down at Gram Panchayats, where majority of women feel that the works are got done by their male counterparts. Surprisingly, the number of such women is less in Eastern region, which is comparatively backward and has low literacy. The women representatives using authority are mostly chairpersons. They are found to be quite authoritative and they get work done in office by authority.

Hence difference in position does play a major role in their style of functioning. In Zila Panchayats women coming from

Table 13
Work done in Panchayat Office
Zila Panchayat

(Percentage Distribution)

Region	*District Auth-ority*	*By Persu-asion*	*By Personal Touch*	*By Rewards & Punis-hment*	*Mixing husband & Family Members*	*Through*	*Total*
Eastern	Varanasi	100.00					100.00
	Gorakhpur	66.68		16.66		16.66	100.00
	Ballia	75.00		12.50		12.50	100.00
Total		75.00		12.50		12.50	100.00
Central	Lucknow	71.44		14.28		14.28	100.00
	Balrampur	40.00		40.00		20.00	100.00
	Sitapur	50.00	25.00			25.00	100.00
Total		55.00	10.00	15.00		20.00	100.00
Western	Bagpat	100.00					100.00
	Mathura	12.50		12.50		50.00	100.00
	Moradabad	75.00	12.50	12.50			100.00
Total		72.23	5.55	11.11		11.11	100.00
Bundelkhand	Banda	33.34	33.33	33.33			100.00
	Hamirpur	60.00				40.00	100.00
	Jhansi	33.33	16.67	33.33		16.67	100.00
Total		41.20	17.64	23.52		17.64	100.00
Grand Total		62.05	7.59	15.18		15.18	100.00

Table 14
Work done in Panchayat Office
Kshetra Panchayat

(Percentage Distribution)

Region	*District Auth-ority*	*By Persu-asion*	*By Personal Touch*	*By Rewards & Punis-hment*	*Mixing husband & Family Members*	*Through*	*Total*
Eastern	Varanasi	25.00	25.00	25.00		25.00	100.00
	Gorakhpur	26.66	26.67	26.67		20.00	100.00
	Ballia	27.27	9.09	36.37		27.27	100.00
Total		26.41	20.58	29.49		23.52	100.00
Central	Lucknow	33.33	11.11	11.11		44.45	100.00
	Balrampur	15.38		53.86		30.76	100.00
	Sitapur	42.87	14.28	14.28		28.57	100.00
Total		31.11	8.88	24.44		35.57	100.00
Western	Bagpat	20.00	20.00	30.00		30.00	100.00
	Mathura	37.50	12.50	25.00	12.50	12.50	100.00
	Moradabad	25.00	8.33	16.67	25.00	25.00	100.00
Total		26.68	13.33	23.33	13.33	23.33	100.00
Bundelkhand	Banda	58.34		8.33	8.33	25.00	100.00
	Hamirpur	50.00	10.00	20.00	10.00	10.00	100.00
	Jhansi	46.17	7.69	15.38	7.69	23.07	100.00
Total		51.44	5.71	14.28	8.57	20.00	100.00
Grand Total		34.05	11.80	22.91	4.86	26.38	100.00

Table 15
Work done in Panchayat Office
Gram Panchayat

(Percentage Distribution)

Region	*District Auth-ority*	*By Persu-asion*	*By Personal Touch*	*By Rewards & Punis-hment*	*Mixing husband & Family Members*	*Through*	*Total*
Eastern	Varanasi	41.18		29.41		29.41	100.00
	Gorakhpur	28.57	4.76	14.28		52.39	100.00
	Ballia	33.34	8.33	8.33		50.00	100.00
Total		33.87	4.83	16.12		45.18	100.00
Central	Lucknow	25.71	5.71	14.28		54.30	100.00
	Balrampur	33.33		5.55		61.12	100.00
	Sitapur	21.42	7.14	7.14		64.30	100.00
Total		25.92	4.93	9.87		59.28	100.00
Western	Bagpat	27.78	11.11	11.11		50.00	100.00
	Mathura	31.57		15.78		52.65	100.00
	Moradabad	36.36		4.54		59.10	100.00
Total		32.20	3.38	10.16		54.26	100.00
Bundelkhand	Banda	23.07	7.69	15.38		53.86	100.00
	Hamirpur	22.72		9.09		68.19	100.00
	Jhansi	17.39	8.69	17.39		56.53	100.00
Total		21.12	5.63	14.08		59.17	100.00
Grand Total		27.83	4.76	12.45		54.96	100.00

strong political background use authority of their own for getting their works done. At Gram Panchayats level the official concerned is fully directed by Pradhan and local women representatives have no scope for using authority, hence works are got done by male family members.

Attitude of Officials

In respect of attitude and behaviour of officials, women feel to get help from officials in discharging their functions frequently. They find officials quite cooperative with them. On probing further, women representatives negate to neglect their new duties but sometimes it does get neglected due to family obligations. It is quite revealing that officials at higher levels are more cooperative, give more recognition to women and are obedient. Contrarily, in lower tier Panchayats, especially in Gram Panchayat, the officials dare to ignore orders of women representatives and many a time their attitude is totally indifferent towards them. This warrants training to rural officials especially at Gram Panchayat and Kshetra Panchayat levels. The women however are found committed towards their duties and responsibilities even they do not get sufficient help from officials. (Tables– 16, 17, 18)

Decision Making

The respective enactments provide to hold regular meetings of Panchayats and all the members are obliged to attend the meetings. It is found that many a times meetings are not held or meetings are not held regularly, but women members claim to attend meetings regularly. At this juncture, just to substantiate their views the officials were asked to reveal whether women attend meetings. Strangely, only one-fifth women are found attending meetings regularly and another one third attend sometimes and three out of ten women attend often and about one tenth seldom. It seems that women are not aware of the importance of attending meetings all the times.

As a part of decision-making powers vested in them, more than half of the women representatives in Panchayats are found not initiating discussions in meetings. But observations reveal

Table 16
Attitudes of Officials
Zila Panchayat

(Percenatage Distribution)

	Co-operation					*Recognition*					*Obedience*					*Ignore Orders*					*Comments*					*Indifference*				
	A	F	ST	R	N	A	F	ST	R	N	A	F	ST	R	N	A	F	ST	R	N	A	F	ST	R	N	A	F	ST	R	N
Eastern	16.67	33.33	33.33	16.67		16.66	8.34	25.00	50.00		8.34	25.00	50.00	16.66				66.67	25.00	8.33			8.33	25.00	66.67		25.00	41.67	25.00	8.33
Central	45.00	5.00	25.00	20.00	5.00	45.00	10.00	25.00	20.00		25.00	10.00	40.00	20.00	5.00		5.00	50.00	25.00	20.00			20.00	20.00	60.00		5.00	35.00	60.00	
Western	16.67	50.00	33.33			16.66	66.68	16.66			11.11	55.56	33.33					61.11	27.78	11.11			5.55	5.55	88.90		16.66	77.79		5.55
Bundel-khand	29.41	47.07	23.52			29.41	29.41	41.18			17.64	23.52	35.32	11.76	11.76			58.83	35.29	5.88					100.00		11.76	58.84	23.52	5.88
Grand Total	26.58	32.93	29.11	10.12	1.26	26.58	26.58	26.58	20.26		15.18	27.84	40.54	12.65	3.79		1.26	59.51	27.84	11.39			8.86	13.93	77.21		15.18	51.92	27.84	5.06

A – Always
F – Frequently
ST – Some Time
R – Rarely
N – Never

Table 17
Attitudes of Officials
Khetra Panchayat

(Percenatage Distribution)

	Co-operation					Recognition					Obedience					Ignore Orders					Comments					Indifference				
	A	F	ST	R	N	A	F	ST	R	N	A	F	ST	R	N	A	F	ST	R	N	A	F	ST	R	N	A	F	ST	R	N
Eastern	26.47	8.82	17.64	14.70	32.37	32.36	11.76	11.76	11.76	32.36		20.58	23.52	11.76	44.14	23.52	11.76	32.38	20.58	11.76				17.64	82.36	20.58	23.52	44.14	5.88	5.88
Central	4.44	4.44	44.48	26.66	20.00	6.66	11.11	40.00	24.26	17.77	4.44	2.22	31.11	37.79	24.44	8.88	24.44	37.80	24.44	4.44			17.77	17.77	64.46	8.88	13.33	57.80	8.88	11.11
Western	3.33	16.66	36.69	26.66	16.66	6.66	6.66	56.69	16.66	13.33		13.33	23.34	50.00	13.33	6.66	10.00	50.00	20.00	13.34		3.33		10.00	86.67	3.33	16.66	53.35	20.00	6.66
Bundel-khand	20.00	20.00	40.00	8.57	11.43	20.00	14.28	31.44	20.00	14.28	5.71	8.58	28.57	28.57	28.57	17.14	22.85	37.16	5.71	17.14				8.57	91.43	11.42	20.00	51.44	8.57	8.57
Grand Total	13.19	11.80	35.43	19.44	20.14	15.97	11.11	34.73	18.75	19.44	2.77	10.41	27.08	31.97	27.77	13.88	18.05	38.91	18.05	11.11		0.69	5.55	13.88	79.88	11.11	18.05	52.10	10.41	8.33

A – Always
F – Frequently
ST – Some Time
R – Rarely
N – Never

Table 18
Attitudes of Officials
Gram Panchayat

(Percenatage Distribution)

	Co-operation					Recognition					Obedience					Ignore Orders					Comments					Indifference				
	A	F	ST	R	N	A	F	ST	R	N	A	F	ST	R	N	A	F	ST	R	N	A	F	ST	R	N	A	F	ST	R	N
Eastern	14.51	9.67	32.25	9.67	33.90	12.90	9.67	32.25	8.06	37.12	4.83	6.45	40.34	12.90	35.48	19.35	30.64	38.73	9.67	1.61			4.83	12.90	82.27	6.45	27.41	51.63	12.90	1.61
Central	7.40	13.58	33.33	7.40	38.29	9.87	7.40	33.33	11.11	38.29	4.93	9.87	27.16	17.28	40.76	24.69	9.87	29.64	22.22	13.58			8.64	34.56	56.80	18.51	19.75	29.65	18.51	13.58
Western	5.08	27.11	30.53	11.86	25.42	6.77	10.16	37.32	16.94	28.81	1.69	23.72	32.20	8.47	33.92	8.47	22.03	52.57	13.55	3.38		1.69	5.08	15.25	77.98	6.77	22.03	47.49	20.33	3.38
Bundel-Khand	11.26	14.08	26.76	11.26	36.64	11.26	7.04	16.90	19.71	45.09	2.81	2.81	22.53	25.35	46.50	23.94	38.04	22.53	7.04	8.45			2.81	11.26	85.93	18.30	25.35	40.87	11.26	4.22
Grand Total	9.52	15.75	30.76	9.89	34.08	10.25	8.42	29.67	13.91	37.75	3.66	10.25	30.03	16.48	39.58	19.78	24.54	34.81	13.55	7.32		0.36	5.49	19.41	74.74	13.18	23.44	41.41	15.75	6.22

A – Always
F – Frequently
ST – Some Time
R – Rarely
N – Never

that generally women representatives hesitate in initiating discussions and the male members are found to be more dominating in meetings. Most of the women representatives either just keep mum or support the move of their male counterparts in meetings. They generally fail to express their views or they do not take their role seriously. Although women representatives claim to initiate discussions, some of them hesitate due to lack of knowledge, confidence and interest in their new functions.

Table 19
Women Attend Meetings

(Percentage Distribution)

Region	*District*	*Regularly*	*Some time*	*Often*	*Seldom*	*Total*
Eastern	Varanasi	9.09	54.55	36.36		100.00
	Gorakhpur	18.18	27.27	45.46	9.09	100.00
	Ballia	20.00	40.00	30.00	10.00	100.00
Total		15.62	40.63	37.50	6.25	100.00
Central	Lucknow	33.33	52.39	9.52	4.76	100.00
	Balrampur	37.50	25.00	25.00	12.50	100.00
	Sitapur	15.38	23.07	53.86	7.69	100.00
Total		30.00	36.00	26.00	8.00	100.00
Western	Bagpat	16.67	33.33	33.33	16.67	100.00
	Mathura		55.56	33.33	11.11	100.00
	Moradabad	25.00	41.67	25.00	8.33	100.00
Total		15.15	42.43	30.30	12.12	100.00
Bundelkhand	Banda		25.00	66.67	8.33	100.00
	Hamirpur	35.72	35.72	21.42	7.14	100.00
	Jhansi	21.42	35.73	28.57	14.28	100.00
Total		20.00	32.50	37.50	10.00	100.00
Grand Total		21.29	37.43	32.25	9.03	100.00

Here lies the importance of training and development. Women representatives should be imparted proper orientation towards their role and responsibilities in new dispensation. It may help bring boldness among them, and they will not feel shy.

It is seen that more than half of the women representatives at Zila Panchayats level take active part in discussion, while this is lowest in the Kshetra Panchayats and more than one-

Table 20
Initiate Discussion
Zila Panchayat

(Percentage Distribution)

Region	*District*	*Always*	*Some time*	*Freq-uently*	*Not Allowed*	*Never*	*Indif-ferent*	*Total*
Eastern	Varanasi		25.00			75.00		100.00
	Gorakhpur		16.67		16.67	66.66		100.00
	Ballia			12.50		87.50		100.00
Total			12.50	4.17	8.33	75.00		100.00
Central	Lucknow	14.29		28.57		14.29	42.85	100.00
	Balrampur		40.00			60.00		100.00
	Sitapur					100.00		100.00
Total		5.00	10.00	10.00		60.00	15.00	100.00
Western	Bagpat	16.67	16.67			66.66		100.00
	Mathura		50.00			50.00		100.00
	Moradabad					100.00		100.00
Total		5.55	16.67			77.78		100.00
Bundelkhand	Banda					100.00		100.00
	Hamirpur		20.00			80.00		100.00
	Jhansi					100.00		100.00
Total			2.88			94.12		100.00
Grand Total		2.53	11.39	3.79	2.50	76.00	3.79	100.00

Table 21
Initiate Discussion
Kshetra Panchayat

(Percentage Distribution)

Region	*District*	*Always*	*Some time*	*Freq-uently*	*Not Allowed*	*Never*	*Indif-ferent*	*Total*
Eastern	Varanasi	12.50	12.50		12.50	50.00	12.50	100.00
	Gorakhpur		13.33			73.34	13.33	100.00
	Ballia		18.18			72.73	9.09	100.00
Total		2.94	14.70		2.94	67.66	11.76	100.00
Central	Lucknow		5.55	5.55		83.35	5.55	100.00
	Balrampur	7.69	30.76		38.46	23.09		100.00
	Sitapur		21.42				78.58	100.00
Total		2.22	17.78	2.22	11.11	40.00	26.67	100.00
Western	Bagpat		30.00			70.00		100.00
	Mathura		12.50		12.50	25.00	50.00	100.00
	Moradabad					83.33	16.67	100.00
Total			13.33		3.33	63.34	20.00	100.00
Bundelkhand	Banda		58.33			25.00	16.67	100.00
	Hamirpur		30.00			70.00		100.00
	Jhansi		7.69		7.69	84.62		100.00
Total			31.43		2.86	60.00	5.71	100.00
Grand Total		1.39	19.44	0.69	5.55	57.26	16.67	100.00

Table 22
Initiate Discussion
Gram Panchayat

(Percentage Distribution)

Region	*District*	*Always*	*Some time*	*Freq-uently*	*Not Allowed*	*Never*	*Indif-ferent*	*Total*
Eastern	Varanasi	5.88	11.76	11.76		58.84	11.76	100.00
	Gorakhpur		19.04			80.96		100.00
	Ballia		4.17			83.33	12.50	100.00
Total		1.61	11.29	3.22		75.82	8.06	100.00
Central	Lucknow		25.71	2.86	5.71	57.15	8.57	100.00
	Balrampur	11.11	27.77		16.67	44.45		100.00
	Sitapur		35.71	7.14	14.28		42.87	100.00
Region Total		2.46	29.63	3.70	11.11	34.58	18.52	100.00
Western	Bagpat		11.11	11.11		72.23	5.55	100.00
	Mathura		36.84		15.80	36.84	10.52	100.00
	Moradabad		9.09			68.19	22.72	100.00
Total			18.64	3.39	5.08	59.34	13.55	100.00
Bundelkhand	Banda	7.69	7.69			76.93	7.69	100.00
	Hamirpur		22.72	4.55		72.73		100.00
	Jhansi	4.35	8.70	4.35	17.39	47.82	17.39	100.00
Total		4.22	12.67	2.81	5.63	66.22	8.45	100.00
Grand Total		2.20	18.68	3.30	5.86	57.51	12.45	100.00

third in Gram Panchayats. Astonishingly, more than one-third of women in Zila Panchayats, more than half in Kshetra Panchayats and little less than half in Gram Panchayats never participate in discussions. At the lower tiers, women are even neither allowed to speak nor heard. This shows the male dominance in meetings as well.

At this level it was thought pertinent to have the views of officials. The officials find more than one-third of women representatives never participating in discussions, however an identical number take part occasionally and about one seventh sometimes. But there are the women, albeit meager in number, who frequently takes part. This is a good beginning. At least Indian rural women are seen coming out of four walls of their houses and are sharing the company of male and have started participating in discussions or at least sitting in meetings in company with male members.

It is disheartening to note that a significant number of women representatives at all the three levels are not encouraged either by their female colleagues or by male colleagues or by Panchayat head or by their family members to put forth their views. Women in large number are allowed to express their opinion in policy making but not allowing them full freedom of expression mars the accomplishment of objectives of their full participation in decision-making at local level. The situation requires to be changed through training and capacity building to all members, especially women members. (Tables– 27, 28, 29)

In respect of taking decisions relating to Panchayat works, largest number (40 percent) of women of Zila Panchayats clearly expresses that decisions are taken by their family members. The number of such women representatives is found increasing while going down the tiers. At Kshetra Panchayat and Gram Panchayat levels they are in majority. If the responses relating to the decisions taken with the help of male family members are added, it converts the myth of decision taken by male counterparts into a reality. This is a major cause of concern. Many a times women representatives feel uncomfortable in taking independent decisions. They work only as rubber stamps for husband and male family members.

Table 23
Participation in Discussion
Zila Panchayat

(Percentage Distribution)

Region	*District*	*Always*	*Sometime*	*Frequently*	*Not-Allowed*	*Never*	*Not Heard*	*Total*
Eastern	Varanasi	50.00	50.00					100.00
	Gorakhpur		50.00			50.00		100.00
	Ballia	12.50	37.50			50.00		100.00
Total		12.50	45.84			41.66		100.00
Central	Lucknow	14.28		28.57		57.15		100.00
	Balrampur		40.00			60.00		100.00
	Sitapur	25.00	75.00					100.00
Total		15.00	40.00	10.00		35.00		100.00
Western	Bagpat	16.67	33.33			50.00		100.00
	Mathura		75.00	25.00				100.00
	Moradabad		50.00	12.50		37.50		100.00
Total		5.55	50.00	11.12		33.33		100.00
Bundelkhand	Banda		50.00			50.00		100.00
	Hamirpur	20.00	80.00					100.00
	Jhansi		33.34	33.33		33.33		100.00
Total		5.88	52.95	11.76		29.41		100.00
Grand Total		10.12	46.85	7.59		35.44		100.00

Table 24
Participation in Discussion
Kshetra Panchayat

(Percentage Distribution)

Region	District	Always	Sometime	Frequently	Not-Allowed	Never	Not Heard	Total
Eastern	Varanasi	12.50	50.00		12.50	25.00		100.00
	Gorakhpur		33.33			66.67		100.00
	Ballia	9.09	18.18			72.73		100.00
Total		5.88	32.35		2.94	58.83		100.00
Central	Lucknow	5.55	16.66	5.55		61.13	11.11	100.00
	Balrampur	7.69	30.77		30.77	30.77		100.00
	Sitapur		42.86		14.28	42.86		100.00
Total		4.44	28.88	2.22	13.33	46.69	4.44	100.00
Western	Bagpat		30.00			60.00	10.00	100.00
	Mathura		37.50		12.50	62.50		100.00
	Moradabad		33.33		16.67	33.33	16.67	100.00
Total			30.00		10.00	50.00	10.00	100.00
Bundelkhand	Banda		50.00			41.67	8.33	100.00
	Hamirpur		10.00	10.00		40.00	40.00	100.00
	Jhansi		23.07			76.93		100.00
Total		28.57	2.85		54.30	14.28	100.00	
Grand Total		2.77	29.86	1.38	6.94	52.11	6.94	100.00

Table 25
Participation in Discussion
Gram Panchayat

(Percentage Distribution)

Region	*District*	*Always*	*Sometime*	*Frequently*	*Not-Allowed*	*Never*	*Not Heard*	*Total*
Eastern	Varanasi	5.88	58.84	5.88		23.52	5.88	100.00
	Gorakhpur	4.76	23.80			71.44		100.00
	Ballia	4.17	33.33			62.50		100.00
Total		4.83	37.09	1.61		54.86	1.61	100.00
Central	Lucknow		34.28		5.71	45.73	14.28	100.00
	Balrampur	22.22	22.22		16.66	38.90		100.00
	Sitapur		42.85			57.15		100.00
Total		4.93	34.56		6.17	48.17	6.17	100.00
Western	Bagpat		11.11	11.11		66.67	11.11	100.00
	Mathura		31.57	15.78	15.78	31.61	5.26	100.00
	Moradabad	9.09	22.72		13.63	40.93	13.63	100.00
Total		3.38	22.07	8.47	10.16	45.76	10.16	100.00
Bundelkhand	Banda		42.32		11.53	38.46	7.69	100.00
	Hamirpur		27.28	4.54		50.00	18.18	100.00
	Jhansi	8.69	47.84			43.47		100.00
Total		2.81	39.43	1.40	4.22	43.69	8.45	100.00
Grand Total		4.02	33.69	2.56	5.12	48.02	6.59	100.00

Table 26
Women Participate in Discussion

(Percentage Distribution)

Region	*District*	*Always*	*Frequently*	*Occasionally*	*Sometime*	*Never*	*Total*
Eastern	Varanasi		9.09	54.55	36.36		100.00
	Gorakhpur			36.36	18.18	45.46	100.00
	Ballia			100.00		100.00	100.00
Total			3.12	46.88	18.75	31.25	100.00
Central	Lucknow		4.76	61.92	14.28	19.04	100.00
	Balrampur			25.00	18.75	56.25	100.00
	Sitapur		7.69	15.38	15.38	61.55	100.00
Total			4.00	38.00	16.00	42.00	100.00
Western	Bagpat			25.00	25.00	50.00	100.00
	Mathura		11.11	44.45	11.11	33.33	100.00
	Moradabad	8.33	33.33	16.68	8.33	33.33	100.00
Total		3.03	15.15	27.27	15.15	39.40	100.00
Bundelkhand	Banda			41.66		58.34	100.00
	Hamirpur			35.71	21.42	42.87	100.00
	Jhansi		7.14	50.00	14.28	28.58	100.00
Total			2.50	42.50	12.50	42.50	100.00
Grand Total		0.64	5.80	38.70	15.48	39.38	100.00

Table 27
Encouraged to Put Forth Views
Zila Panchayat

(Percentage Distribution)

Region	*By Female Colleagues*				*By Male Colleagues*				*By Adhyaksha*				*By Family Members*			
	Yes	*No*	*Some time*	*Always*	*Yes*	*No*	*Some time*	*Always*	*Yes*	*No*	*Some time*	*Always*	*Yes*	*No*	*Some time*	*Always*
Eastern	8.33	41.67	12.50	37.50	8.33	41.67	50.00		12.50	29.17	50.00	8.33	12.50	29.16	16.66	41.68
Central	10.00	5.00	65.00	20.00	10.00	15.00	55.00	20.00	10.00	10.00	60.00	20.00	10.00	15.00	55.00	20.00
Western	11.11	11.11	38.89	38.89		66.68	16.66	16.66		16.66	72.23	11.11	22.23	11.11	50.00	16.66
Bundelkhand	17.64	11.76	35.30	35.30	11.76	23.52	47.08	17.64	11.76	17.64	41.19	29.41	23.52	11.76	41.20	23.52
Grand Total	11.39	18.98	36.72	32.91	7.59	36.70	43.06	12.65	8.86	18.98	55.71	16.45	16.45	17.72	39.25	26.58

Table 28
Encouraged to put forth Views
Kshetra Panchayat

(Percentage Distribution)

Region	*By Female Colleagues*				*By Male Colleagues*				*By Adhyaksha*				*By Family Members*			
	Yes	*No*	*Some time*	*Always*	*Yes*	*No*	*Some time*	*Always*	*Yes*	*No*	*Some time*	*Always*	*Yes*	*No*	*Some time*	*Always*
Eastern	23.52	38.25	29.41	8.82		64.74	32.35	2.91	8.82	52.95	32.35	5.88	8.82	44.13	38.23	8.82
Central	13.33	33.33	48.90	4.44	2.22	64.45	33.33		6.66	44.45	44.45	4.44	11.11	33.33	51.12	4.44
Western	3.33	30.00	50.00	16.67		53.34	43.33	3.33	6.66	46.67	46.67		3.33	36.67	40.00	20.00
Bundelkhand	8.57	28.57	42.86	20.00		51.44	45.71	2.85	8.57	48.58	37.14	5.71	22.86	20.00	40.00	17.14
Grand Total	12.50	31.94	43.06	12.50	0.69	59.04	38.19	2.08	7.63	47.94	40.27	4.16	11.80	33.33	43.07	11.80

Table 29
Encouraged to put forth Views
Gram Panchayat

(Percentage Distribution)

	By Female Colleagues				*By Male Colleagues*				*By Adhyaksha*				*By Family Members*			
Region	*Yes*	*No*	*Some time*	*Always*	*Yes*	*No*	*Some time*	*Always*	*Yes*	*No*	*Some time*	*Always*	*Yes*	*No*	*Some time*	*Always*
Eastern	19.35	37.11	35.48	8.06	1.61	59.69	37.09	1.61	1.61	51.62	40.32	6.45	14.51	53.24	30.64	1.61
Central	19.75	33.33	37.05	9.87	6.17	53.10	35.80	4.93	3.70	55.57	32.09	8.64	17.28	45.69	25.92	11.11
Western	16.94	23.72	35.62	23.72	8.47	54.25	28.81	8.47	8.47	57.65	30.50	3.38	20.33	33.89	35.62	10.16
Bundelkhand	12.67	30.98	35.23	21.12	2.81	57.76	30.98	8.45	2.81	47.90	43.66	5.63	5.63	23.94	50.72	19.71
Grand Total	17.21	31.50	35.91	15.38	4.76	56.05	33.33	5.86	4.02	53.13	36.63	6.22	14.28	39.21	35.53	10.98

Surprisingly active family members who have been in politics for many years, take decisions independently on behalf of female representatives, sometimes even without their knowledge. It is in tune to the old Indian village traditions that a woman cannot take any decision independently. She is governed by the decisions of husband. She is not free to defy. This social myth needs to be erased and woman is to be empowered to take decisions independently or give suggestions to husband. (Tables– 30, 31, 32)

Table 30
Decisions in Panchayat work are taken
Zila Panchayat

(Percentage Distribution)

Region	*Independently by Women*	*With the help of Male Family Member*	*Concurrence with Male Member*	*Consult with Female Colleagues*	*By Family Member*	*With the Advice from Officials*	*Total*
Eastern		58.34			41.66		100.00
Central	10.00	10.00	30.00		50.00		100.00
Western		11.11	38.89		50.00		100.00
Bundelkhand	11.76	35.31	29.41		23.52		100.00
Grand Total	5.06	30.37	22.78		41.79		100.00

Table 31
Decisions in Panchayat work are taken
Kshetra Panchayat

(Percentage Distribution)

Region	*Independently by Women*	*With the help of Male Family Member*	*Concurrence with Male Member*	*Consult with Female Colleagues*	*By Family Member*	*With the Advice from Officials*	*Total*
Eastern	2.94	23.52	17.64		55.90		100.00
Central		35.55	11.11		53.34		100.00
Western		26.66	6.66	66.68			100.00
Bundelkhand		22.85	25.71		51.42		100.00
Grand Total	69.00	27.77	15.27		56.27		100.00

In Indian village scenario, more in northern part of the country, women are not allowed to go outside all-alone. They are allowed to move outside either in-group or in company of a male. In this context, it was thought obvious to know whether women representations are also accompanied by male or not. Surprisingly, half of the officials find males accompanying women representatives always. Almost a negligible number of officials feel otherwise. A significant number have no opinion and prefer not to respond.

Table 32
Decisions in Panchayat work are taken
Gram Panchayat

(Percentage Distribution)

Region	*Independently by Women*	*With the help of Male Family Member*	*Concurrence with Male Member*	*Consult with Female Colleagues*	*By Family Member*	*With the Advice from Officials*	*Total*
Eastern		14.51	16.12	1.61	66.15	1.61	100.00
Central	2.46	22.22	19.75		53.11	2.46	100.00
Western		30.50	16.94		52.56		100.00
Bundelkhand		11.26	18.30		70.44		100.00
Grand Total	0.73	19.41	17.94	0.36	60.47		100.00

In this context the officials were asked whether males accompanying women members are allowed to sit and attend meetings. Strangely, on record majority of the officials refute the male members attending the meeting either along with the women members or in place of women members. However, they admit the males attending the meeting and many times discharging the duties and even putting the signature of women representatives. Every seventh official admits that only males (in place of women, in many cases) attend meetings, whereas one-fifth officials confess the males (along with women) attending the meetings. On further probing one-tenth of officials accept males always attending meetings and, an identical number confess occasional attending, while about

Table 33

Women Members Accompanied by Male

(Percentage Distribution)

Region	*District*	*Always*	*Frequently*	*Occasionally*	*Some Time*	*Never*	*NR*	*Total*
Eastern	Varanasi	45.46	36.36	9.09	9.09			100.00
	Gorakhpur	81.82	18.18					100.00
	Ballia	60.00	10.00				30.00	100.00
Total		62.50	21.89	3.12	3.12		9.37	100.00
Central	Lucknow	42.88	14.28		23.80	4.76	14.28	100.00
	Balrampur	75.00			6.25		18.75	100.00
	Sitapur	38.48	7.69		30.76		23.07	100.00
Total		52.00	8.00		20.00	2.00	18.00	100.00
Western	Bagpat	66.68	8.33		8.33		16.66	100.00
	Mathura	44.45	22.22		11.11		22.22	100.00
	Moradabad	66.68	8.33	8.33		8.33	8.33	100.00
Total		60.61	12.12	3.03	6.06	3.03	15.15	100.00
Bundelkhand	Banda	41.68	16.66		8.33		33.33	100.00
	Hamirpur	50.00	21.44		14.28		14.28	100.00
	Jhansi	35.74	14.28	14.28	21.42		14.28	100.00
Total		42.50	17.50	5.00	15.00		20.00	100.00
Grand Total		53.57	14.19	2.58	12.25	1.29	16.12	100.00

NR– No Response

Table 34
Male Attend Meetings

(Percentage Distribution)

Region	*District*	*Yes*	*No*	*Always*	*Occa-sionally*	*Some time*	*Forced Entry*	*Only Male Attend*	NR
Eastern	Varanasi	54.54	45.46	9.09	27.27	18.18		–	45.46
	Gorakhpur	45.46	54.54	9.09		36.36		–	54.55
	Ballia	20.00	80.00	20.00	10.00	30.00	10.00	30.00	–
Total		21.87	78.13	12.50	12.50	28.14	3.12		
Central	Lucknow	4.76	95.24	9.52	14.28	23.80	19.04	14.28	19.08
	Balrampur	6.25	93.75	18.75	18.75	25.00	12.50	18.75	6.25
	Sitapur	30.79	69.21		15.38	23.07	7.69	23.07	30.79
Total		12.00	88.00	10.00	16.00	24.00	14.00	18.00	18.00
Western	Bagpat	8.34	91.66	25.00		50.00	8.33	16.66	–
	Mathura	55.56	44.44		11.11	22.22		22.22	44.45
	Moradabad	33.33	66.67			25.00		8.33	66.67
Total		30.31	69.69	9.09	3.03	33.33	3.03	15.15	36.37
Bundelkhand	Banda	33.34	66.66	8.33	8.33	33.34	8.33	33.33	8.34
	Hamirpur	7.14	92.86	7.14	7.14	35.73	28.57	14.28	7.14
	Jhansi	14.28	85.72	14.28	7.14	35.74	7.14	14.28	21.42
Total		17.50	82.50	10.00	7.50	35.00	15.00	20.00	12.50
Grand Total		19.35	80.65	10.32	10.32	29.70	9.67	16.12	23.87

NR– No Response

one-third accept that males attend sometimes. A significant number admit forced entry of male members. It is not a healthy sign for country's democracy. Ironically, officials on promise of anonymity, confess that despite their best efforts they fail to pursue male members not to attend meetings but they cannot report officially or cannot ask males to go outside the meetings, because they (official) have to live with them only and at local level they (male) are strong and influential persons.

Out of curiosity, the officials were asked as to whether male family members only attend meetings or discharge official functions as well. The responses are quite revealing. Majority of the officials find male family members discharging official duties on behalf of women representatives in most cases. They cannot take any action as they are afraid of local leaders or sometimes develop rapport for their own benefits.

Table 35
Male Work on Behalf of Women

(Percentage Distribution)

Region	*District*	*Yes*	*No*	*Total*
Eastern	Varanasi	90.91	9.09	100.00
	Gorakhpur	81.82	18.18	100.00
	Ballia	100.00		100.00
Total		90.63	9.37	100.00
Central	Lucknow	76.20	23.80	100.00
	Balrampur	100.00		100.00
	Sitapur	76.93	23.07	100.00
Total		84.00	16.00	100.00
Western	Bagpat	91.67	8.33	100.00
	Mathura	88.89	11.11	100.00
	Moradabad	66.67	33.33	100.00
Total		81.82	18.18	100.00
Bundelkhand	Banda	83.34	16.66	100.00
	Hamirpur	92.86	7.14	100.00
	Jhansi	78.58	21.42	100.00
Total		85.00	15.00	100.00
Grand Total		85.17	14.83	100.00

Relationship with Chairperson

Women representatives generally try to maintain good relations with their chairperson. However, at times there are adjustment problems with male chairperson. Women members do not get due importance and do not feel free to express their views and problems in presence of male chairperson. But where there is woman chairperson, women members feel quite free to initiate and participate in discussions. They are able to communicate freely and put forth their problems and suggestions.

It is encouraging that woman representatives at Zila Panchayat level receive cooperation and support from the Adhyaksha. Their advice is recognized and appreciated. The Adhyakshas are generally encouraging and rarely indifferent. The same story is written in other two tiers as well. Pramukh of Kshetra Panchayats and Pradhan of Gram Panchayats are found fully cooperative, appreciative and encouraging towards their women members. Whatever negativity in their attitude is it may be because of other reasons. The cordial relationship is in tune to the Indian tradition where nobody is generally rude to women. (Tables– 36, 37, 38)

The women members having experience and knowledge of administration and aware about their roles and responsibilities, unhesitatingly express their views even with male chairpersons. The number of such members is of course not much. Most of the women representatives just come when they are specially required and go unconcerned. They do not bother much and many of them leave the problems to their family members. Majority of them enjoy their new role as a ritual and not as a challenge and opportunity. There is a need to bring attitudinal change among the women. The chairpersons should also be encouraging and supportive.

Relationship with Peers

Interestingly, most of the times female colleagues are found to be co-operative and supportive. They always encourage and appreciate one another and seldom pass teasing comments. In few cases political affiliation may lead to differences temporarily. (Tables– 39, 40, 41)

Table 36
Behaviour of Adhayaksha
Zila Panchayat

(Percenatage Distribution)

Region	Co-operation/Support					Recognition for Advice					Appreciation					Comments for Mistakes					Encouragement					Indifference				
	A	F	ST	R	N	A	F	ST	R	N	A	F	ST	R	N	A	F	ST	R	N	A	F	ST	R	N	A	F	ST	R	N
Eastern	16.66	25.00	41.68		16.66	8.33	25.00	41.68	8.33	16.66	8.33	33.34	33.34	8.33	16.66			29.16	54.18	16.66		8.33	41.68	33.33	16.66		16.66	50.00	33.34	
Central	55.00		15.00	25.00	5.00	45.00	5.00	25.00	20.00	5.00	50.00		25.00	20.00	5.00			15.00	60.00	25.00	10.00	25.00	30.00	30.00	5.00		5.00	45.00	50.00	
Western	27.78	50.00	11.11		11.11	11.11	72.23	5.55		11.11	22.22	55.57	16.66	5.55				38.90	33.33	27.77		27.77	33.35	22.22	16.66		11.11	55.57	27.77	5.55
Bundel-khand	35.29	47.07	5.88		11.76	11.76	11.76	58.84	5.88	11.76	17.64	47.07	23.53		11.76	5.88	5.88	17.64	52.96	17.64	5.88	23.53	23.53	29.42	17.64	5.88	17.64	41.19	23.53	11.76
Grand Total	32.93	29.11	20.25	6.32	11.39	18.98	27.84	32.93	8.86	11.39	24.04	32.93	25.31	8.86	8.86	1.26	1.26	1.26	25.31	50.66	21.51	3.79	20.25	32.93	13.92	1.26	12.66	48.13	34.17	3.79

A – Always
F – Frequently
ST – Some Time
R – Rarely
N – Never

Table 37
Behaviour of Pramukh
Kshetra Panchayat

(Percenatage Distribution)

Region	Co-operation/Support					Recognition for Advice					Appreciation					Comments for Mistakes					Encouragement					Indifference				
	A	F	ST	R	N	A	F	ST	R	N	A	F	ST	R	N	A	F	ST	R	N	A	F	ST	R	N	A	F	ST	R	N
Eastern	44.14	11.76	20.58	5.88	17.64	17.64	20.58	17.64	20.58	23.56	23.52	14.70	20.58	14.70	26.50	2.94	8.22	17.64	41.19	29.41		29.41	14.70	17.64	28.25	5.88	32.36	32.35	29.41	
Central	17.77	8.88	55.60	8.88	8.88	13.33	11.11	42.24	15.55	17.77	20.00	4.44	37.79	15.55	22.22	2.22		35.55	44.46	17.77		15.55	33.35	24.44	26.66	6.66	11.11	44.46	26.66	11.11
Western	20.00	16.66	33.35	23.33	6.66	20.00	23.33	13.33	36.68	6.66	23.33	13.33	30.01	23.33	10.00		3.33	26.66	36.68	33.33		3.33	20.00	40.00	36.66	3.33	13.33	30.01	40.00	13.33
Bundel-khand	22.85	28.57	31.43	5.71	11.42	5.71	8.57	37.16	37.14	11.42	17.14	22.85	31.45	14.28	14.28			34.28	37.15	28.57		2.85	25.71	42.87	28.57	2.85	22.85	45.74	22.85	5.71
Grand Total	25.69	15.97	36.82	10.41	11.11	13.88	15.27	29.25	26.38	15.22	20.83	13.19	30.57	16.66	18.75	1.38	2.77	29.16	40.31	26.38		13.19	24.30	30.55	31.96	4.86	19.44	38.91	29.16	7.63

A – Always
F – Frequently
ST – Some Time
R – Rarely

Table 38
Behaviour of Pradhan
Gram Panchayat

(Percenatage Distribution)

Region	Co-operation/Support					Recognition for Advice					Appreciation					Comments for Mistakes					Encouragement					Indifference				
	A	F	ST	R	N	A	F	ST	R	N	A	F	ST	R	N	A	F	ST	R	N	A	F	ST	R	N	A	F	ST	R	N
Eastern	33.90	27.41	16.12	9.67	12.90	16.12	17.74	22.58	30.66	12.90	17.74	14.51	43.56	11.29	12.90		1.61	35.50	32.25	30.64		8.06	17.74	46.79	27.41	12.90	25.80	38.73	20.96	1.61
Central	12.34	20.98	27.19	18.51	20.98	8.64	16.04	20.98	29.65	24.69	8.64	16.04	16.04	39.53	16.04	2.46	1.23	29.62	43.24	23.45	3.70	14.81	14.81	39.52	27.16	7.40	7.40	46.94	17.28	20.98
Western	6.77	20.33	32.24	16.94	23.72	1.69	15.25	39.00	22.03	22.03	3.38	15.25	42.40	16.94	22.03			27.11	47.47	25.42		6.77	23.72	35.62	33.89	5.08	20.33	39.01	27.11	8.47
Bundel-khand	11.26	16.90	36.64	14.08	21.12	8.45	8.45	25.35	32.42	25.35	8.45	14.08	40.86	11.26	25.35	5.63	8.45	23.94	39.45	22.53		2.81	19.71	29.57	47.91	15.49	26.76	39.45	16.90	1.40
Grand Total	15.75	21.24	28.22	15.01	19.78	8.79	14.28	26.37	28.95	21.61	9.52	15.01	35.56	20.87	19.04	2.19	2.93	28.93	40.68	25.27	1.09	8.42	18.68	37.75	34.06	10.25	19.41	41.41	20.14	8.79

A – Always
F – Frequently
ST – Some Time
R – Rarely

Table 39
Behaviour of Female Colleagues
Zila Panchayat

(Percenatage Distribution)

Region	Co-operation/Support					Recognition for Advice					Appreciation					Teasing Comments					Encouragement					Indifference				
	A	F	ST	R	N	A	F	ST	R	N	A	F	ST	R	N	A	F	ST	R	N	A	F	ST	R	N	A	F	ST	R	N
Eastern	83.33	16.67				83.34		16.66			83.34		16.66						8.33	91.67	12.50	20.83	16.67	25.00	25.00	16.66	12.50	37.52	16.7	16.66
Central	50.00	35.00	10.00	5.00		50.00	35.00	10.00	5.00		50.00	35.00	10.00	5.00					40.00	60.00	15.00	45.00	25.00	15.00			5.00	65.00	30.00	
Western	55.56	44.44				66.68	27.77	5.55			50.00	27.28	22.22						33.33	66.67		16.66	16.66	61.13	5.55			77.79	16.66	5.55
Bundel-khand	64.71	35.29				58.83	41.17				35.29	47.07	17.64						29.41	70.59	11.76	11.76	47.07	29.41			23.52	52.96	17.64	5.88
Grand Total	64.57	31.64	2.53	1.26		65.83	24.05	8.86	1.26		56.98	25.31	16.45	1.26					26.58	73.42	10.12	24.05	25.31	26.58	8.86	5.06	10.12	56.98	20.25	7.59

A – Always
F – Frequently
ST – Some Time
R – Rarely
N – Never

Table 40
Behaviour of Female Colleagues
Kshetra Panchayat

(Percenatage Distribution)

Region	Co-operation/Support					Recognition for Advice					Appreciation					Teasing Comments					Encouragement					Indifference				
	A	*F*	*ST*	*R*	*N*	*A*	*F*	*ST*	*R*	*N*	*A*	*F*	*ST*	*R*	*N*	*A*	*F*	*ST*	*R*	*N*	*A*	*F*	*ST*	*R*	*N*	*A*	*F*	*ST*	*R*	*N*
Eastern	29.42	20.58	29.42	14.70	5.88	29.41	17.64	38.25	11.76	2.94	29.42	20.58	29.42	5.88	14.70	2.94			20.47	76.49		11.76	38.25	26.47	23.52	14.70	20.00	44.14	14.70	5.88
Central	24.44	24.44	28.91	8.88	13.33	22.22	24.44	35.58	8.88	8.88	6.66	28.88	33.37	15.55	15.55			13.33	51.12	35.55	2.22	22.22	31.11	33.34	11.11	4.44	13.33	37.79	40.00	4.44
Western	40.00	16.67	40.00	3.33		53.34	23.33	23.33			56.68	20.00	16.66	6.66					43.33	56.67	10.00	3.33	26.66	46.68	13.33		10.00	56.67	30.00	3.33
Bundel-khand	31.45	22.85	34.28		11.42	37.15	14.28	37.15	2.85	8.57	31.45	17.14	25.71	14.28	11.42			5.71	25.71	68.58			34.29	40.60	25.71	8.57	25.71	37.16	25.71	2.85
Grand Total	30.55	21.52	32.66	6.94	8.33	34.02	20.16	34.02	6.25	5.55	28.48	22.22	27.08	11.11	11.11	0.69		5.55	36.11	57.65	2.77	10.41	32.63	36.14	18.05	6.94	17.36	43.07	28.47	4.16

A = Always
F = Frequently
ST= Some Times
R = Rarely
N = Never

Table 41
Behaviour of Female Colleagues
Gram Panchayat

(Percenatage Distribution)

Region	Co-operation/Support					Recognition for Advice					Appreciation					Teasing Comments					Encouragement					Indifference				
	A	F	ST	R	N	A	F	ST	R	N	A	F	ST	R	N	A	F	ST	R	N	A	F	ST	R	N	A	F	ST	R	N
Eastern	25.80	32.27	29.03	12.90		25.80	35.50	27.41	11.29		25.80	27.41	30.67	11.29	4.83			4.83	24.19	70.98	4.83	12.90	24.19	32.28	25.80	8.06	32.28	37.09	17.7	4.83
Central	19.75	24.69	29.65	18.51	7.40	23.45	29.65	22.22	14.81	9.87	11.11	23.45	39.52	14.81	11.11			8.64	41.97	49.39	7.40	9.87	23.45	35.83	23.45	4.93	12.34	24.69	32.12	25.92
Western	47.48	23.72	25.42	1.69	1.69	50.87	15.25	25.42	6.77	1.69	50.88	10.16	16.94	5.08	16.94			1.69	32.20	66.11	8.47	23.72	33.92	25.42	8.47	16.94	28.85	23.72	27.11	3.38
Bundel-khand	22.53	29.60	22.53	7.04	18.30	25.37	23.94	21.12	15.49	14.08	22.53	15.49	26.76	16.90	18.32			5.63	26.76	67.61	7.04	9.85	14.08	26.76	42.27	11.26	23.94	53.55	9.85	1.40
Grand Total	27.86	27.47	26.73	10.62	7.32	30.43	26.37	23.80	12.45	6.95	26.00	19.41	29.32	12.45	12.82			5.49	31.86	62.65	6.96	13.55	23.46	30.4	25.64	9.89	23.44	34.81	21.97	9.89

A = Always
F = Frequently
ST= Some Times
R = Rarely
N = Never

The women chairpersons also express getting full support and cooperation from female members. It is because of their support that they feel confident and are able to perform their role effectively, as claimed by them.

As regards behaviour of male colleagues, female members find them cooperative and supportive in words but actually they do not give them importance, the women members deserve, as felt by many respondents. Male members have apprehensions about the ability of female members, hence their relationships are not always good. Though women members get cooperation and support but rarely get recognition, appreciation and encouragement. They some times receive teasing comments also from male members. Ironically, traditional male dominance still prevails and the male members have not changed their mindset. (Tables - 42, 43, 44)

At this level the officials were requested to give their opinion as to whether female members get cooperation from male colleagues or not. Surprisingly, about half of the officials find male members not cooperating with female representatives, whereas about one fourth admit that male representatives cooperate with female representatives. It may be that sometimes division may be made on political lines and male members would extend cooperation with female members belonging to same political outfit. The male members seek cooperation of women representatives where there is a need on political ground.

Scope for Conflicts and Adjustments

Demands of the political role are quite contradictory to the basic nature and societal role expectations of a woman. Because of this woman representatives have to make a lot of adjustments and bring changes both in their attitude, behaviour and lifestyle. Woman's familial role as a wife, mother, daughter-in-law and, the political role as a representative of the people are quite incompatible in nature. Hence to bring balance between both the roles and for making them more compatible, lot of adjustments both inside and outside the home are required. The incompatible demands

Table 42
Behaviour of Male Colleagues
Zila Panchayat

(Percenatage Distribution)

	Co-operation/Support					*Recognition for Advice*					*Appreciation*					*Teasing Comments*					*Encouragement*					*Indifference*				
Region	*A*	*F*	*ST*	*R*	*N*	*A*	*F*	*ST*	*R*	*N*	*A*	*F*	*ST*	*R*	*N*	*A*	*F*	*ST*	*R*	*N*	*A*	*F*	*ST*	*R*	*N*	*A*	*F*	*ST*	*R*	*N*
Eastern	33.33	8.33	58.34			33.33	25.00	25.00		16.67	33.33	16.67	25.00	8.33	16.67				25.00	75.00		8.33	41.68	33.33	16.66		16.66	58.34	25.00	
Central	25.00	10.00	25.00	40.00		30.00	5.00	20.00	45.00		30.00	5.00	25.00	40.00					10.00	90.00	10.00	10.00	25.00	30.00	25.00		10.00	55.55	35.00	
Western	22.22	61.12	16.66			33.33	39.90	22.22	5.55		33.33	44.46	16.66	5.55					5.55	94.45		16.66	44.46	33.33	5.55		16.66	38.90	33.33	11.11
Bundel-khand	29.41	41.18	29.41			23.52	29.41	47.07			23.52	11.76	41.20	17.64	5.88				17.64	82.36		23.52		52.96	23.52		11.76	41.19	35.29	11.76
Grand Total	27.84	27.84	34.20	10.12		30.40	24.05	27.84	12.65	5.06	30.40	18.98	26.58	17.72	6.32				15.18	84.82	2.53	13.92	29.11	36.70	17.72		13.92	49.36	31.64	5.06

A = Always
F = Frequently
ST= Some Times
R = Rarely
N = Never

Table 43
Behaviour of Male Colleagues
Kshetra Panchayat

(Percenatage Distribution)

Region	Co-operation/Support					Recognition for Advice					Appreciation					Teasing Comments					Encouragement					Indifference				
	A	F	ST	R	N	A	F	ST	R	N	A	F	ST	R	N	A	F	ST	R	N	A	F	ST	R	N	A	F	ST	R	N
Eastern	38.26	8.82	14.70	17.64	20.58	32.37	2.94	20.58	17.64	26.47	29.41	8.82	20.58	8.82	32.37			2.94	26.47	70.59		14.70	8.82	20.58	55.90	14.70	26.48	35.29	20.59	2.94
Central	4.44	2.22	37.79	33.33	22.22	4.44	4.44	42.24	24.44	24.44	2.22		44.46	26.66	26.66			20.00	33.33	46.67	2.22		26.66	40.00	31.12	13.33	15.58	37.77	24.44	8.88
Western	36.69	16.66	13.33	26.66	6.66	33.33	16.66	13.33	23.35	13.33	36.68	13.33	13.33	26.66	10.00			6.66	26.66	66.68		3.33	23.34	33.33	40.00	6.67	23.33	30.00	33.33	6.67
Bundel-khand	17.14	25.71	22.86	11.42	22.87	14.28	22.85	28.59	17.14	17.14	14.28	22.85	25.74	14.28	22.85			2.85	11.42	85.73			20.00	25.71	54.29	5.71	20.00	54.30	14.28	5.71
Grand Total	22.22	12.50	23.62	22.91	18.75	19.44	11.11	27.79	20.83	20.83	18.75	10.41	27.79	19.44	23.61			9.02	25.00	65.98	0.69	4.16	20.13	30.55	44.47	10.41	20.83	39.60	22.91	6.25

A = Always
F = Frequently
ST = Some Times
R = Rarely
N = Never

Table 44
Behaviour of Male Colleagues
Gram Panchayat

(Percenatage Distribution)

	Co-operation/Support					*Recognition for Advice*					*Appreciation*					*Teasing Comments*					*Encouragement*					*Indifference*				
Region	*A*	*F*	*ST*	*R*	*N*	*A*	*F*	*ST*	*R*	*N*	*A*	*F*	*ST*	*R*	*N*	*A*	*F*	*ST*	*R*	*N*	*A*	*F*	*ST*	*R*	*N*	*A*	*F*	*ST*	*R*	*N*
Eastern	12.90	14.51	24.19	22.58	25.82	12.90	14.51	25.80	17.74	29.05	11.29	9.67	25.80	14.51	38.73			3.22	27.41	69.37		6.45	16.12	25.80	51.63	11.29	37.09	38.72	11.3	1.61
Central	3.70	14.81	22.22	32.11	27.16	3.70	19.75	25.94	22.22	28.39	2.46	14.83	14.82	32.09	35.80		6.17	22.22	30.86	40.75	2.46	12.34	9.87	34.56	40.77	7.40	11.11	41.99	19.75	19.75
Western	13.55	20.33	28.85	13.55	23.72	11.86	16.94	30.53	22.03	18.64	11.86	11.86	32.20	20.33	23.75			8.47	28.81	62.72			25.42	30.50	44.08	5.08	16.95	30.50	37.28	10.19
Bundel-khand	8.45	14.08	19.71	26.76	31.00	7.04	15.49	25.35	22.53	29.59	4.22	15.49	19.71	16.90	43.68			9.85	19.71	70.44		2.81	7.04	16.90	73.25	19.71	25.35	36.64	11.26	7.04
Grand Total	9.15	15.75	23.44	24.54	27.12	8.42	16.84	26.75	21.24	26.8	6.95	13.18	22.34	21.61	35.92		1.83	11.72	26.73	59.72	0.73	5.86	13.91	27.10	52.40	10.98	21.97	37.39	19.41	10.25

A = Always
F = Frequently
ST = Some Times
R = Rarely
N = Never

from both fronts are the major reason for role conflict among women representatives.

Surprisingly, every fourth women representatives took up this role because of compulsion form her husband or family members (probably because of revolutionary provisions (73rd Constitution Amendment Act), whereas one-fifth women entered into local politics for maintaining the family traditions. Since seats are reserved for women, husband and other male family members interested in politics bring their wives, daughters-in-law etc. to fulfill their own political ambition. However, there are about one-seventh women representatives who opted for this role because of their own interest in politics. Such women are found to be more active and they take independent decisions on all aspects. About one-fifth of women chose the political role for sake of personality development and also for engaging themselves in social service. This may however be a cover as the politicians at all the levels claim to practice politics for rendering social service. Social service in their view covers in real sense all they claim to do.

Table 45
Male Members Cooperate with Female Members

(Percentage Distribution)

Region	*District*	*Yes*	*No*	*NR*	*Total*
Eastern	Varanasi	36.36	36.36	27.28	100.00
	Gorakhpur	45.45	45.45	9.10	100.00
	Ballia	20.00	40.00	40.00	100.00
Total		25.00	50.00	25.00	100.00
Central	Lucknow	38.10	33.33	28.57	100.00
	Balrampur	18.75	68.75	12.50	100.00
	Sitapur	23.07	61.55	15.38	100.00
Total		28.00	62.00	20.00	100.00
Western	Bagpat	33.33	33.33	33.34	100.00
	Mathura	22.22	66.67	11.11	100.00
	Moradabad	41.67	50.00	8.33	100.00
Total		33.33	48.49	18.18	100.00
Bundelkhand	Banda	8.33	41.67	50.00	100.00
	Hamirpur	42.87	35.71	21.42	100.00
	Jhansi	28.58	50.00	21.42	100.00
Total		27.50	42.50	30.00	100.00
Grand Total		28.38	48.40	23.22	100.00

Table 46
Ranking Reasons for Entering into the New Role

(Percentage Distribution)

Factors	*1*	2	3	4	5
Interest in politics	15.75	12.50	10.75	10.00	6.25
Maintaining family tradition	20.00	17.50	13.00	16.75	5.00
Under compulsion	25.00	15.50	21.25	12.75	12.50
On moral conscience	6.25	7.50	5.00	6.50	8.50
Enjoy new role	3.75	10.00	5.00	16.00	10.75
Free from home work	8.50	8.75	8.75	8.50	12.50
Feel freedom & Independence	–	5.30	5.00	12.50	12.50
Scope for personality development	7.75	12.30	15.00	12.50	8.50
Scope for social service	13.00	10.65	16.25	12.50	12.50
Fear of in-laws/parents	–	–	–	6.00	10.00
Total	100.00	100.00	100.00	100.00	100.00

The further analyses region-wise and panchayat wise are quite informative. More than one-fifth women in Zila Panchayats show 'interest in politics'as reason for accepting the new role, whereas the number of such women is found reducing at lower tiers of panchayats. Surprisingly, 'maintaining family tradition' and 'under compulsion' are the reasons scoring highest at all the three levels. Unfortunately, women have not suffered from lack of participation in development but, rather, from their enforced but asymmetric participation in it, by which they bear the costs but are excluded from the benefits.

Here officials were asked as to whether women representatives work ever as a pressure group in panchayats. The responses show the disinterest of women towards their new roles and responsibilities. Majority of the officials do not find any pressure group of women representatives. Had they been interested in getting the official roles done and establishing themselves in panchayats, and their voices heard, the women representatives would have formed a pressure group. This would be an indicator of their getting empowered. It is therefore necessary that women representatives should come out of their political garb and form a group of their own. It would help them in getting their voices heard by all–other representatives, officials, citizen, their family members and the State government.

Table 47
Highest Preference–Zone Wise

Response	*Zila Panchayat*					*Kshetra Panchayat*					*Gram Panchayat*				
	E	*C*	*W*	*B*	*State*	*E*	*C*	*W*	*B*	*State*	*E*	*C*	*W*	*B*	*State*
Interest in politicts	33.33	20.00	8.88	29.41	22.98	8.82	6.66	–	20.00	8.87	11.29	16.04	8.47	18.30	13.52
Maintain family tradition	50.00	40.00	64.70	35.29	47.49	47.05	17.77	30.00	42.85	36.91	59.67	20.98	27.11	26.80	33.64
Under compulsion	41.66	35.00	38.88	23.52	34.76	41.11	46.66	50.00	34.28	43.01	58.00	38.27	49.15	53.52	49.73
Moral conscience	8.33	10.00	5.56	23.52	11.85	5.85	4.44	–	2.85	3.28	11.61	6.70	5.08	4.22	6.77
Fear in-laws/parents	–	5.00	–	–	1.25	14.70	8.88	–	2.85	6.60	23.20	17.28	5.08	5.63	12.79
Enjoy this new role	8.33	5.00	22.22	29.41	16.24	11.76	6.66	6.66	17.14	7.93	11.29	8.64	–	14.08	8.50
Free from home work	–	10.00	–	–	2.50	–	–	6.66	–	1.67	–	1.23	3.38	–	1.15
Feel freedom & Independence	–	5.00	–	–	1.25	–	–	–	–	–	–	–	–	–	–
Scope for personality development	29.63	15.00	22.20	23.52	22.58	17.64	4.44	10.00	11.42	10.90	17.74	11.11	5.08	12.67	11.65
Scope for social services	16.66	25.00	27.77	29.41	**24.71**	11.76	6.66	13.38	14.28	**11.52**	17.72	17.28	28.81	14.08	**19.47**

E – Eastern Zone
C – Central Zone
W – Western Zone
B – Bundelkhand

Table 48
Women Forming a Pressure Group

(Percentage Distribution)

Region	*District*	*Yes*	*No*	*Total*
Eastern	Varanasi		100.00	100.00
	Gorakhpur	18.18	81.82	100.00
	Ballia	10.00	90.00	100.00
Total		9.37	90.63	100.00
Central	Lucknow	19.04	80.96	100.00
	Balrampur		100.00	100.00
	Sitapur	15.38	84.62	100.00
Total		12.00	88.00	100.00
Western	Bagpat	33.33	66.67	100.00
	Mathura	11.11	88.89	100.00
	Moradabad	8.33	91.67	100.00
Total		18.18	81.82	100.00
Bundelkhand	Banda	16.66	83.34	100.00
	Hamirpur	7.14	92.86	100.00
	Jhansi	7.14	92.86	100.00
Total		10.00	90.00	100.00
Grand Total		12.25	87.75	100.00

In connection with continuing with this new role, majority of the women representatives want to continue in this role for getting enhanced social status. By accepting this new role their status has raised, both in the society as well as in the family. The next reason identified by women representatives at all the levels is to prepare political background for their family. Interestingly, the responses are found increasing from 69.62 per cent at Zila Panchayat to 79.17 per cent at Kshetra Panchayat and further to 81.02 percent at Gram Panchayat levels. This illustrates their intention of treating local public office as their family fiefdom. A substantial number of women members wish to continue in this new role for shaping a career in politics, while some finds it a proper platform for utilizing their time and making use of their education.

Overall, most of the women feel good about their new role and wish to continue. It seems that they have tasted the fruits of political role and are not willing to go back within the four walls of home, despite constraints and problems. Financial benefit may be one attraction, but a good number of the women members like independence and wish to increase their mental faculty through this challenging role. This indicates the initiation of process of empowerment among women, although in a confusing state of affairs.

Table 49
Reasons for Continuing in New Role
Zila Panchayat

(Percentage Distribution)

Region	*Financial Gain*	*Indepe-ndence*	*To get Social Status*	*Shaping a Career*	*Utilise Education*	*Utilise Time Properly*	*Increase Mental Faculty*	*Prepare Background for Family*
Eastern	41.67	4.17	79.17	8.33	4.17	–	4.17	66.67
Central	30.00	10.00	90.00	10.00	30.00	30.00	10.00	75.00
Western	–	22.22	75.00	33.33	22.22	16.67	27.78	88.89
Bundelkhand	5.88	–	100.00	41.17	47.06	29.41	52.94	47.06
Grand Total	21.52	8.86	83.54	21.52	24.05	17.72	21.52	69.62

Table 50
Reasons for Continuing in New Role
Kshetra Panchayat

(Percentage Distribution)

Region	*Financial Gain*	*Indepe-ndence*	*To get Social Status*	*Shaping a Career*	*Utilise Education*	*Utilise Time Properly*	*Increase Mental Faculty*	*Prepare Background for Family*
Eastern	26.47	8.82	70.58	–	17.64	8.82	23.52	82.35
Central	33.33	8.89	71.11	–	2.22	6.67	8.89	84.44
Western	20.00	10.00	96.67	3.33	13.33	6.67	16.67	80.00
Bundelkhand	22.85	8.57	–	28.57	8.57	25.71	57.14	68.57
Grand Total	26.39	9.03	–	7.64	9.72	11.81	25.69	79.17

Table 51
Reasons for Continuing in New Role
Gram Panchayat

(Percentage Distribution)

Region	*Financial Gain*	*Indepe-ndence*	*To get Social Status*	*Shaping a Career*	*Utilise Education*	*Utilise Time Properly*	*Increase Mental Faculty*	*Prepare Background for Family*
Eastern	40.32	8.06	87.09	4.83	6.45	6.45	25.80	88.70
Central	51.85	18.51	67.90	11.11	3.70	2.46	12.34	82.71
Western	61.01	23.72	79.66	23.72	6.77	6.77	10.16	83.05
Bundelkhand	46.47	5.63	80.28	16.90	7.04	12.67	14.08	67.60
Grand Total	50.31	13.91	78.02	13.91	5.86	6.95	15.38	81.02

Despite all the constraints and criticisms, the women representatives do not feel going back. They wish to continue with the political role because they enjoy their new role. The extent of enjoyment may differ from tier to tier, but the extent is highest (88.04 per cent) at Zila Panchayats level. Surprisingly, it is found decreasing to 68.75 percent at Kshetra Panchayats and further to 58.98 at Gram Panchayats. Contrarily, the number of women representatives not enjoying their new avatar is recorded increasing from one-tenth at Zila Panchayats to three out of ten at Kshetra Panchayats and further to two-fifths in Gram Panchayats.

This shows that women having accepted this new role under compulsion belong to this category. Those who were brought in this role under compulsion find the responsibilities very demanding hence do not enjoy their role very much. Surprisingly, a large number of women representatives in Gram Panchayats are not enjoying their role. It may be because of prevailing non-conducive working environment there in or in real sense most of them are not playing any role.

Table 52
Role Enjoyment
Zila Panchayat

(Percentage Distribution)

Region	*Great Extent*	*Some Extent*	*Not At All*	*Total*
Eastern	33.34	50.00	16.66	100.00
Central	30.00	50.00	20.00	100.00
Western	33.33	61.12	5.55	100.00
Bundelkhand	52.95	47.05		100.00
Grand Total	36.70	51.91	11.39	100.00

Table 53
Role Enjoyment
Kshetra Panchayat

(Percentage Distribution)

Region	*Great Extent*	*Some Extent*	*Not At All*	*Total*
Eastern	11.76	61.77	26.47	100.00
Central	6.66	53.34	40.00	100.00
Western	6.66	60.00	33.34	100.00
Bundelkhand	22.85	54.30	22.85	100.00
Grand Total	11.80	56.95	31.25	100.00

Table 54
Role Enjoyment
Gram Panchayat

(Percentage Distribution)

Region	*Great Extent*	*Some Extent*	*Not At All*	*Total*
Eastern	4.83	46.77	48.40	100.00
Central	9.87	46.93	43.20	100.00
Western	15.25	49.16	35.59	100.00
Bundelkhand	15.49	47.90	36.61	100.00
Grand Total	11.35	47.63	41.02	100.00

As regards contesting local elections again in future, a good number of the women representatives wish to contest elections and come back. But those on whom the political role appears to have been imposed (they are in majority) lack independent opinion and leave the decision of contesting elections in future on their male family members. It reflects that women in general are not allowed to be empowered, less by circumstances, more by male chauvinism, even after a decade of initiating the new dispensation. Further, women not enjoying their new roles intend either not to contest elections in future or leave the matter to their family members. Such a situation indicates the existence of scope of representation by proxy. This needs to be eliminated, as number of such women is found increasing from half at Zila Panchayats to two-thirds and more at lower panchayat levels. All the regions in the state present the same colour.

Table 55
Contesting Elections in Future
Zila Panchayat

(Percentage Distribution)

Region	*Yes*	*No*	*Depends Upon Family*	*Total*
Eastern	33.33		66.67	100.00
Central	35.00		65.00	100.00
Western	55.57	5.55	38.88	100.00
Bundelkhand	76.48		23.52	100.00
Grand Total	48.10	1.26	50.64	100.00

Table 56
Contesting Elections in Future
Kshetra Panchayat

(Percentage Distribution)

Region	*Yes*	*No*	*Depends Upon Family*	*Total*
Eastern	23.52	11.76	64.72	100.00
Central	26.66	8.88	64.46	100.00
Western	30.00	13.33	56.67	100.00
Bundelkhand	31.42	11.42	57.16	100.00
Grand Total	27.77	11.11	61.12	100.00

Table 57
Contesting Elections in Future
Gram Panchayat

(Percentage Distribution)

Region	*Yes*	*No*	*Depends Upon Family*	*Total*
Eastern	14.51	20.96	64.53	100.00
Central	22.22	8.64	69.14	100.00
Western	23.72	15.25	61.03	100.00
Bundelkhand	25.35	14.08	60.57	100.00
Grand Total	21.61	14.28	64.11	100.00

Surprisingly, even after becoming representatives in Panchayati Raj Institution, for women there is no concession in responsibilities and duties towards their family, children and husband. They are expected to perform these duties and responsibilities in perfection, while the political role creates obstacles and leads to conflicting situations. In Indian society, home and family are the sole responsibility of a woman and her all other roles come later on. The women belonging to middle and lower classes having higher ambitions are being crushed in between their traditional and imposed roles. The male dominated society and family both are the culprits for creating such a situation.

When the women representatives are unable to manage the demands of both family and panchayats, they experience lot of stress and strain. This is the major cause of role conflict among them. Many a times they are found unconcerned and

Table 58
Impact of New Role
Zila Panchayat

(Percentage Distribution)

Region	*Health Deterioration*	*Mental Tension*	*Heavy Work Load*	*Rigid Social Norms*	*Ugly Situation*	*Pressure of Husband*	*Pressure of Family*	*Pressure from Acquaintances*	*Pressure of Children*
Eastern	29.17	12.50	12.50	45.83	41.67	29.17	54.17	-	12.50
Central	35.00	10.00	25.00	75.00	25.00	-	60.00	50.00	25.00
Western	44.44	33.33	22.22	27.78	38.89	16.67	77.78	38.89	11.11
Bundelkhand	23.52	70.58	41.17	29.41	29.41	29.41	52.94	52.94	17.64
Grand Total	34.17	29.11	24.05	45.57	34.18	18.98	60.75	-	16.46

Table 59
Impact of New Role
Kshetra Panchayat

(Percentage Distribution)

Region	*Health Deteri-oration*	*Mental Tension*	*Heavy Work Load*	*Rigid Social Norms*	*Ugly Situ-ation*	*Pressure of Husband*	*Pressure of Family*	*Pressure from Acqua-intances*	*Pressure of Children*
Eastern	41.17	32.35	17.64	55.88	38.23	14.70	32.35	55.88	8.82
Central	26.67	24.44	15.55	62.22	33.33	15.55	60.00	60.00	13.33
Western	23.33	6.67	12.33	43.33	46.67	26.67	76.67	43.33	20.00
Bundelkhand	45.71	20.00	40.00	22.85	28.57	37.14	62.85	68.57	17.14
Grand Total	34.03	21.53	21.53	47.22	36.11	22.92	57.64	57.64	14.58

Table 60
Impact of New Role
Gram Panchayat

(Percentage Distribution)

Region	*Health Deteri-oration*	*Mental Tension*	*Heavy Work Load*	*Rigid Social Norms*	*Ugly Situ-ation*	*Pressure of Husband*	*Pressure of Family*	*Pressure from Acqua-intances*	*Pressure of Children*
Eastern	45.16	25.80	17.74	54.84	33.87	19.35	53.22	74.19	12.90
Central	14.81	29.63	28.39	60.49	40.74	9.88	62.96	37.04	17.28
Western	6.78	16.94	28.81	69.49	64.41	18.64	74.58	44.07	15.25
Bundelkhand	26.76	18.30	29.57	39.43	28.16	35.21	81.69	54.92	8.45
Grand Total	20.87	23.07	26.37	55.67	41.02	20.51	68.13	51.64	13.55

apathetic with local administration to the extent that their familial role is not at all disturbed. Scope of conflict arises when the women members perform their new role actively. Most of them are found not sincere about their new role, hence less scope for role conflict.

It has become necessary for women representatives to devote lot of time towards Panchayat functions in addition to pressure on them for managing the family affairs. Those who take both the roles seriously (one-fourth) face heavy workload, pressure from husband (one-fifth), pressure from children (one-tenth) and mental tension (one-fourth), which affect their performance in their new role as representative and also as home manager. Contrarily for those who enjoy the political role because of imposition, it is a ritual and hence no conflict. They seldom feel any pressure of work and tension in life. They take it easy without any botheration. The serious players face problems at both the ends if family members are not cooperative and positive. It is observed that with the passage of time they have reconciled with the situation and adjustments have been made in most of the cases, exceptions are there but rare.

The situation warrants training and development for women representatives. The development workshops should be organised exclusively for women representatives, away form home for a few days and no male family member should be allowed. Staying alone away from home would certainly develop confidence among women, they would initiate thinking independently. Such programmes are more necessary for women at Gram Panchayat and Kshetra Panchayat levels.

Women representatives do feel that though their new role has brought them good status, but it has adversely affected their family. It is presumed that due to involvement in the new role, the women are unable to pay full attention towards family needs. The reality is however quite contrary. At Zila Panchayat level women representatives (about half) do feel that their joining the political role has hampered, to varying extent, the education of children, the health of children and development of their family besides curtailing sometime for husband and parents (in-laws). But the women at Kshetra and Gram Panchayats have belied by majority all these myths. The analysis of responses analysed on regional and district levels are quite encouraging. The differing extent and contrary opinions may be due to their level of active involvement in new role and also the workload. (Tables – 61, 62, 63)

The women representatives should be subjected to attitudinal change programmes. They need to be made aware that being home manager family is their prime responsibility but not their role responsibility. Husband and all other members also have to play their role. Managing the home is a collective responsibility of all the family members and not of women alone. The women should be oriented to enter into roles other than their familial roles.

The active involvement in new role may cause lot of grievances and disputes within the family, which may affect the harmony and create stressful situations. This may be one of the reasons that many women in general prefer not to take their new role seriously. They don't want to vitiate their family atmosphere because of their joining politics. However, instances are available where women have shown brevity and are playing new role in a serious manner with commitment without caring for criticism from family members, sometime from husband also. They are truthful and sincere to their new role.

While turning the leaf containing negative aspects, women representatives overall are found quite happy with their new role. Earlier they were confined only to the four walls of their house and did not have any identity of their own but after joining the local politics they have gained high status in family, command more respect, get love and affection and security and protection of the family.

It is quite pleasant that women representatives at all the tiers feel to have acquired increased social awareness and enriched their mental faculty. They feel proud in helping the society and also elevating their family standard. Truly, they feel having gained a lot as a result of their new role.

Table 61
Joining the Politics Hamperd
Zila Panchayat

(Percentage Distribution)

Region	Children's Education					Children's Health					Husband's Love					Parent's Care					Family Development					Family Harmony					Social Life				
	F	GE	P	L	NA	F	GE	P	L	NA	F	GE	P	L	NA	F	GE	P	L	NA	F	GE	P	L	NA	F	GE	P	L	NA	F	GE	P	L	NA
Eastern			50.00	16.67	33.33			41.67	33.33	25.00		8.34		25.00	66.66		22.22	33.33	44.45					41.66	58.34				33.33	66.67			8.34	41.66	50.00
Central			15.00	55.00	30.00			15.00	55.00	30.00				70.00	30.00		7.69	23.07	38.48	30.76				45.55	55.55				25.00	75.00	5.00	15.00	10.00	40.00	30.00
Western			22.22	22.22	55.56			16.66	11.11	72.23				5.88	94.12				42.85	57.15				16.67	83.33				16.66	83.34			44.44	5.56	50.00
Bundelkhand			11.78	23.52	64.70			17.64	29.42	52.94				25.00	75.00				20.00	80.00			11.78	33.52	64.70					100.00			17.64	47.07	35.29
Grand Total			26.58	29.11	44.31			24.05	32.91	43.04		2.59		32.46	64.95		6.52	13.04	36.95	43.49			2.53	32.91	64.56				20.25	79.75	1.26	3.79	18.98	34.17	41.80

F = Fully
GE = Great Extent
P = Partially
L = Little
NA = Not at All

Table 62
Joining the Politics Hamperd
Kshetra Panchayat

(Percentage Distribution)

Region	Children's Education					Children's Health					Husband's Love					Parent's Care					Family Development					Family Harmony					Social Life				
	F	GE	P	L	NA	F	GE	P	L	NA	F	GE	P	L	NA	F	GE	P	L	NA	F	GE	P	L	NA	F	GE	P	L	NA	F	GE	P	L	NA
Eastern				8.82	91.18			2.94	8.82	88.24			6.07	18.18	75.75				37.50	62.50				14.70	85.30			11.76	2.94	85.30			17.65	17.65	64.70
Central				22.22	77.78				24.44	75.56			2.22	20.00	77.78			3.70	29.62	66.68	2.22			20.00	77.78	2.22			22.22	75.56	4.44	2.22	6.66	24.44	62.24
Western			20.00	20.00	60.00			6.66	30.00	73.34				16.66	83.34				33.33	66.67			3.33	20.00	76.67			3.34	16.66	80.00			16.66	23.34	60.00
Bundel-khand		2.85	17.14	28.57	51.44		2.85	20.00	25.71	51.44		2.86	5.71	11.43	80.00			7.69	46.15	46.16		2.85	5.71	2.85	88.59			8.57	5.71	85.72		2.85	17.14	31.42	48.59
Grand Total		0.69	8.33	20.13	70.85		0.69	6.94	20.13	72.24		0.69	3.49	16.78	79.04	1.61	1.61	3.22	33.87	59.69	0.69	0.69	2.08	14.58	81.96	0.69		5.55	12.50	81.26	1.38	1.38	13.88	24.30	59.06

F = Fully
GE = Great Extent
P = Partially
L = Little
NA = Not at All

Table 63
Joining the Politics Hamperd
Gram Panchayat

(Percentage Distribution)

Region	Children's Education					Children's Health					Husband's Love					Parent's Care					Family Development					Family Harmony					Social Life				
	F	GE	P	L	NA	F	GE	P	L	NA	F	GE	P	L	NA	F	GE	P	L	NA	F	GE	P	L	NA	F	GE	P	L	NA	F	GE	P	L	NA
Eastern		1.61	3.22	22.58	72.59			4.83	17.74	77.43		1.63	3.27	21.31	73.79		3.70	22.22	18.51	55.57			3.22	17.74	79.04			3.22	19.35	77.43		1.61	17.74	14.51	66.14
Central			16.04	20.98	62.98			12.34	28.39	59.27				29.48	70.52		7.89	23.68	26.31	42.12	1.23	6.17	12.34	14.81	65.45		1.23	9.87	12.34	76.56	4.93	4.93	9.87	25.92	54.35
Western			23.72	33.89	42.39			23.72	32.20	44.08			3.44	15.51	81.05			25.00	18.75	56.25			13.55	30.50	55.95			15.25	30.50	54.25		6.77	18.64	32.20	42.39
Bundelkhand	1.40	1.40	7.04	23.94	66.22		1.40	8.45	18.30	71.85	1.40	1.40	2.81	12.67	81.72			16.66	20.84	62.50			5.63	7.04	87.33				1.40	98.60			7.04	22.53	70.43
Grand Total	0.36	0.73	12.45	24.90	61.56		0.36	12.08	24.17	63.39	0.37	0.74	2.23	20.14	76.52		3.30	22.31	21.48	52.91	0.36	1.83	8.79	16.84	72.18		0.36	6.95	15.01	77.68	1.46	3.29	12.82	23.80	58.63

F = Fully
GE = Great Extent
P = Partially
L = Little
NA = Not at All

Table 64
Feeling in the Family with New Role
Zila Panchayat

(Percentage Distribution)

Region	District	Honour & Respect				Love & Affection				Security & Protection			
		Always	*Some time*	*Rarely*	*Never*	*Always*	*Some time*	*Rarely*	*Never*	*Always*	*Some time*	*Rarely*	*Never*
Eastern	Varanasi	50.00	50.00	-	-	-	100.00	-	-	-	50.00	50.00	-
	Gorakhpur	16.66	41.67	41.67	-	16.66	33.34	16.66	33.34	16.66	33.34	16.66	33.34
	Ballia	-	62.50	37.50	-	-	75.00	25.00	-	-	25.00	25.00	50.00
Total		16.67	50.00	33.33	-	8.33	58.35	16.66	16.66	8.33	33.34	25.00	33.33
Central	Lucknow	51.15	42.85	-	-	57.15	28.57	14.28	-	57.15	28.57	14.28	-
	Balrampur	20.00	40.00	40.00	-	20.00	-	80.00	-	20.00	80.00	-	-
	Sitapur	-	62.50	25.00	12.50	37.50	37.50	25.00	-	-	25.00	50.00	25.00
Total		25.00	50.00	20.00	5.00	40.00	25.00	35.00	-	25.00	40.00	25.00	10.00
Western	Bagpat	16.66	-	66.68	16.66	-	33.33	33.33	33.34	16.66	-	66.68	16.66
	Mathura	25.00	50.00	25.00	-	25.00	50.00	25.00	-	-	25.00	50.00	25.00
	Moradabad	-	75.00	25.00	-	-	-	75.00	25.00	-	25.00	25.00	50.00
Total		11.11	44.46	38.88	5.55	5.55	22.23	50.00	22.22	5.55	16.66	44.46	33.33
Bundelkhand	Banda	33.33	33.33	33.34	-	-	33.33	33.33	33.34	-	-	50.00	50.00
	Hamirpur	20.00	40.00	40.00	-	-	40.00	40.00	20.00	-	40.00	20.00	40.00
	Jhansi	66.68	16.66	16.66	-	-	33.33	33.33	33.34	-	16.66	50.00	33.34
Total		41.18	29.41	29.41	-	-	35.30	35.29	29.41	-	17.64	41.18	41.18
Grand Total		22.78	44.32	30.37	2.53	13.92	36.72	32.91	16.45	10.12	27.84	32.93	29.11

Table 65
Feeling in the Family with New Role
Kshetra Panchayat

(Percentage Distribution)

		Honour & Respect				Love & Affection				Security & Protection			
Region	*District*	*Always*	*Some time*	*Rarely*	*Never*	*Always*	*Some time*	*Rarely*	*Never*	*Always*	*Some time*	*Rarely*	*Never*
Eastern	Varanasi	25.00	50.00	25.00	-	25.00	50.00	25.00	-	25.00	50.00	25.00	-
	Gorakhpur	6.66	13.33	33.33	46.68	6.66	-	46.67	46.67	6.66	-	20.00	73.34
	Ballia	-	18.18	36.36	45.46	-	9.09	27.27	63.64	-	-	18.18	81.82
Total		8.82	23.52	32.35	35.31	8.82	14.70	35.29	41.19	8.82	11.76	20.58	58.84
Central	Lucknow	16.66	22.22	33.35	27.77	5.55	16.66	44.46	33.33	5.55	11.11	38.88	44.46
	Balrampur	30.76	15.38	38.48	15.38	38.48	15.38	30.76	15.38	23.10	15.38	30.76	30.76
	Sitapur	28.57	57.15	14.28	-	-	42.86	28.57	28.57	14.28	21.44	50.00	14.28
Total		24.44	31.13	28.88	15.55	13.33	24.44	35.57	26.66	13.33	15.56	40.00	31.11
Western	Bagpat	-	10.00	40.00	50.00	-	10.00	20.00	70.00	10.00	10.00	20.00	60.00
	Mathura	62.50	25.00	12.50	-	-	37.50	50.00	12.50	25.00	25.00	25.00	25.00
	Moradabad	8.33	8.33	50.00	33.34	-	16.66	33.34	50.00	-	16.66	16.66	66.68
Total		20.00	13.33	36.67	30.00	-	20.00	33.33	46.67	10.00	16.66	20.00	53.34
Bundelkhand	Banda	16.66	58.34	25.00	-	-	16.66	41.67	41.67	-	8.33	41.67	50.00
	Hamirpur	-	50.00	-	50.00	-	10.00	50.00	40.00	10.00	10.00	20.00	60.00
	Jhansi	7.69	38.46	38.47	15.38	-	7.69	53.85	38.46	-	7.69	38.46	53.85
Total		8.57	48.58	22.85	20.00	-	11.42	48.58	40.00	2.85	8.57	34.28	54.30
Grand Total		15.97	29.87	29.86	24.30	6.25	18.05	38.20	37.50	9.02	13.19	29.86	47.93

Table 66
Feeling in the Family with New Role
Gram Panchayat

(Percentage Distribution)

		Honour & Respect				*Love & Affection*				*Security & Protection*			
Region	*District*	*Always*	*Some time*	*Rarely*	*Never*	*Always*	*Some time*	*Rarely*	*Never*	*Always*	*Some time*	*Rarely*	*Never*
Eastern	Varanasi	47.08	23.52	23.52	5.88	29.41	35.31	23.52	11.76	23.52	23.52	41.20	11.76
	Gorakhpur	-	9.52	80.96	9.52	-	9.52	19.04	71.44	-	4.76	42.85	52.39
	Ballia	-	4.16	37.50	58.34	-	-	41.66	58.34	-	-	37.50	62.50
Total		12.90	11.29	48.40	27.41	8.06	12.90	29.04	50.00	6.45	8.06	40.32	45.17
Central	Lucknow	28.57	20.00	14.28	37.15	25.72	20.00	14.28	40.00	22.85	17.14	28.57	31.44
	Balrampur	50.00	11.11	5.55	33.34	27.78	27.78	16.66	27.78	27.78	22.22	22.22	27.78
	Sitapur	28.57	7.14	28.57	35.72	-	35.72	35.72	28.56	-	3.57	35.72	60.71
Total		33.33	13.58	17.28	35.81	17.28	27.16	22.22	33.34	16.04	13.58	29.62	40.76
Western	Bagpat	-	16.66	16.66	66.68	-	5.55	22.22	72.23	-	11.11	11.11	77.78
	Mathura	52.65	26.31	10.52	10.52	26.31	26.31	10.52	36.86	21.05	26.31	10.52	42.12
	Moradabad	27.29	40.90	22.72	9.09	27.28	27.28	22.72	22.72	9.09	18.18	18.18	54.55
Total		27.11	28.84	16.94	27.11	18.64	20.33	18.64	42.39	10.16	18.64	13.55	57.65
Bundelkhand	Banda	19.23	30.78	23.07	26.92	-	3.84	23.07	73.09	-	3.84	15.38	80.78
	Hamirpur	9.09	13.63	18.18	59.10	-	9.09	18.18	72.73	4.54	-	22.72	72.74
	Jhansi	17.39	34.80	21.73	26.08	4.34	8.69	43.49	43.48	13.04	4.34	30.43	52.19
Total		15.49	26.76	21.12	36.63	1.40	7.04	28.16	63.40	5.63	2.81	22.53	69.03
Grand Total		22.71	19.78	25.27	32.24	11.35	17.21	24.54	46.90	9.89	10.62	26.73	52.76

Table 67
Benefits of New Role
Zila Panchayat

(Percentage Distribution)

Region	*High Status in Family*	*Social Prestige*	*Help to Society*	*Help to Family*	*Social Awar-eness*	*Total*
Eastern	62.50	70.83	70.83	16.66	37.50	100.00
Central	45.00	80.00	55.00	20.00	35.00	100.00
Western	33.33	83.33	77.77	33.33	38.88	100.00
Bundelkhand	11.76	64.70	94.11	11.76	76.47	100.00
Gramd Total	79.66	97.16	73.41	20.25	45.56	100.00

Table 68
Benefits of New Role
Kshetra Panchayat

(Percentage Distribution)

Region	*High Status in Family*	*Social Prestige*	*Help to Society*	*Help to Family*	*Social Awar-eness*	*Total*
Eastern	38.23	55.88	41.17	41.17	35.29	100.00
Central	33.33	84.44	42.22	26.66	31.11	100.00
Western	43.33	70.00	66.66	43.33	33.33	100.00
Bundelkhand	-	74.28	57.14	34.28	54.28	100.00
Gramd Total	28.47	72.22	50.69	35.41	38.19	100.00

Table 69
Benefits of New Role
Gram Panchayat

(Percentage Distribution)

Region	*High Status in Family*	*Social Prestige*	*Help to Society*	*Help to Family*	*Social Awar-eness*	*Total*
Eastern	56.45	75.80	70.96	37.09	14.51	100.00
Central	37.03	74.07	39.50	35.80	32.09	100.00
Western	55.93	61.01	55.93	40.67	45.76	100.00
Bundelkhand	22.53	76.05	64.78	28.16	43.66	100.00
Gramd Total	41.75	72.16	56.77	35.16	34.06	100.00

On enquiry as to how would they feel without this role, the women representatives of all the three tiers express that they would become again victim of tradition, lose their self confidence and development, lose freedom and would feel

Table 70
Feelings without this New Role
Zila Panchayat

(Percentage Distribution)

	Victim of Tradition				*Lack of Self Development*				*Lack of Freedom*				*Insecurity*				*Under Pressure*			
Region	*A*	*ST*	*R*	*N*	*A*	*ST*	*R*	*N*	*A*	*ST*	*R*	*N*	*A*	*ST*	*R*	*N*	*A*	*ST*	*R*	*N*
Eastern		33.33	45.84	20.83		33.33	41.67	25.00	8.33	25.00	61.67	25.00		37.50	29.17	33.33		50.00	16.67	33.33
Central	20.00	20.00	35.00	25.00	15.00	20.00	35.00	30.00	10.00	25.00	35.00	30.00	10.00	10.00	50.00	30.00	10.00	10.00	55.00	25.00
Western	11.11	27.78	50.00	11.11	11.11	22.22	27.77	38.90	5.55	33.33	33.33	27.79	5.55	11.11	44.46	38.88	5.56	27.78	33.33	33.33
Bundelkhand		47.06	35.29	17.65	11.76	23.52	41.20	23.52		11.76	47.05	41.19		5.88	35.29	58.83	5.88	47.05	29.42	17.65
Grand Total	7.59	31.64	41.79	18.98	8.86	25.31	36.72	29.11	6.32	24.05	39.24	30.37	3.79	17.73	39.24	39.24	5.06	34.19	32.91	27.84

A - Always
ST - Sometime
R - Rarely
N - Never

Table 71
Feelings without this New Role
Kshetra Panchayat

Percentage Distribution)

	Victim of Tradition				*Lack of Self Development*				*Lack of Freedom*				*Insecurity*				*Under Pressure*			
Region	*A*	*ST*	*R*	*N*	*A*	*ST*	*R*	*N*	*A*	*ST*	*R*	*N*	*A*	*ST*	*R*	*N*	*A*	*ST*	*R*	*N*
Eastern	5.88	32.35	14.70	47.07	2.94	35.29	17.64	44.13	5.88	35.30	8.82	50.00		20.58	23.52	55.90		29.41	17.64	52.95
Central	8.89	24.44	20.00	46.67	4.45	17.77	31.11	46.67	4.45	20.00	22.22	53.33	4.45	11.11	24.44	60.00	2.22	15.55	28.89	53.34
Western	10.00	30.00	26.67	33.33	13.33	16.67	40.00	30.00	10.00	16.66	43.34	30.00		26.66	36.67	36.67		26.67	30.00	43.33
Bundelkhand	8.57	20.00	48.58	22.85	8.57	17.14	40.00	34.29	5.70	14.28	37.14	42.88	2.85	8.57	22.85	65.73	2.85	17.14	45.73	34.28
Grand Total	8.33	26.39	27.09	38.19	6.94	21.53	31.94	39.59	6.25	21.53	27.09	45.13	2.08	15.97	26.39	55.56	1.39	21.53	30.55	46.53

A - Always
ST - Sometime
R - Rarely
N - Never

Table 72
Feelings without this New Role
Gram Panchayat

(Percentage Distribution)

	Victim of Tradition				*Lack of Self Development*				*Lack of Freedom*				*Insecurity*				*Under Pressure*			
Region	*A*	*S T*	*R*	*N*	*A*	*S T*	*R*	*N*	*A*	*S T*	*R*	*N*	*A*	*S T*	*R*	*N*	*A*	*S T*	*R*	*N*
Eastern	11.29	43.56	16.12	29.03	6.45	43.56	12.90	37.09	8.06	40.33	17.74	33.87	6.45	22.58	29.03	41.94	4.83	17.77	38.70	38.70
Central	12.34	18.52	25.92	43.22	11.11	16.04	29.63	43.22	3.70	27.16	22.20	46.94	7.40	27.16	23.45	41.99	3.70	20.98	30.88	44.44
Western	13.55	20.34	32.20	33.91	8.47	13.55	38.99	38.99	8.47	11.86	37.28	42.39	5.08	22.03	30.50	42.39	5.08	22.03	30.50	42.39
Bundelkhand	4.22	14.08	33.80	47.90	2.82	18.30	30.98	47.90	2.82	8.44	39.45	49.29	2.82	14.08	30.98	52.12		25.35	28.16	46.49
Grand Total	10.25	23.44	27.10	39.21	7.32	22.34	28.20	42.14	5.49	21.96	28.94	43.61	5.49	21.61	28.20	44.7	3.30	21.61	31.9	43.22

A - Always
ST - Sometime
R - Rarely
N - Never

insecure and under pressure. This seems that women in general are found enjoying this role despite having lot of conflicts and problems. (Tables - 70, 71, 72)

In last few decades Indian politics has become a dirty game and it often involves violence, muscle power and money. Women representatives of grassroot level institutions find them difficult to adjust in such an atmosphere and very often feel prone to outside risk, associated with game of power and politics. They realize that due to new role they are likely to lose their feminism and very often become victim of character assassination and social impeachment. But all these factors are found helpful in creating, confidence and developing capacity amongst many of the women to fight these evils. They feel that once they stabilize in new role, nobody can touch them. In their opinion, that is the main reason that male dominated society does not want the women, in general to establish them in politics. Actually males are afraid of females, they feel.

Table 73
Costs of New Role
Zila Panchayat

(Percentage Distribution)

Region	*Loss of Feminism*	*Outside Risk*	*Character Assassination*	*Social Impeachment*
Eastern	37.50	66.66	50.00	25.00
Central	35.00	85.00	50.00	25.00
Western	44.44	72.22	44.44	50.00
Bundelkhand	29.41	100.00	41.17	41.17
Grand Total	35.44	79.74	46.83	34.17

Table 74
Costs of New Role
Kshetra Panchayat

(Percentage Distribution)

Region	*Loss of Feminism*	*Outside Risk*	*Character Assassination*	*Social Impeachment*
Eastern	11.76	67.64	35.29	26.47
Central	31.11	82.35	38.23	20.00
Western	26.66	70.00	40.00	40.00
Bundelkhand	62.85	74.28	48.57	28.57
Grand Total	33.33	68.05	37.50	27.77

Table 75
Costs of New Role
Gram Panchayat

(Percentage Distribution)

Region	*Loss of Feminism*	*Outside Risk*	*Character Assassination*	*Social Impeachment*
Eastern	45.16	90.32	66.13	27.41
Central	32.10	86.42	33.33	22.22
Western	22.03	74.57	23.72	25.31
Bundelkhand	49.29	77.46	45.07	43.66
Grand Total	38.47	83.24	41.76	31.82

While disclosing their major cause of dissatisfaction towards Panchayat administration, women representatives find low work culture, low privileges, non-cooperative colleagues and non-cooperative staff, problems of citizen and personal problems as major factors of concern. Despite these problems and conflicts, majority of the women representatives are not thinking to quit the politics and they want to continue with this new role. This indicates the level of confidence among women. This is a healthy sign for the country and its democracy in the long run. (Tables - 76, 77, 78)

As regards political role, half of the women representatives find their role satisfactory and challenging. In spite of problems, they are found to be sensitive towards the needs and problems of citizens. Over all their performance level is found to be higher than their male counterparts, and citizens are quite happy and satisfied with their performance. It is surprising that women who enter into new role due to circumstances also feel satisfied and are found happy with new role. Surprisingly, women in Gram Panchayats in significant numbers feel the new role imposed on them and found themselves burdened and thus unhappy. This indicates their more involvement in Panchayat activities because of their ready availability in village all the time. The situation is not such in other two tiers where women assemble when there is some meeting.

Actually, notice of meeting is not given personally to women representatives. It is the male family members who

Table 76
Cause of Dissatisfaction/Concerns
Zila Panchayat

(Percentage Distribution)

	Low Privileges					*Low Work Culture*					*Non Cooperating Staff*					*Non Cooperating Colleagues*						
Region	*A*	*F*	*ST*	*R*	*N*	*A*	*F*	*ST*	*R*	*N*	*A*	*F*	*ST*	*R*	*N*	*A*	*F*	*ST*	*R*	*N*	*A*	*F*
Eastern	25.00	16.66	33.35	16.66	8.33	33.34	25.00	29.16	12.50		12.50	20.86	50.00	12.50	4.16	12.50	16.66	45.84	25.00		25.00	20.84
Central	25.00	25.00	30.00	20.00		25.00	25.00	35.00	15.00		20.00	15.00	35.00	25.00	5.00	20.00	10.00	25.00	25.00	20.00		
Western	27.78	22.23	27.78	16.66	5.55	38.90	22.22	27.77	11.11		44.45	22.22	22.22	11.11		5.55	27.77	38.91	22.22	5.55	5.55	5.55
Bundel-khand	11.76	35.31	41.17	11.76		41.17	29.41	29.41			5.88	29.41	47.07	17.64		11.76	29.41	41.19	17.64		11.76	17.64
Grand Total	22.78	24.05	32.93	16.45	3.79	34.20	25.31	30.37	10.12		20.25	21.51	39.26	16.45	2.53	12.65	20.25	38.00	22.76	6.32	11.39	11.39

Contd.

	Authorition Adha./ Pramukh/Pradh.			*Away from Husband/Family*					*Low Prosp‿cts in Politics*					*Personal Problems*					*Problems of Community*				
Region	*ST*	*R*	*N*	*A*	*F*	*ST*	*R*	*N*	*A*	*F*	*ST*	*R*	*N*	*A*	*F*	*ST*	*R*	*N*	*A*	*F*	*ST*	*R*	*N*
Eastern	29.16	20.84	4.16			12.50	33.33	54.17	8.33	8.33	33.34	25.00	25.00		4.16	33.34	25.00	37.50	16.66	29.16	33.35	12.50	8.33
Central	40.00	30.00	30.00			10.00	35.00	55.00		10.00	55.00	25.00	10.00			20.00	50.00	30.00	20.00	30.00	45.00	5.00	
Western	33.36	27.77	27.77		11.11	22.22	38.90	27.77		11.11	33.33	33.33	22.23		11.11	44.46	27.77	16.66	16.66	22.22	44.46	16.66	
Bundel-khand	41.30	17.64	11.76		5.88	23.52	35.30	35.30		5.88	41.18	41.18	11.76			29.41	41.18	29.41	5.88	35.29	47.07	5.88	5.88
Grand Total	35.45	24.05	17.72		3.79	16.45	36.44	44.32	2.53	8.86	40.52	30.37	17.72		3.79	31.64	35.46	29.11	15.18	29.11	41.79	10.12	3.79

A = Always
F= Frequently
ST= Some Times
R= Rarely
N= Never

Table 77
Cause of Dissatisfaction/Concerns
Kshetra Panchayat

(Percentage Distribution)

	Low Privileges					*Low Work Culture*					*Non Cooperating Staff*					*Non Cooperating Colleagues*						
Region	*A*	*F*	*ST*	*R*	*N*	*A*	*F*	*ST*	*R*	*N*	*A*	*F*	*ST*	*R*	*N*	*A*	*F*	*ST*	*R*	*N*	*A*	*F*
Eastern	11.76	14.70	35.32	23.52	14.70	23.52	23.52	38.28	14.70		2.94	26.47	47.07	17.64	5.88	14.70	14.70	44.14	14.70	11.76	5.88	11.76
Central	11.11	22.22	37.79	20.00	8.88	13.33	24.44	42.24	15.55	4.44	8.88	15.55	28.88	31.14	15.55	15.55	22.22	33.35	17.77	11.11	2.22	13.33
Western	20.00	26.66	33.34	20.00		26.66	23.33	36.68	10.00	3.33	13.33	26.68	40.00	13.33	6.66	10.00	23.34	30.00	33.33	3.33	3.33	20.00
Bundel-khand	20.00	22.85	34.30	22.85		14.28	22.85	28.59	25.71	8.57	11.42	22.85	28.60	22.85	14.28	17.15	20.00	28.57	28.57	5.71	14.28	14.28
Grand Total	15.27	21.52	35.44	21.52	6.25	18.75	23.61	36.82	16.66	4.16	9.02	22.22	35.44	22.22	11.11	14.58	20.13	34.05	22.91	8.33	6.25	14.58

Contd.

	Authorition Adha./ Pramukh/Pradh.			*Away from Husband/Family*					*Low Prospects in Politics*					*Personal Problems*					*Problems of Community*				
Region	*ST*	*R*	*N*	*A*	*F*	*ST*	*R*	*N*	*A*	*F*	*ST*	*R*	*N*	*A*	*F*	*ST*	*R*	*N*	*A*	*F*	*ST*	*R*	*N*
Eastern	38.25	17.64	26.47			14.70	29.41	55.89	5.88	14.70	35.32	20.58	23.52	2.94	8.82	29.41	32.36	26.47	11.76	26.47	44.11	17.64	
Central	31.13	15.55	37.77		6.66	26.66	15.55	51.13	4.44	15.55	44.46	24.44	11.11		11.11	28.88	33.35	26.66	24.47	28.88	28.88	13.33	4.44
Western	30.34	20.00	23.33		3.33	30.00	30.00	36.67		13.33	33.33	36.68	16.66	6.66	6.66	33.34	33.34	20.00	36.67	26.66	36.67		
Bundel-khand	25.74	22.85	22.85		14.28	20.00	22.85	42.87	14.28	20.00	25.78	25.78	14.28	8.57	11.42	20.00	34.30	25.71	28.57	28.57	34.29	8.57	
Grand Total	31.95	18.75	28.47		6.25	22.91	23.61	47.23	6.25	15.97	35.43	26.38	15.97	4.16	9.72	27.77	38.35	25.00	25.00	27.77	35.44	10.41	1.38

A = Always
F= Frequently
ST= Some Times
R= Rarely
N= Never

Table 78
Cause of Dissatisfaction/Concerns
Gram Panchayat

(Percentage Distribution)

	Low Privileges					*Low Work Culture*					*Non Cooperating Staff*					*Non Cooperating Colleagues*						
Region	*A*	*F*	*ST*	*R*	*N*	*A*	*F*	*ST*	*R*	*N*	*A*	*F*	*ST*	*R*	*N*	*A*	*F*	*ST*	*R*	*N*	*A*	*F*
Eastern	33.87	22.58	35.49	6.45	1.61	27.41	22.58	33.89	9.67	6.45	29.03	24.19	30.66	12.90	3.22	33.89	22.58	32.25	8.06	3.22	37.11	22.58
Central	27.16	19.75	32.11	13.58	7.40	20.98	23.45	38.29	11.11	6.17	32.11	23.45	28.40	13.58	2.46	29.62	27.16	33.37	7.40	2.46	28.41	24.7
Western	37.31	23.72	32.20	6.77		25.45	28.81	28.81	13.55	3.38	28.81	27.11	30.53	13.55		32.20	25.42	30.52	11.86		39.90	23.72
Bundel-khand	28.16	22.53	36.64	8.45	4.22	23.94	19.71	32.42	12.67	11.26	23.94	21.12	33.82	15.49	5.63	33.82	23.94	29.57	7.04	5.63	28.16	28.16
Grand Total	31.13	21.97	34.09	9.15	3.66	24.17	23.44	33.72	11.72	6.95	28.57	23.80	30.79	13.91	2.93	32.25	24.90	31.50	8.42	2.93	32.60	24.90

Contd.

	Authorition Adha./ Pramukh/Pradh.			*Away from Husband/Family*					*Low Prospects in Politics*					*Personal Problems*					*Problems of Community*				
Region	*ST*	*R*	*N*	*A*	*F*	*ST*	*R*	*N*	*A*	*F*	*ST*	*R*	*N*	*A*	*F*	*ST*	*R*	*N*	*A*	*F*	*ST*	*R*	*N*
Eastern	25.80	8.06	6.45	11.29	17.74	32.27	19.35	19.35	24.19	29.03	32.28	9.67	4.83	8.06	14.51	38.73	19.35	19.35	4.83	19.35	41.96	17.74	16.12
Central	25.92	11.11	9.87	13.58	18.57	24.69	27.18	16.04	22.22	22.22	32.11	13.58	9.87	8.64	19.8	35.81	24.69	11.11	11.11	18.51	33.35	22.22	14.81
Western	28.81	8.47		10.16	8.47	28.81	25.42	27.18	22.03	33.91	28.81	15.25		10.16	15.25	32.23	25.42	16.94	10.16	15.25	32.23	23.72	18.64
Bundel-khand	23.97	8.45	11.26	18.30	25.38	30.98	14.08	11.26	22.53	25.35	33.82	9.85	8.45	9.85	12.67	36.65	19.71	21.12	12.67	16.90	43.68	15.49	11.26
Grand Total	26.00	9.15	7.32	13.55	17.94	28.96	21.61	17.94	22.71	27.1	31.89	12.08	6.22	9.15	15.75	35.92	22.34	16.84	9.89	17.58	37.74	19.78	15.01

A = Always
F= Frequently
ST= Some Times
R= Rarely
N= Never

Table 79
Satisfaction with New Role
Zila Panchayat

(Percentage Distribution)

Region	*Fully Satisf-actory*	*Satis-factory*	*Indif-ferent*	*Dis-satisfied*	*Happy*	*Imposed*	*Un-happy*	*Bur-dened*	*Total*
Eastern	37.50	41.67			20.83				100.00
Central	50.00	20.00			25.00		5.00		100.00
Western	50.00	33.34			16.66				100.00
Bundelkhand	29.41	35.31	11.76	5.88	17.64				100.00
Grand Total	41.80	32.91	2.53	1.26	20.25		1.26		100.00

Table 80
Satisfaction with New Role
Kshetra Panchayat

(Percentage Distribution)

Region	*Fully Satisf-actory*	*Satis-factory*	*Indif-ferent*	*Dis-satisfied*	*Happy*	*Imposed*	*Un-happy*	*Bur-dened*	*Total*
Eastern	17.64	47.07	5.88	2.94	26.47				100.00
Central	20.00	46.69	8.88	6.66	17.77				100.00
Western	23.33	43.34	10.00		23.33				100.00
Bundelkhand	11.42	57.17	2.85	2.85	25.71				100.00
Grand Total	18.05	48.63	6.94	3.47	22.91				100.00

Table 81
Satisfaction with New Role
Gram Panchayat

(Percentage Distribution)

Region	*Fully Satisf-actory*	*Satis-factory*	*Indif-ferent*	*Dis-satisfied*	*Happy*	*Imposed*	*Un-happy*	*Bur-dened*	*Total*
Eastern	14.51	24.22	11.29	12.90	12.90	8.06	16.12		100.00
Central	17.28	25.95	13.58	8.64	19.75	2.46	11.11	1.23	100.00
Western	11.86	18.64	15.25	10.16	25.46	5.08	8.47	5.08	100.00
Bundelkhand	11.26	18.30	12.67	22.59	22.59	11.26	9.85	2.81	100.00
Grand Total	13.91	21.97	13.18	20.19	20.19	6.59	11.35	2.19	100.00

Table 82
Performance Rating of Women Members

(Percentage Distribution)

Region	*Excellent*	*Satis-factory*	*Coope-rative*	*Innocent*	*Leaner*	*Disin-terested*	*Have no Full Freedom*	*Family Member not Couraging /Supportive*	*Total*
Eastern		3.12	6.25	3.12	12.50		53.14	21.87	100.00
Central		2.00	8.00		34.00	2.00	36.00	18.00	100.00
Western		6.06	15.15	3.03	21.22	3.03	33.33	18.18	100.00
Bundelkhand		7.50	10.00	2.50	20.00	7.50	32.50	20.00	100.00
Grand Total		4.51	9.67	1.93	23.22	3.22	38.10	19.35	100.00

are informed and they themselves attend the meeting and never bother to inform the real member, unless and until specific instructions for attending the meeting by real members are given.

At this stage officials were asked to rate the performance of women representatives. In view of officials women members are found cooperative (one-fourth), learner (more than one fifth), have no full freedom (more than one-third), family members not supportive (one-fifth).

In sum, there are a number of areas causing conflicts, but women members are more or less satisfied and happy in their new role. It seems that either they are not very serious about their role and their reluctance or easy going make them satisfied or they are not allowed to act freely nor willing to act independently. The women members seem to have reconciled and adapted the new situations. They are learners and want to excel, if proper support and enabling environment is created for them. (Table-82)

It is heartening to find that majority of women representatives aspire to excel is political role, if given a free hand and proper working environment and family support. They however feel that they are in transition and male dominated Indian society is not willing to make space for women, because they are afraid of them. Males want females to be confined to the home responsibilities as that they (male) can freely enjoy outside life. Therefore they are deliberately not allowing women especially from middle and lower classes, to come forward and join political mainstream. But they feel that cast has been drawn and one day women will be able to make their place in the society.

4

CONFLICTS AND ADJUSTMENTS IN FAMILY

Problems and their specific solutions are always rooted in the socio-cultural context of the society concerned. Hence the problems of elected women representatives need to be examined at micro-level from a socio-cultural perspective. It is equally important to find as to how they adjust themselves to the problematic situations in order to lead a happy marital life.

Women of today are assuming different roles besides the role within their homes. In the role relationship term, a married working or professional woman is a wife, mother, daughter-in-law, neighbour, worker, subordinate, peer and so on. She has to play all these roles i.e. traditional roles and modern or imposed role of a professional/politician, simultaneously, and expectations of these roles and demands might lead her to conflicting situations because of their built-in-antagonism. According to Halahan and Gilbert (1979), "women in dual, career- marriage, roles are experiencing higher role conflict than their spouses since they are now actively involved in adding a role (i.e. professional) which may require attitude and behaviour that are in consistent with those of their more traditional roles i.e. parent and spouse".

In the inter-role situation, family relation is of significance (Dahlstrom, 1917, Powell, 1963, Hoffman, 1961, Sullerat, 1971, D'souza 1968, Kala Rani, 1967, Singh, 1972, Nevill & Demico

1975a, 1975b). Since married women are a member of a family, their decision to work or refrain from work depends upon the views and the needs of their husband and other family members and presupposes a series of practical adjustments, some degree of cooperation and support for the role, by the husband and the family members. Presence of in-laws and size of family are some of the contributing factors in the role conflict among working women.

The attitude of husband is often a decisive factor in his wife's decision to take up a job. Whereas a favourable attitude of husband towards his wife's employment facilitates her career choice, unfavourable attitude of husband hinders her employment. Hence the attitude of husband is one of the major role conflicting factors (Blood & Hamblin, 1958, Blood, 1963, Bailyn 1970). Most of women in political role are not prone to such problems as they are in their new role not because of their choice but because of their husband or family members to fulfill the constitutional mandates.

The negative attitude of men can be attributed, in part to their general family ideology and opinion of social prestige. There is a serious risk of conflict and tension in the marriage, particularly when the wife's employment/profession creates a change in earlier habits (Dahlstrom, 1967, Nischal, 1975). Wife's work participation can create a potential status problem for husband. Arora et. al. (1963) conclude that traditional attitudes of husbands always produce role conflict among working wives. Women in political role are victim of a new tendency. Husbands/male members bring women in fore but want them to continue with the traditional role inside house and hand over the baton of political role to husband or male members of family to play that role in their name. Theoretically, women are in role but the real role players, in most cases, are husband and their male family members (Singh, 2004).

A working wife canot manage effectively the household job, and employment if her husband does not extend his help in the household work (D'Souza, 1968, Kapur, 1974, Dhingra, 1972, Tripathi, 1967, Kala Rani, 1976). Dhingra (1972) found that almost half of the married women of his sample were experiencing substantial difficulty in carrying out their household duties of their wife role adequately, including the care and attention given to the husband, along with their jobs. Conflict is felt among those working/professional women who need and expect help from their husband but do not get assistance in carrying out these responsibilities. Satyanand (1973) found that "husband was still quite not prepared to relinquish his patriarchal privileges." But want to enjoy the privileges linked with the new role of his wife (Singh, 2004).

Adjustment refers to "the state of accommodation which is achieved in different areas where conflict may exist in marriage". Lock and Williamson have defined marital adjustment as "the presence of such characteristic in a marriage as a tendency to avoid or resolve conflicts, a feeling of satisfaction with the marriage and with each other, the sharing of common interests and activities and the fulfilling of marital expectations of the husband and wife".

Green states that the "target of adjustment in a marriage are habits, attitudes and values of the spouses. Satisfaction in marriage depends upon the degree to which the spouses interact with each other. But conflicting expectations of marriage constitute a problem in adjustment....."

Adjustment includes all those actions, which tend to bring about functional changes in a relationship. Adjustment is a process rather than a stable phenomenon which means there is continuous interaction between the spouses, an interaction determined by the institutional specifications of the relationship, by the nature of the partners themselves and by the quality of relationship between them.

Thus in married life both the 'intra personal' and 'inter personal' relationships are liable to affect marital adjustment. In this process both husband and wife as well as all other family members, are supposed to extend their helping hand in order to strengthen the bond. This may lead to establish a harmonious relationship resulting in adjustment in the conjugal life.

Women in India whatever may be their status visualize themselves primarily as mother and housewife and consider these traditional roles as the most significant ones. Whatever they do or achieve is an extension of this primary (wife/mother) image. She imbibes life, gladly sacrifices everything and because of their sacrificing and forgiving nature, she is able to adjust better in adverse situations than her counterpart i.e. man.

STATUS WITHIN THE FAMILY

Family is the most important place that determines status and role. In the traditional middle class and upper middle class families, women earlier had practically no other role and their whole life had been spent within the family. With the change of time, family and home still hold their position as the focus of their activities, though to a considerable extent a woman has outside roles. Any change in their position will no doubt affect the members of the family. Decision making in the family is a critical element in the status of family members, since it involves allocation of resources and the distribution of roles within the family. The role of women in the decision making process can be assessed by considering her influence on all the family decisions.

The data show that every seventh household is a woman. This trend, of course, is not much encouraging but indicates initiation of granting status to women in a male dominated traditional society like ours. Such a social status may provide a firm base for sustaining other roles including political one granted under the aegis of the supreme law of the land.

The Constitution empowers women to take part in decision making in local governance, but at the family level it is observed that maximum decisions in family matters are taken either both by husband and wife or by husband only. Decision relating to family budget, purchase of assets, rationing, schooling of children and social relations are generally taken jointly. But comparative analysis suggests that husband has a major say in relation to family decisions, woman as a decision maker in family matters has a very little say. In many matters parents/in-laws take decisions. It seems that all the decisions are taken by husband or male members and made known to

Table 1
Decision Making Power
Zila Panchayat

(Percentage Distribution)

	Family Budgeting				Purchase of Assets				Rationing				Schooling of Children				On Social relation			
Region	Self	Husband	Both	In-laws/	Self	Husband	Both	In-laws/ Parents	Self	Husband	Both	In-laws/ Parents	Self	Husband	Both	In-laws/ Parents	Self	Husband	Both	In-laws/ Parents
Eastern	8.33	25.00	41.67	25.00		41.67	50.00	8.33	8.33	25.00	58.33	8.33		50.00	50.00			37.50	45.83	16.66
Central		25.00	40.00	35.00		30.00	50.00	20.00		25.00	45.00	30.00		35.00	40.00	25.00	5.00	25.00	45.00	25.00
Western	11.12	50.00	16.66	22.22	5.55	66.68	16.66	11.11	11.12	16.66	50.00	22.22	5.55	44.46	16.66	33.33	5.56	38.88	11.11	44.45
Bundelkhand	5.88	47.07	41.17	5.88	5.88	64.71	29.41		5.88	35.30	29.41	29.41	17.64	47.07	29.41	5.88	5.88	64.72	5.88	23.52
Grand Total	6.32	35.45	35.45	22.78	2.53	49.38	37.97	10.12	6.32	25.31	46.86	21.51	5.06	44.31	35.45	15.18	3.79	40.52	29.11	26.58

Table 2
Decision Making Power
Kshetra Panchayat

(Percentage Distribution)

	Family Budgeting				*Purchase of Assets*				*Rationing*				*Schooling of Children*				*On Social relation*			
Region	*Self*	*Husband*	*Both*	*In-laws/*	*Self*	*Husband*	*Both*	*In-laws/ Parents*	*Self*	*Husband*	*Both*	*In-laws/ Parents*	*Self*	*Husband*	*Both*	*In-laws/ Parents*	*Self*	*Husband*	*Both*	*In-laws/ Parents*
Eastern	8.82	64.72	20.58	5.88	5.88	82.36	8.82	2.94	11.76	35.29	47.07	5.88		79.42	11.76	8.82	2.94	76.48	5.88	14.7
Central		55.56	24.44	20	4.44	48.91	28.88	17.77		53.34	22.22	24.44		71.12	17.77	11.11		60	13.33	26.67
Western	6.66	33.33	26.68	33.33		56.67	23.33	20		33.33	30	36.67		60	30	10		36.67	30	33.33
Bundelkhand	2.85	42.87	25.71	28.57		77.15	2.85	20	5.71	34.29	25.71	34.29		71.43	20	8.57		51.43	8.57	40
Grand Total	4.16	50	24.32	21.52	2.77	65.3	16.66	15.27	4.16	40.29	30.55	25		70.84	19.44	9.72	0.69	56.96	13.88	28.47

Table 3
Decision Making Power
Gram Panchayat

(Percentage Distribution)

	Family Budgeting				Purchase of Assets				Rationing				Schooling of Children				On Social relation			
Region	*Self*	*Hus-band*	*Both*	*In-laws/*	*Self*	*Hus-band*	*Both*	*In-laws/ Parents*	*Self*	*Hus-band*	*Both*	*In-laws/ Parents*	*Self*	*Hus-band*	*Both*	*In-laws/ Parents*	*Self*	*Hus-band*	*Both*	*In-laws/ Parents*
Eastern	6.45	59.68	11.29	22.58	3.22	87.11	6.45	3.22	12.90	33.88	29.03	24.19	1.61	77.43	8.06	12.90	3.22	64.53	3.22	29.03
Central	3.70	64.21	12.34	19.75	3.70	66.68	9.87	19.75	6.17	69.14	11.11	13.58	3.70	72.85	12.34	11.11	3.70	60.51	9.87	25.92
Western	1.69	62.73	22.03	13.55	1.69	59.34	27.11	11.86	1.69	47.48	30.50	20.33	1.69	59.34	32.20	6.77	1.69	57.64	28.81	11.86
Bundelkhand		63.40	18.30	18.30		76.07	12.67	11.26	4.22	40.86	35.21	19.71		74.66	11.26	14.08		61.98	11.26	26.76
Grand Total	2.93	62.64	15.75	18.68	2.19	72.18	13.55	12.08	6.22	49.10	25.64	19.04	1.83	71.44	15.38	11.35	2.19	61.19	12.82	23.80

woman (wife/mother/daughter-in-law) to act accordingly. The decision taking power being utilized by husband is more prevalent at Kshetra and Gram Panchayat levels. (Tables -1, 2, 3)

With regard to spending of family income, it is observed that husband spends maximum family income. Majority of the women representatives are of opinion that income of both husband and wife is controlled by the husband (Table 4). Such a situation is not in good taste. Male dominated society should transfer some financial powers to the better half of the society. Economic empowerment may achieve its aim only when women enjoy great financial powers at home. It is a social irony that woman, known as house manager, is denied of power of spending family income.

Table 4
Spending Powers
Jila Panchayat

(Percentage Distribution)

Region	*Self*	*Husband*	*In-laws/ Parents*	*Total*
Eastern		83.33	16.67	100.00
Central		70.00	30.00	100.00
Western	5.55	61.12	33.33	100.00
Bundelkhand	5.88	76.48	17.64	100.00
Grand Total	2.53	73.42	24.05	100.00

Table 5
Spending Powers
Kshetra Panchayat

(Percentage Distribution)

Region	*Self*	*Husband*	*In-laws/ Parents*	*Brothers*	*Total*
Eastern	2.94	85.30	8.82	2.94	100.00
Central		75.56	24.44		100.00
Western		73.34	26.66		100.00
Bundelkhand		85.72	14.28		100.00
Grand Total	0.69	79.87	18.75	0.69	100.00

Not only that, the income of wife is also spent by her husband, as it seems, a woman in our traditional society has no separate entity of her own. She being an idol of patience and sacrifice is ready to sacrifice everything for the happiness of husband and children. In the process, she is ignored, her desires and ambitions do not find any place in family desires. She assimilates herself in her husband. This needs to be broken. Woman should be recognized as a separate human being and a partner of husband and not a slave to him.

Table 6
Spending Powers
Gram Panchayat

(Percentage Distribution)

Region	*Self*	*Husband*	*In-laws/ Parents*	*Brothers/ Children*	*Total*
Eastern	4.83	69.37	19.35	6.45	100.00
Central	3.70	67.91	24.69	3.70	100.00
Western		79.67	18.64	1.69	100.00
Bundelkhand		84.51	15.49		100.00
Grand Total	2.19	75.11	19.78	2.92	100.00

ADJUSTMENTS AT HOME

A woman representative has to meet the expectations and obligations corresponding to her various roles within the family, whether nuclear or joint. In addition, she has also to perform her political role, which lies outside the family purview. The political role compels a woman to step out of the limited spheres of the house and thereby makes her over-burdened with work load. The political role demands very social and active life outside home, hence she has to adjust herself both at home and outside in order to avoid conflicting situations and run a smooth family life. The familial problem multiplies if a woman lives with their in-laws or the family is too large.

It further complicates, if the woman takes its imposed role sincerely and devotes some time for her new role in the office and in the community. Her independent decisions, without consulting husband and other family member may create problem for her. More so, she is not fully conversant with her new role. Thus, she is easy to be moulded by husband to confine herself to the familial role and not bother for her political role, which is often taken care by husband and family members.

The data illustrate that about half of the women representatives live with their in-laws. In many cases elderly in-laws create problems in the name of maintraining social and family traditions.

Table 7
Living with In-Laws
Zila Panchayat

(Percentage Distribution)

Region	*Yes*	*No*	*Total*
Eastern	37.50	62.50	100.00
Central	65.00	35.00	100.00
Western	77.78	22.22	100.00
Bundelkhand	58.83	41.17	100.00
Grand Total	58.23	41.77	100.00

Table 8
Living with In-Laws
Kshetra Panchayat

(Percentage Distribution)

Region	*Yes*	*No*	*Total*
Eastern	23.52	76.48	100.00
Central	60.00	40.00	100.00
Western	40.00	60.00	100.00
Bundelkhand	42.85	57.15	100.00
Grand Total	43.05	56.95	100.00

Table 9
Living with In-Laws
Gram Panchayat

(Percentage Distribution)

Region	*Yes*	*No*	*Total*
Eastern	43.54	56.46	100.00
Central	46.92	53.08	100.00
Western	54.24	45.76	100.00
Bundelkhand	33.80	66.20	100.00
Grand Total	44.32	55.68	100.00

Size of family is an important factor of conflict for women stepping outside home. The responses in this regard show that majority of the women representatives at all the three levels live in a quite large family, consisting of 6 to 15 members. A sizeable number of women are found living even in larger family. Such a situation demands spending more time by women in household chores.

Table 10
Size of Family
Zila Panchayat

(Percent Distribution)

Region	*1-5*	*6-10*	*11-15*	*16-20*	*>-20*	*Total*
Eastern	33.34	25.00	25.00	16.66		100.00
Central	20.00	30.00	25.00	15.00	10.00	100.00
Western		33.33	22.22	38.90	5.55	100.00
Bundelkhand	17.64	47.08	17.64	17.64		100.00
Grand Total	18.98	32.94	22.78	21.51	3.79	100.00

Table 11
Size of Family
Kshetra Panchayat

(Percent Distribution)

Region	*1-5*	*6-10*	*11-15*	*16-20*	*>-20*	*Total*
Eastern	5.88	50.00	35.30	2.94	5.88	100.00
Central	11.11	60.00	26.67		2.22	100.00
Western	23.34	40.00	30.00	6.66		100.00
Bundelkhand	8.57	57.15	20.00	14.28		100.00
Grand Total	11.80	52.80	27.77	5.55	2.08	100.00

Table 12
Size of Family
Gram Panchayat

(Percent Distribution)

Region	*1-5*	*6-10*	*11-15*	*16-20*	*>-20*	*Total*
Eastern	6.45	45.18	32.25	11.29		100.00
Central	13.58	69.15	13.58	2.46	1.23	100.00
Western	11.86	61.04	18.64	5.08	3.38	100.00
Bundelkhand	11.26	50.72	26.76	8.45	2.81	100.00
Grand Total	10.98	57.16	22.34	6.59	2.93	100.00

In nuclear family, a woman has to concentrate her familial roles only to her husband and one or two children. The adjustment in small and nuclear family is easy in comparison to large family consisting of in-laws and other members. The homogeneity of nuclear family is missing in larger (joint or extended) family. This affects the time allotment by a woman. However, a mother in-law in political role is better placed than her daughter-in-law.

Table 13
Domestic Servant Available
Zila Panchayat

(Percentage Distribution)

				If Yes			
Region	*Yes*	*No*	*Total*	*Full Time*	*Part Time*	*No. of Hours*	*Total*
Eastern	100.00		100.00	45.83	45.83	8.34	100.00
Central	100.00		100.00	80.00	20.00		100.00
Western	100.00		100.00	72.23	16.66	11.11	100.00
Bundelkhand	94.12	5.88	100.00	37.50	37.50	25.00	100.00
Grand Total	98.74	1.26	100.00	58.99	30.76	10.25	100.00

For effective management of household works women representatives living in large family may require domestic help. It is found that almost all women representatives at Zila Panchayats, irrespective of the regions, employ a servant. Majority of the women at this level having domestic help have full time servant. But the situation at other tiers is quite different. A little more than one-third of women responsdents at Kshetra Panchayat level have servant and out of them, less than half employ the servant for full time. At the Gram Panchayat level, even less than one-third women have a servant and only a half of them have full time servant.

This reflects the level of affordability and social status of women representatives. The women representatives at Zila Panchayats probably enjoy good status in the society, hence they can afford a servant. At the Kshetra Panchayats and Gram Panchayats level probably it is the Pramuk or Pradhan who can afford a servant. The women respondents who are not having any domestic help have to manage all the household responsibilities themselves. In village life, even if a family engage a servant he helps in jobs outside home and not to women in discharging their household responsibilities. Women at Gram and Kshetra Panchayats level belong to that category. Management of entire household responsibility by themselves, most of the time, overburdens them and creates stressful situations for them.

Table 14
Domestic Servant Available
Kshetra Panchayat

(Percentage Distribution)

				If Yes			
Region	*Yes*	*No*	*Total*	*Full Time*	*Part Time*	*No. of Hours*	*Total*
Eastern	44.12	55.88	100.00	46.67	53.33		100.00
Central	11.11	88.89	100.00	60.00	40.00		100.00
Western	53.34	46.66	100.00	25.00	56.25	18.75	100.00
Bundelkhand	54.29	45.71	100.00	57.90	36.84	5.26	100.00
Grand Total	38.19	61.81	100.00	45.45	47.28	7.27	100.00

Table 15
Domestic Servant Available
Gram Panchayat

(Percentage Distribution)

				If Yes			
Region	*Yes*	*No*	*Total*	*Full Time*	*Part Time*	*No. of Hours*	*Total*
Eastern	41.93	58.07	100.00	57.69	42.31		100.00
Central	16.04	83.96	100.00	46.15	53.85	10.00	100.00
Western	37.28	62.72	100.00	50.00	45.46	4.54	100.00
Bundelkhand	28.76	73.24	100.00	57.90	36.84	5.26	100.00
Grand Total	29.30	70.70	100.00	53.75	43.75	2.50	100.00

For proper management of household responsibilities and also for saving time for other roles, modern time saving amenities can play a very important role and may prove very beneficial for women in managing household work effectively. Most of the women in general and in villages in particular have to spend much of their time in cooking and related activities. They may be able to devote their time to jobs other than cooking, if modern amenities are available with them. Most of the respondents have many of the modern time saving amenities like pressure cooker, mixer/grinder, LPG stove, scooter/car, fridge, washing machine. The responses in this connection clearly reflect the financial situation of the women representatives. The women in Zila Panchayats have many more amenities in comparison to their counterparts at lower levels. (Tables -16, 17, 18)

In respect of management of household responsibilities, like cooking, purchase of crockery, washing clothes, caring of in-laws, cleaning of house, helping children in study etc., majority of the elected women manage it themselves. For effective management of these household responsibilities, they often take help from husband or in-laws and servant.

It is really a social stigma that women representatives have to perform all the household responsibilities even after they have another important role granted under the Constitution. The male dominated traditional society is not ready to share the household responsibilities with women, whereas male members are making use of the provisions of the supreme law of the land in keeping women in front row, but not allowing them to perform that role freely and independently. Male members want to enjoy privileges associated with the role of women. This needs to be changed. Managing household should be a joint responsibility and all the family members should have some role to play. Management of household responsibilities often creates conflicting situations as the women representatives have to devote large amount of time and energy towards political role also. Hence management of dual responsibilities often overburdens them and creates conflicting situations. (Tables -19, 20, 21)

In connection with primary duties towards husband, children and family, elected women feel that their husband, home and children often get neglected because of their new avatar in the form of political role and consequently raised status in society for which they have to devote some time. It is

Table 16

Availability of Modern Time Saving Amenities

Zila Panchayat

(Percentage Distribution)

Region	*Pressure Cooker*	*Mixer/ Grinder*	*LPG Stove*	*Scooter/ Moter-cycle/Car*	*VCR/ VCP*	*Kitchen Oven*	*Refrig-erator*	*Vacum Cleaner*	*Washing Machine*
Eastern	100.00	45.83	100.00	95.83	87.50	12.50	54.16	4.16	50.00
Central	100.00	55.00	90.00	90.00	55.00	10.00	60.00	10.00	30.00
Western	100.00	55.55	94.44	100.00	77.77		100.00		44.44
Bundelkhand	100.00	41.17	100.00	100.00	58.82		76.47		35.29
Grand total	100.00	49.36	96.20	96.20	70.88	6.32	70.88	3.79	40.50

Table 17
Availability of Modern Time Saving
Kshetra

(Percentage Distribution)

Region	*Pressure Cooker*	*Mixer/ Grinder*	*LPG Stove*	*Scooter/ Moter-cycle/Car*	*VCR/ VCP*	*Kitchen Oven*	*Refrig-erator*	*Vacum Cleaner*	*Washing Machine*
Eastern	61.76	8.82	50.00	55.88	32.35		23.52		5.88
Central	71.11	4.44	51.11	60.00	28.88		28.88		6.66
Western	90.00	16.66	80.00	93.33	40.00		40.00		10.00
Bundelkhand	97.14	11.42	68.57	80.00	25.71		28.57		5.71
Grand total	79.16	9.72	61.11	70.83	31.25		29.86		6.94

Table 18
Availability of Modern Time Saving Amenities
Gram Panchayat

(Percentage Distribution)

Region	*Pressure Cooker*	*Mixer/ Grinder*	*LPG Stove*	*Scooter/ Moter-cycle/Car*	*VCR/ VCP*	*Kitchen Oven*	*Refrig-erator*	*Vacum Cleaner*	*Washing Machine*
Eastern	70.96	4.83	61.29	61.29	24.19		6.45		
Central	66.66	3.70	41.97	50.61	17.28		11.11		
Western	91.52		55.93	67.79	15.25		10.16		
Bundelkhand	57.74		19.71	32.39	5.63		2.81		
Grand total	70.69	2.19	43.58	52.01	15.38		7.69		0.73

observed that less than half of the women representatives in Zila Panchayats, and two-thirds at other tiers negate that their husband is ever neglected because of their new role. So is the case regarding neglect of children and society. But every sixth woman at Zila Panchayats and every fifth at Kshetra Panchayats accept that some time panchayat works are neglected because of family load. It leads to conclude that woman who take some interest in their political role are facing problem in maintaining balance between both the roles. But they are of the view that in spite of the dual burden they try their best and are able to fulfill their family duties most of the time. In the process family may be neglected, knowingly or unknowingly. However, neglect is compensated by gaining the status in the society. (Tables - 22, 23, 24)

At this stage, family members of women representatives were asked as to whether she devotes some time in household activities. Majority of the women are found spending full time to home management, attending the children, husband and in laws. But family members are of the opinion that women many a times, do not care for themselves. (Table -25)

It is clear that women respondents who are not allowed to perform their political role and thus are confined to the home and devote full time to household chores. There is therefore an imperative need to create interest in women towards their new role. They may be exposed to various situations in different states and thus be acquainted with responsibilities.

The respondents were further asked to classify whether their political role creates obstacles in family life. The responses are quite satisfactory. Majority of the women representatives find no obstacles because of their new role. Surprisingly a significant number of women representatives at Zila Panchayats level feel that their joining politics sometime creates problems in running the household properly or care to husband, children or parents/in-laws. It seems that women at Zila Panchayats level being more educated are able to take their new role seriously and thus devote time more than their counterparts at lower levels and hence face obstacles. Those who are not serious about their new role are free from any obstacles. (Tables - 26, 27, 28)

Table 19

Managing House Holds Responsibilities

Zila Panchayat

(Percentage Distribution)

	Cooking					*Serving Food*					*Purchase of Grocery*					*Washing Clothes/Utensils*			
Region	*Servants*	*J/Sister*	*J/Servant*	*Self*	*D-In*	*Servants*	*J/Sister*	*J/Servant*	*Self*	*D-In*	*Servants*	*Husband*	*J/H*	*J/Sister*	*J/Servant*	*Servants*	*J/Sister*	*Self*	*D-In*
Eastern	8.33	16.66	41.68	8.33	25.00	8.33	16.67	25.00	25.00	25.00	33.33	25.00	41.67			91.67			8.33
Central	30.00	20.00		45.00	5.00	20.00	25.00		50.00	5.00	45.00	25.00	20.00		10.00	60.00		40.00	
Western	11.12	22.22	22.22	22.22	22.22	22.22	27.78	22.22		27.78	61.12	27.77	11.11			77.78		11.11	11.11
Bundelkhand		23.52	17.64	47.08	11.76	17.64	29.41	5.88	35.31	11.76	52.95	11.76	29.41	5.88		58.84	23.52	17.64	
Grand Total	12.65	20.25	21.51	29.14	16.45	16.45	24.05	13.92	27.86	17.72	46.85	22.78	26.58	1.26	2.53	73.43	5.06	16.45	5.06

Contd...

	Cleaning House					*Nurshing Sick Children*					*Caring Parents*				*Helping Children in Study*				
Region	*Servants*	*J/Sister*	*Self*	*D-In*	*Husband*	*J/H*	*J/Sister*	*J/Servant*	*Self*	*D-In*	*Servants*	*Husband*	*J/Sister*	*Self*	*Husband*	*J/H*	*J/Sister*	*Self*	*D-In*
Eastern	58.33	16.66		25.00		45.84			33.33	20.83	25.00			75.00	33.35	16.66	16.66	8.33	25.00
Central	65.00	5.00	30.00			10.00	15.00		75.00				47.05	52.95	10.00	40.00	40.00	10.00	
Western	77.78		11.11	11.11	5.55		44.46		22.22	27.77		16.66	50.00	33.34	11.11	11.11	16.66	38.90	22.22
Bundelkhand	47.07	29.41	23.52				52.95	5.88	29.41	11.76			70.00	30.00	5.88	11.76	35.29	47.07	
Grand Total	62.05	12.65	15.18	10.12	1.26	16.45	25.31	1.26	40.54	15.18	4.25	4.25	44.68	46.82	16.45	20.25	26.60	24.05	12.65

Table 20
Managing House Holds Responsibilities
Kshetra Panchayat

(Percentage Distribution)

	Cooking					*Serving Food*					*Purchase of Grocery*					*Washing Clothes/Utensils*			
Region	*Servants*	*J/Sister*	*J/Servant*	*Self*	*D-In*	*Servants*	*J/Sister*	*J/Servant*	*Self*	*D-In*	*Servants*	*Husband*	*J/H*	*J/Sister*	*Self*	*Servants*	*J/Sister*	*J/Servant*	*Self*
Eastern		11.76		50.00	38.24	2.94	14.70		50.00	32.36	26.47	55.89	8.82		8.82	14.70	17.64	2.94	38.25
Central		20.00		62.63	17.77	2.22	15.55		71.12	11.11	22.22	28.88	31.13	4.44	13.33	4.44	22.22	2.22	53.35
Western			10.00	53.34	36.66		26.67	3.33	30.00	40.00	40.00	30.00	23.34	6.66		20.00	20.00	3.33	20.00
Bundelkhand	5.71	22.85		62.87	8.57	5.71	28.57		51.44	14.28	25.71	37.16	34.28	2.85		8.57	34.28		45.73
Grand Total	1.38	14.58	2.08	57.66	24.30	2.77	20.13	0.69	52.80	23.61	27.78	37.50	25.00	3.47	6.25	11.11	23.61	2.08	40.98

Contd...

	Cleaning House					*Nurshing Sick Children*					*Caring Parents*					*Helping Children in Study*				
Region	*D-In*	*Servant*	*J/Sister*	*J/Servant*	*Self*	*D-In*	*J/H*	*J/Sister*	*Self*	*D-In*	*J/H*	*J/Sister*	*J/Servant*	*Self*	*D-In*	*Husband*	*J/H*	*J/Sister*	*Self*	*D-In*
Eastern	26.47	8.82	23.52	5.88	46.47	35.31	2.94	23.52	44.13	29.41		33.33		55.56	11.11	29.41	8.82	2.94	20.58	38.25
Central	17.77	4.44	26.66		51.13	17.77	15.55	15.55	51.13	17.77	14.28	42.86		42.86		26.68	17.77	20.00	15.55	20.00
Western	36.37	23.33	23.33	3.34	20.00	30.00	10.00	23.33	30.00	36.37	14.28	28.57	14.28	35.73	7.14	40.00	23.34	20.00	13.33	3.33
Bundelkhand	11.42	5.71	34.28		42.87	17.14	11.42	25.71	51.45	11.42		50.00	13.63	36.37		34.28	14.28	37.16	8.57	5.71
Grand Total	22.22	9.72	27.08	2.08	36.82	24.30	10.41	21.52	45.16	22.91	8.21	41.11	6.84	41.11	2.74	31.96	15.97	20.13	14.28	17.36

Table 21
Managing House Holds Responsibilities
Gram Panchayat

(Percentage Distribution)

Region	Cooking					Serving Food					Purchase of Grocery					Washing Clothes/Utensils			
	Servants	J/Sister	J/Servant	Self	D-In	Servants	J/Sister	J/Servant	Self	D-In	Servants	Husband	J/H	J/Sister	Self	D-In	Servant	J/Sister	J/Sevant
Eastern	1.61	11.29	6.45	45.17	35.48	1.61	24.19	8.06	38.73	27.41	22.58	59.69	9.67		8.06		16.12	19.35	
Central		17.28		62.97	19.75		22.22		59.27	18.51	7.40	53.11	18.51	8.64	12.34		6.17	30.86	1.23
Western		20.33		54.25	25.42		22.03		50.86	27.11	3.38	37.33	30.50	10.16	13.55	5.08	8.47	18.64	8.47
Bundelkhand		12.67		61.98	25.35		22.53		57.76	19.71	1.40	56.37	22.53	9.85	9.85			25.35	
Grand Total	0.36	15.38	1.46	56.80	26.00	0.36	22.71	1.83	52.39	22.71	8.42	52.05	20.14	7.32	19.98	1.09	7.32	24.17	2.19

Contd...

Region	Cleaning House					Nurshing Sick Children						Caring Parents					Helping Children in Study				
	Self	D-In	Servant	J/Sister	J/Servant	Self	D-In	Husband	J/H	J/Sister	J/Servant	Self	D-In	Husband	J/H	J/Sister	Self	D-In Husband	J/H	Self	D/In
Eastern	40.34	24.19	16.12	17.75	1.61	32.26	32.26	1.61	4.83	16.12		51.64	25.8	4.00		56.00	36.00	4.0048.41	1.61	20.96	16.12
Central	48.16	13.58	7.40	38.39		46.93	17.28		28.39	16.04		41.99	13.58	7.89	23.68	31.57	34.23	2.6348.16	17.28	11.11	11.11
Western	33.98	25.44	3.38	18.64	1.69	52.57	23.72		32.23	18.64	5.08	30.50	13.55		37.93	37.93	17.25	6.8932.23	30.50	10.16	8.47
Bundelkhand	54.94	19.71	1.40	21.12		54.95	22.53		14.08	15.49		56.35	14.08		31.03	31.03	37.94	47.91	18.30	8.45	9.85
Grand Total	46.18	20.14	6.95	21.97	0.73	46.91	23.44	0.36	20.14	16.48	1.09	45.45	16.48	3.30	23.96	38.04	31.40	3.3044.71	16.84	12.45	11.35

Table 22
Familial Duties Neglected
Zila Panchayat

(Percentage Distribution)

Region	Husband					Children					Family					Society					Panchayat				
	A	F	ST	R	N	A	F	ST	R	N	A	F	ST	R	N	A	F	ST	R	N	A	F	ST	R	N
Eastern			8.33	50.00	41.67			25.00	33.33	41.67			25.00	33.33	41.67			16.66	58.34	25.00			16.66	66.68	16.66
Central			10.00	55.00	35.00			15.00	35.00	50.00			10.00	35.00	55.00	5.00		15.00	35.00	45.00	5.00	10.00	25.00	30.00	30.00
Western	5.55		16.66	27.79	50.00			38.88	16.66	44.46			16.66	50.00	33.34	5.55		11.11	55.57	27.77	5.55		16.66	27.79	50.00
Bundel-khand			17.64	17.64	64.72			35.29	64.71				5.88	29.41	64.71			17.64	41.18	41.18			5.88	52.94	41.18
Grand Total	1.26		12.65	39.24	46.85			20.25	30.37	49.38			15.18	36.70	48.12	2.53		15.18	48.12	34.17	2.53	2.53	16.45	45.58	32.91

A – Always
F – Frequently
ST – Some Time
R – Rarely
N – Never

Table 23
Familial Duties Neglected
Kshetra Panchayat

(Percentage Distribution)

	Husband					Children					Family					Society					Panchayat				
Region	A	F	ST	R	N	A	F	ST	R	N	A	F	ST	R	N	A	F	ST	R	N	A	F	ST	R	N
Eastern			18.18	18.18	63.64			2.94	32.35	64.71				32.35	67.65	2.94	11.76	20.58	26.47	38.25		11.76	20.58	23.52	44.14
Central				17.77	82.23				13.33	86.67				11.11	88.89	2.22		11.11	31.11	55.56	2.22		11.11	31.11	55.56
Western			3.33	40.00	56.67			10.00	33.33	56.67			3.33	33.33	63.34	3.33		36.67	40.00	20.00	3.33		40.00	33.34	23.33
Bundel-khand	5.71		22.85	20.00	51.44		2.85	14.28	14.28	68.59			11.42	22.85	65.73		5.71	22.85	25.71	45.73		11.42	22.85	22.85	42.88
Grand Total	1.39		10.48	23.1	65.07		0.69	6.25	22.22	70.84			3.47	23.61	72.92	2.08	4.16	21.52	30.55	41.69	1.38	5.55	22.22	27.77	43.08

A – Always
F – Frequently
ST – Some Time
R – Rarely
N – Never

Table 24
Familial Duties Neglected
Gram Panchayat

(Percentage Distribution)

	Husband					Children					Family					Society					Panchayat				
Region	A	F	ST	R	N	A	F	ST	R	N	A	F	ST	R	N	A	F	ST	R	N	A	F	ST	R	N
Eastern			9.83	14.75	75.42			6.45	20.96	72.59		1.61	4.83	12.90	80.66	3.22	9.67	27.41	20.96	38.74	3.22	4.83	32.25	14.51	45.19
Central			3.84	37.17	58.99		1.23	2.46	35.80	60.51			1.23	35.80	62.97		2.46	13.58	29.62	54.34		2.46	17.28	28.39	51.87
Western			15.51	29.31	55.18			13.55	32.20	54.25			13.55	40.67	45.78	3.38	1.69	32.21	32.21	30.51	3.50	1.75	42.13	29.82	22.8
Bundel-khand			11.26	19.71	69.03			7.04	28.16	64.80			8.69	20.28	71.03	1.40	8.45	19.71	21.12	49.32	1.40	5.63	11.26	36.98	50.73
Grand Total			9.70	25.74	64.56		0.36	6.95	29.67	63.02		0.36	6.64	27.67	65.33	1.83	5.49	22.34	26	44.34	1.84	3.69	24.35	26.19	43.93

A – Always
F – Frequently
ST – Some Time
R – Rarely
N – Never

Table 25
Women Devote Desired Time

(Percentage Distribution)

Region	Home Management					Care of Children					Care of Parents/in-laws					Care of Husband				
	F	GE	SE	N	DT	F	GE	SE	N	DT	F	GE	SE	N	DT	F	GE	SE	N	DT
Eastern	84.19	9.16	3.33	1.66	1.66	85.00	8.35	4.16	1.66	0.83	69.70	6.06	18.18		6.06	80.00	12.50	5.84		1.66
Central	76.06	15.75	4.10	1.36	2.73	73.31	18.49	6.16	1.36	0.68	71.29	21.83	5.74		1.14	72.62	15.75	10.95		0.68
Western	78.52	13.08	7.47	0.93		82.25	13.08	4.67			85.30	13.23		1.47		75.71	20.56	3.73		
Bundelkhand	74.00	15.44	8.94	1.62		69.94	18.69	9.75	1.62		51.18	37.20	4.65	2.32	4.65	67.49	20.32	11.38	0.81	
Grand Total	78.05	13.50	5.84	1.41	1.20	77.24	14.91	6.25	1.20	0.40	71.44	19.91	6.06	0.43	2.16	73.81	17.13	8.26	0.20	0.60

Contd.

Region	Family Functions					Social Functions					For-herself				
	F	GE	SE	N	DT	F	GE	SE	N	DT	F	GE	SE	N	DT
Eastern	72.50	17.50	10.00			41.68	15.00	20.83	4.16	18.3	10.00	15.00	43.34	10.83	20.83
Central	52.07	23.97	22.60		1.36	39.75	16.43	28.76	3.42	11.64	26.71	15.75	32.21	11.66	13.69
Western	63.57	22.42	14.01			28.03	28.97	30.86	3.73	8.41	11.21	27.10	43.94	6.54	11.21
Bundelkhand	66.68	22.76	9.75	0.81		43.92	13.82	18.69	6.50	17.07	16.26	25.20	30.91	14.13	13.00
Grand Total	63.12	21.77	14.51	0.20	0.40	38.73	18.14	24.79	4,43	23.91	16.76	20.36	37.09	11.08	14.71

Table 26
Political Role Creates Obstacle
Zila Panchayat

(Percentage Distribution)

Region	Maintaining Family					Personal Care to Husband					Keeping As Ideal Wife					Being Good Mother					Being Good Daughter In-Law				
	A	F	ST	R	N	A	F	ST	R	N	A	F	ST	R	N	A	F	ST	R	N	A	F	ST	R	N
Eastern			16.66	41.67	41.67			8.33	50.00	41.67			8.33	50.00	41.67			8.33	50.00	41.67			25.00	50.00	25.00
Central			35.00	25.00	40.00			30.00	25.00	45.00		10.00	20.00	30.00	40.00			35.00	25.00	40.00		14.28	42.87	7.14	35.71
Western	22.23		16.66	11.11	50.00			29.41	17.64	52.95			5.88	41.17	52.95				44.44	55.56			16.66	33.67	50.00
Bundelkhand			23.54	11.76	64.70			6.25	25.00	68.75				25.00	75.00			17.64	11.76	70.60			9.09	18.18	72.73
Grand Total	5.06		22.78	24.05	48.11			18.18	31.16	50.66		3.84	8.97	37.19	50.00			15.18	34.17	50.65		4.44	24.44	24.44	46.68

F = Frequently
ST = Some Time
R = Rarely
N = Never

Table 27
Political Role Creates Obstacle
Kshetra Panchayat

(Percentage Distribution)

	Maintaining Family					Personal Care to Husband					Keeping As Ideal Wife					Being Good Mother					Being Good Daughter In-Law				
Region	*A*	*F*	*ST*	*R*	*N*	*A*	*F*	*ST*	*R*	*N*	*A*	*F*	*ST*	*R*	*N*	*A*	*F*	*ST*	*R*	*N*	*A*	*F*	*ST*	*R*	*N*
Eastern			11.76	11.76	76.48			11.76	23.52	64.72			15.15	21.21	63.64			8.82	26.47	64.71				17.64	82.36
Central	2.22		4.44	28.88	64.46			2.22	33.33	64.45			2.22	31.11	66.67			2.22	28.88	68.90			7.14	28.57	64.29
Western			13.33	33.33	53.34			3.33	36.67	60.00			3.33	40.00	56.67				33.33	66.67			15.38	53.84	30.78
Bundelkhand	14.28		11.42	31.42	42.88			11.42	31.42	57.16	2.85	8.57	5.71	28.57	54.30		2.85	5.71	25.71	65.73		6.66	26.67	26.67	40.00
Grand Total	4.16		9.72	26.38	59.74			6.94	31.25	61.81	0.69	2.09	6.29	30.06	60.87		0.69	4.16	28.47	66.68		2.70	10.81	29.72	56.77

F = Frequently
ST = Some Time
R = Rarely
N = Never

Table 28
Political Role Creates Obstacle
Gram Panchayat

(Percentage Distribution)

	Maintaining Family					*Personal Care to Husband*					*Keeping As Ideal Wife*					*Being Good Mother*					*Being Good Daughter In-Law*				
Region	*A*	*F*	*ST*	*R*	*N*	*A*	*F*	*ST*	*R*	*N*	*A*	*F*	*ST*	*R*	*N*	*A*	*F*	*ST*	*R*	*N*	*A*	*F*	*ST*	*R*	*N*
Eastern			12.90	16.12	76.98		1.63	9.83	24.59	63.95		1.63	6.55	29.50	62.32		3.32	8.06	25.80	62.92		8.69	13.04	34.78	43.49
Central	2.46	1.23	13.58	34.56	48.17	1.26		7.59	48.10	43.05	1.28	1.28	6.41	41.03	50.00	1.23	1.23	11.11	30.86	55.57	5.40	2.70	21.62	27.02	43.26
Western			15.25	45.77	38.98			1.69	58.66	39.65				62.07	37.93			18.64	44.08	37.28			3.12	56.25	40.63
Bundelkhand			14.08	11.26	74.66		1.40	12.67	18.30	67.63			8.45	21.12	70.43			12.67	18.30	69.03			21.73	34.78	43.49
Grand Total	0.73	0.36	13.97	26.83	58.11	0.37	0.74	8.17	37.17	53.55	0.37	0.74	5.59	37.68	55.62	0.36	1.09	12.45	29.3	56.80	1.73	2.60	14.78	38.26	42.63

F = Frequently
ST = Some Time
R = Rarely
N = Never

Now comes the time management by women representatives. Earlier women were busy all the time in their household works, but now the women joining the politics have to divide time for both the roles. As regards management of time, it is observed that majority of elected women spend most of their time in household responsibilities including caring the children, husband and in-laws.

Interestingly, women representatives at Kshetra and Gram Panchayats devote more time on their traditional roles. They have little time left for their new role or for themselves. It is seen that probably women as Adyaksha, Pramukh and Pradhan have to devote more time to their official duties and some time to society as well.

In real sense, women have no time management plan. They just guess the time devoted to different activities. The women visit Panchayat office only for attending meetings etc and most of the time they remain confined to their home. Actually, their new role does not require full time.

Table 29
Distribution of Time

(Percentage Distribution)

	Most Time	*More Time*	*Little*	*No Husband/ in-laws/ Children*	*No Res-ponse*	*Total*
For Husband	38.46	29.51	24.10	7.93		100.00
For Children	55.34	31.85	5.63	2.18	5.00	100.00
For In-laws	43.48	25.10	14.27	7.15	10.00	100.00
For House Work	75.38	8.39	5.18		11.05	100.00
For Office Work	28.20	23.99	9.68		38.13	100.00
For hobby/Recreation	9.30	8.48	8.23		73.99	100.00
For Society	19.56	17.09	14.20		49.15	100.00
For shopping	6.66	3.44	2.20		87.70	100.00
For friends	5.22	1.79	2.89			100.00
For Self	9.66	7.92	5.15		77.27	100.00

But the women are not at all repentant about their time spent on various activities. Overall observations reveal that women respondents feel satisfied with the time they give to various roles, both in the family and outside. However a significant number of women representatives find the time devoted in office, to discharge official duties, and to community not sufficient. More than one-fifth of the respondents are not satisfied with time left for themselves. This is a good indication that Indian women have now at least started thinking in terms of devoting sometime for themselves also. (Tables - 30, 31, 32)

The analysis depicts that women representatives, despite their dual responsibilities, try to fulfill their familial responsibilities and duties towards husband and children. They spare sufficient time for their children and husband. Children always approach them when there is a need. The elected women are found making both the ends meet successfully. They always try to fulfill their family obligations along with discharging their role as people's representatives. At initial stage, they feel some problem of adjustment but due to passage of time they succeed in allotting time for each work and family members also extend helping hands. Surprisingly, about one-fourth of women do not find time or opportunity to dine with their husband and/or children. It seems that still women in general in rural areas take their meals after all the male members finish. This practice needs to be broken. Women who enjoy equal status should have their meals alongwith other male family members. (Tables-33, 34, 35)

CONFLICT AND ADJUSTMENT WITH HUSBAND

Adoption of the demands of dual career life – style requires much flexibility as well as willingness to experiment and innovate by both the partners. Indian society having been all along guided and guarded by traditions is now getting ready, of course at snail's pace, to accept women in new role (a role beyond their traditional familial role).

A woman has to fulfill the demands and wishes of different members of the family because of the role she plays and the status she occupies.

Table 30
Satisfaction with Time Alloted
Zila Panchayat

(Percentage Distribution)

	Husband		Children		In-Laws (Parents)		Brother/Sister (in-laws)		Relation		Neighbours		Society		At Office		Official Obligations		Ward/ Village		Self	
Region	Yes	No	Yes	No	Yes	No	Yes	No	Yes	No	Yes	No	Yes	No	Yes	No	Yes	No	Yes	No	Yes	No
Eastern	91.67	8.33	100.00		66.67	33.33	100.00		66.67	33.33	75.00	25.00	100.00		100.00		100.00		91.67	8.33	75.00	25.00
Central	85.00	15.00	80.00	20.00	84.22	15.78	80.00	20.00	65.00	35.00	65.00	35.00	85.00	15.00	85.00	15.00	90.00	10.00	90.00	10.00	70.00	30.00
Western	100.00		77.78	22.22	100.00		100.00		83.34	16.66	61.18	38.88	55.56	44.44	55.56	44.44	55.56	44.44	61.18	38.88	55.56	44.44
Bundelkhand	81.25	18.75	76.48	23.52	100.00		100.00		88.24	11.76	94.12	5.88	64.71	35.29	76.48	23.52	76.48	23.52	76.48	23.52	70.59	29.41
Grand Total	89.62	10.38	84.82	15.18	87.50	12.50	94.94	5.06	74.69	25.31	73.42	26.58	78.49	21.51	81.02	18.98	82.28	17.72	81.02	18.98	69.38	31.64

Table 31
Satisfaction with Time Alloted
Kshetra Panchayat

(Percentage Distribution)

	Husband		*Children*		*In-Laws (Parents)*		*Brother/Sister (in-laws)*		*Relation*		*Neighbours*		*Society*		*At Office*		*Official Obligations*		*Ward/ Village*		*Self*	
Region	*Yes*	*No*	*Yes*	*No*	*Yes*	*No*	*Yes*	*No*	*Yes*	*No*	*Yes*	*No*	*Yes*	*No*	*Yes*	*No*	*Yes*	*No*	*Yes*	*No*	*Yes*	*No*
Eastern	96.97	3.03	94.12	5.88	88.89	11.11	94.12	5.88	85.30	14.70	82.36	17.64	88.24	11.76	94.12	5.88	91.18	8.82	85.30	14.70	73.53	26.47
Central	100.00		100.00		96.78	3.22	100.00		97.78	2.22	95.56	4.44	91.12	8.88	91.12	8.88	91.12	8.88	91.12	8.88	88.89	11.11
Western	100.00		96.67	3.33	100.00		100.00		93.34	6.66	93.34	6.66	90.00	10.00	93.34	6.66	93.34	6.66	90.00	10.00	86.67	13.33
Bundelkhand	97.15	2.85	80.00	20.00	80.00	20.00	97.15	2.85	68.58	31.42	71.43	28.57	82.86	17.14	82.86	17.14	85.72	14.28	77.15	22.85	62.86	37.14
Grand Total	98.60	1.40	93.06	6.94	92.65	7.35	97.92	2.08	86.89	13.19	86.12	13.88	88.20	11.80	90.28	9.72	90.28	9.72	86.12	13.88	78.48	21.52

Table 32
Satisfaction with Time Alloted
Gram Panchayat

(Percentage Distribution)

	Husband		Children		In-Laws (Parents)		Brother/Sister (in-laws)		Relation		Neighbours		Society		At Office		Official Obligations		Ward/ Village		Self	
Region	Yes	No	Yes	No	Yes	No	Yes	No	Yes	No	Yes	No	Yes	No	Yes	No	Yes	No	Yes	No	Yes	No
Eastern	96.73	3.27	88.71	11.29	92.00	8.00	98.39	1.61	90.33	9.67	93.55	6.45	95.17	4.83	91.94	8.06	93.55	6.45	87.10	12.90	85.49	14.51
Central	94.88	5.12	87.66	12.34	96.37	3.63	100.00		86.42	13.58	88.89	11.11	86.42	13.58	91.36	8.64	88.89	11.11	97.54	2.46	85.19	14.81
Western	100.00		83.06	16.94	100.00		94.92	5.08	79.67	20.33	83.06	16.94	83.06	16.94	74.58	25.42	76.28	23.72	74.58	25.42	69.50	30.50
Bundelkhand	95.78	4.22	88.74	11.26	100.00		100.00		84.51	15.49	90.15	9.85	85.92	14.08	84.51	15.49	76.06	23.94	73.24	26.76	70.43	29.57
Grand Total	96.65	3.35	87.18	12.82	97.34	2.66	98.54	1.46	85.35	14.65	89.02	10.98	87.55	12.45	86.09	13.91	83.89	16.11	83.89	16.11	78.03	21.97

Table 33
Time-Use
Zila Panchayat

(Percentage Distribution)

	Children Approach					*You Dine with Husband & Children*					*You Move with Children*					*Move with Husband*				
Region	*A*	*F*	*ST*	*R*	*N*	*A*	*F*	*ST*	*R*	*N*	*A*	*F*	*ST*	*R*	*N*	*A*	*F*	*ST*	*R*	*N*
Eastern	8.33	41.67	50.00					58.34	33.33	8.33	29.16	20.84	50.00			8.34	25.00	62.50	4.16	
Central	60.00	20.00	20.00			10.00	20.00	35.00	25.00	10.00	25.00	20.00	55.00			50.00	15.00	25.00	10.00	
Western	44.45	33.33	22.22			22.22	27.79	22.22	16.66	11.11	22.22	38.89	38.89			47.07	29.41	23.52		
Bundelkhand	47.05	52.95					23.52	35.29	41.19		23.52	58.84	17.64			25.00	68.75	6.25		
Grand Total	37.99	36.70	25.31			7.59	16.45	39.26	29.11	7.59	25.31	32.91	41.78			31.19	32.46	32.46	3.89	

A = Always
F = Frequently
ST = Some Times
R = Rarely
N = Never

Table 34
Time-Use
Kshetra Panchayat

(Percentage Distribution)

Region	Children Approach					You Dine with Husband & Children					You Move with Children					Move with Husband				
	A	F	ST	R	N	A	F	ST	R	N	A	F	ST	R	N	A	F	ST	R	N
Eastern	32.37	29.41	17.64	20.58			8.82	26.47	17.64	47.07	5.88	32.35	55.89	2.94	2.94	18.75	25.00	56.25		
Central	24.45	60.00	11.11	4.44			26.66	42.23	20.00	11.11	28.90	40.00	22.22	6.66	2.22	40.00	31.12	28.88		
Western	56.68	20.00	16.66	3.33	3.33	23.33	23.33	13.33	26.68	13.33	20.00	26.67	26.67	23.33	3.33	27.62	24.13	41.37	3.44	3.44
Bundelkhand	51.44	28.57	8.57	11.42			5.71	42.87	28.57	22.85	20.68	20.68	41.41	6.89	10.34	34.50	31.03	31.03	3.44	
Grand Total	39.60	36.80	13.19	9.72	0.69	4.86	16.66	32.66	22.91	22.91	19.56	31.15	35.53	9.42	4.34	31.11	28.14	38.53	1.48	0.74

A = Always
F = Frequently
ST = Some Times
R = Rarely
N = Never

Table 35
Time-Use
Gram Panchayat

(Percentage Distribution)

	Children Approach					*You Dine with Husband & Children*					*You Move with Children*					*Move with Husband*				
Region	*A*	*F*	*ST*	*R*	*N*	*A*	*F*	*ST*	*R*	*N*	*A*	*F*	*ST*	*R*	*N*	*A*	*F*	*ST*	*R*	*N*
Eastern	37.11	29.03	19.35	11.29	3.22	4.83	6.45	16.12	38.73	33.87	19.35	33.89	40.32	4.83	1.61	26.22	14.75	49.21	6.55	3.27
Central	22.22	38.27	24.71	9.87	4.93	11.11	20.98	18.51	19.78	29.62	16.04	25.92	44.47	9.87	3.70	30.00	23.75	35.00	7.50	3.75
Western	38.99	38.99	20.33	1.69		20.36	13.55	45.76	8.47	11.86	38.98	13.55	44.09	3.38		24.13	17.24	56.91	1.72	
Bundelkhand	39.43	26.79	21.12	11.26	1.40		5.63	32.39	38.04	23.94	34.78	26.08	33.35	5.79		27.54	31.89	31.89	7.24	1.44
Grand Total	33.71	33.33	21.61	8.79	2.56	8.79	12.08	27.49	26.37	25.27	26.56	25.09	40.61	6.27	1.47	27.23	22.38	42.19	5.97	2.23

A = Always
F = Frequently
ST = Some Times
R = Rarely
N = Never

Acquisition of an additional role and status by a married woman is likely to induce a change in her role and expectations in relation to her husband and other family members. She is found making every effort to bridge new roles and responsibilities with her traditional roles. However often the working woman becomes tensed and confused because of the clash between her changed attitudes and traditional attitudes of her husband and family members.

Indian men generally picture an ideal woman as "a modest, shy, submissive, reserved and untouched" object. This stereotype concept seems to lead to marital frustration and disappointments which ultimately find expression in marital disharmony of the working women. Combining the two roles is not an easy and smooth task, especially for those in politics due to their active social and political life.

It requires not only additional physical strength but also psychological adjustment to the changes brought about by this combination. The moment the wife commits herself to work outside home, the husband feels that he loses a part of his wife's active support. The time and energy a wife can give to the emotional, social and physical needs of her husband are lessened. Here the scenario is totally different. Women have been virtually pushed to the new role (just to fulfill the constitutional requirement). Their problems are even more pronounced as the women representatives have greater responsibility towards society. Being representatives of the people in local governance, they are expected to devote more time towards the problems of community at large.

A woman does have a responsibility towards her husband as well as society. She tries her best to overcome the difficulties in handling both these roles to run a smooth political as well as family life. But if the husband being influenced by the traditional female role, irrespective of the wife's political commitments and status, does not cooperate and resent to share household work with wife, and, if wife has less time for home management, then marital life is likely to be affected resulting in tension and conflicting situations.

There are different areas of conflict where the woman representative has to make adjustment with the husband. Most of the women representatives experience dispute with their husband on various issues. Though women representatives feel that their husband are cooperative, as they support them in their new role; because of their stereotypical attitude towards women role, more often husband dispute with them.

Since women in the political role have active social life, they have to interact on regular basis with officials and other male members as well as citizens, hence they have to be more social and open, which, most of the time, is not liked by their husbands and other male members of the family. Male members of the family some times even instigate husband against wife. It is observed that dispute with husband is mainly related to the freedom of the wife due to her new political role. As a people's representative she wants to be out of the home frequently, which husband most of the times does not appreciate and wants more attention of wife towards home and family. With their new role women representatives are now becoming modern in their views and attitudes, which has its effect on their behaviour as well. This change in behaviour and attitudes as a result of their modernity is not always appreciated by husbands who have stereotype image of women.

It is seen that women in general are facing dispute with husband on their new role, which compels women to come out of house and take part in decision making at local level. The freedom thus being enjoyed by women is another cause for husband disputing with them. Negligence of family, spending their income independently, their changed behaviour, not following all the time family decorum (as standardized by traditional male society) and modernity are the other reasons of dispute in family. Women at all the tiers, irrespective of the region or district, are facing this problem. This reveals the unchanged fundamental male mentality towards fair sex. Male members seem to be using women representatives as their political mascot. They are mentally not ready to tolerate women as an equally respectable human being. They want to grab the political position by putting women in the role, but feel uncomfortable in allowing her to perform political role independently. The husband and other family members should encourage and support her in new role rather snatching the baton from her and using her as a showcase. In many cases women themselves are responsible for their plight. They feel happy in their familial role and hesitate in coming forward. A proper awareness campaign can change their mentality and attitude. (Tables-36, 37, 38)

But it is observed that in case of women representatives who were deliberately brought in politics by their husband and who work just as rubber stamps for their husband, have lesser chances of dispute with their husband and such husbands also have lesser grievances because wife devotes full time at home and the entire official work is done by the husband or other male members of the family.

As regards reaction of husbands on joining the wife her political role, it is found that husbands appreciate their wives joining the new role. One-third of the husbands appreciate their wives joining politics, because women have been able to acquire this new role due to support of their husband. About half of the women representatives discharge their official functions with the help of their husband. In many cases it is found that women only confine themselves to attending meetings while the rest of the official works are handled by the husband. Hence in these cases husband seems to be very supportive and cooperative. (Tables - 39, 40, 41)

At this level, family members of women respondents were asked to reveal as to whether women representatives require the help of either husband or other male family members in discharging official duties. Ironically only about one-tenth of family members contacted negated the established thesis that women cannot do anything independently, hence require help. Majority of the family members were of the opinion that women representatives do require help in performing their political responsibilities. They help them in attending the meetings, and dealing with the officials and discharging official duties. It warrants the need of orienting the women towards their changed roles and responsibilities. (Table-42)

Table 36
Dispute with Husband
Zila Panchayat

(Percentage Distribution)

Region	Over New Role			On Freedom			Negligence for Family			On Spending			On Behaviour			On Family Tradition/Decorum			On Social Liaison			On Modernity		
	Yes	No	Some time	Yes	No	Some time	Yes	No	Some time	Yes	No	Some time	Yes	No	Some time	Yes	No	Some time	Yes	No	Some time	Yes	No	Some time
Eastern		100			100.00			58.33	41.67		91.67	8.33		91.67	8.33		100.00			91.67	8.33		100.00	
Central	5.00	95.00		5.00	95.00			95.00	5.00		95.00	5.00		10.00			95.00	5.00	5.00	95.00			100.00	
Western		77.78	22.22		100.00	6.25		88.24	11.76		100.00			10.00			100.00			100.00			100.00	
Bundelkhand		100.00			93.75	1.29		93.75	6.25		100.00			93.75	6.25		100.00			100.00			100.00	
Grand Total	1.28	93.60	5.12	1.29	97.42			81.82	18.18		96.11	3.89		96.21	3.79		98.71	1.29	2.53	96.21	1.26		100.00	

Table 37
Dispute with Husband
Kshetra Panchayat

(Percentage Distribution)

	Over New Role			*On Freedom*			*Negligence for Family*			*On Spending*			*On Behaviour*			*On Family Tradition/Decorum*			*On Social Liaison*			*On Modernity*		
Region	*Yes*	*No*	*Some time*	*Yes*	*No*	*Some time*	*Yes*	*No*	*Some time*	*Yes*	*No*	*Some time*	*Yes*	*No*	*Some time*	*Yes*	*No*	*Some time*	*Yes*	*No*	*Some time*	*Yes*	*No*	*Some time*
Eastern		96.97	3.03		100.00			93.34	6.06		100.00			100.00			96.97	3.03		96.97	3.03		100.00	
Central		93.34	6.66		97.78	2.22		95.56	4.44		100.00			97.78	2.22		93.34	6.66		93.34	6.66		100.00	
Western		78.58	21.42		100.00			86.67	13.33		86.67	13.33		100.00			83.34	16.66		96.67	3.33		96.67	3.33
Bundelkhand	2.86	82.86	14.28		88.58	11.42		91.43	8.57	5.71	88.58	5.71	5.71	94.29	5.71		88.58	5.71	2.86	97.14		2.86	91.42	5.72
Grand Total	0.70	88.67	10.63		96.51	3.49		92.31	7.69	1.39	94.42	4.19	1.39	97.91	2.09		90.92	7.69	0.69	95.82	3.49	0.69	97.22	2.09

Table 38
Dispute with Husband
Gram Panchayat

(Percentage Distribution)

Region	Over New Role			On Freedom			Negligence for Family			On Spending			On Behaviour			On Family Tradition/Decorum			On Social Liaison			On Modernity		
	Yes	No	Some time	Yes	No	Some time	Yes	No	Some time	Yes	No	Some time	Yes	No	Some time	Yes	No	Some time	Yes	No	Some time	Yes	No	Some time
Eastern		95.09	4.91		98.37	1.63		95.09	4.91		100.00			96.73	3.27		100.00			100.00			100.00	
Central		78.21	21.79		100.00			80.77	19.23		98.72	1.28		100.00			93.59	6.41		98.72	1.28		97.44	2.56
Western		89.29	10.71		98.28	1.72		84.49	15.51		94.83	5.17		100.00			100.00			100.00			96.56	3.44
Bundelkhand		84.51	15.49		94.37	5.63		92.96	7.04		98.60	1.40		97.19	2.81		98.60	1.40		100.00			98.60	1.40
Grand Total		86.10	13.90		97.77	2.23		88.06	11.94		98.14	1.86		98.51	1.49		97.77	2.23		99.63	0.37		98.14	1.86

This is a wrong notion that women are good only in household and cannot do any work outside their traditional role. The growing literacy and education and awareness have helped brought great change in capacity and capability of women. They are equally good even on outside jobs if given a chance.

The women having support of their husband on their joining politics feel that in most cases they have been brought into politics by their husband. But few women representatives, who have come in politics on their own for personal independence and elevated status feel that their husband, most of the time, do not appreciate their joining politics. Their number is quite less. The women in political role feel that their duties towards husband and family some times get neglected despite their best effort to fulfill the requirements at both the fronts. They always keep family, children and husband on top priority and politics for them comes later on. The husband is always helpful in performing the official responsibilities.

The women getting full support from their husbands and are appreciated by their husbands for their new role are the one who are assisted in performing the role. Thus many of these women are dummy. The political role has just been imposed upon them by virtue of new dispensation and the husbands are playing the real game. This is prevalent in Gram Panchayats and Kshetra Panchayats, in majority of cases and, in few cases in Zila Panchayats as well. Such a situation makes the mockery of the Constitution and can not help bring empowerment of women. In spite of constitutional obligations, the women in many places at all the tiers are treated by their husband like puppets.

Surprisingly, grievance level of family members with women representatives is higher at Zila Panchayats in comparison to their counterparts at lower levels. The children of women at Kshetra Panchayats are least aggrieved because of their mother joining the politics. Husband of women representatives at Kshetra Panchayats and Gram Panchayats are least aggrieved. However, grievance level of in-laws and other family members is recorded more. It reflects that husband

Table 39
Family Member Like Joining Politics
Zila Panchayat

(Percentage Distribution)

				Children				Father/Mother (in- laws)				Relations				Sister/Brother (in-laws)				Neighbours			
Region	*ST*	*R*	*N*	*A*	*ST*	*R*	*N*	*A*	*ST*	*R*	*N*	*A*	*ST*	*R*	*N*	*A*	*ST*	*R*	*N*	*A*	*ST*	*R*	*N*
Eastern	33.33			58.35	16.66	8.33	16.66		33.33		66.67	66.67	8.33	25.00		66.68	8.33	8.33	16.66	66.67		33.33	
Central	10.00	5.00		70.00	20.00	10.00		76.93		15.38	7.69	80.00	10.00	5.00	5.00	75.00	5.00	15.00	5.00	65.00	15.00	15.00	5.00
Western	29.41			27.79	50.00	16.66	5.55	42.87	35.71	21.42		22.22	66.67	11.11		38.88	44.46	11.11	5.55	11.11	55.56	33.33	
Bundelkhand	12.50			35.29	52.95	11.76		10.00	70.00	20.00		17.64	64.72	17.64		41.18	41.18	5.88	11.76	23.52	47.08	23.52	5.88
Grand Total	22.07	1.29		49.38	32.91	11.39	6.32	36.98	32.60	15.21	15.21	49.39	34.17	15.18	1.26	57	22.78	10.1	10.12	44.31	26.58	26.58	2.53

Table 40
Family Member Like Joining Politics
Kshetra Panchayat

(Percentage Distribution)

				Children				Father/Mother (in- laws)				Relations				Sister/Brother (in-laws)				Neighbours			
Region	*ST*	*R*	*N*	*A*	*ST*	*R*	*N*	*A*	*ST*	*R*	*N*	*A*	*ST*	*R*	*N*	*A*	*ST*	*R*	*N*	*A*	*ST*	*R*	*N*
Eastern	18.18			55.89	38.23	5.88		12.50	50.00	25.00	12.50	41.18	41.18	14.70	2.94	38.23	41.19	14.70	5.88	44.13	35.29	14.70	5.88
Central	17.77	11.11	4.44	64.45	20.00	11.11	4.44	37.04	37.04	18.52	7.40	48.91	28.88	13.33	8.88	48.90	33.33	13.33	4.44	46.68	24.44	15.55	13.33
Western	30.00		6.66	50.00	16.66	10.00	23.34	63.64	9.09	18.18	9.09	10.00	53.34	16.66	20.00	13.33	46.68	16.66	23.33	10.00	56.67	13.33	20.00
Bundelkhand	22.85	2.85	5.71	31.44	28.57	17.14	22.85	26.68	46.66	13.33	13.33	20.00	45.73	22.85	11.42	22.86	40.00	22.86	14.28	14.28	34.30	28.57	22.85
Grand Total	20.97	4.89	4.19	51.40	25.69	11.11	11.80	36.07	36.07	18.03	9.83	31.94	40.99	16.66	10.41	32.63	39.60	16.66	11.11	30.55	36.13	18.05	15.27

ST – Sometime
R – Rarely
N – Never

Table 41
Family Member Like Joining Politics
Gram Panchayat

(Percentage Distribution)

				Children				Father/Mother (in- laws)				Relations				Sister/Brother (in-laws)				Neighbours			
Region	ST	R	N	A	ST	R	N	A	ST	R	N	A	ST	R	N	A	ST	R	N	A	ST	R	N
Eastern	44.26	1.63		58.07	33.87	8.06		44.46	37.03	18.51		30.64	43.56	17.74	8.06	35.48	40.34	16.12	8.06	33.87	37.10	17.74	11.29
Central	16.66	2.56	1.28	67.92	8.64	16.04	7.40	65.80	7.89	5.26	21.05	58.03	19.75	11.11	11.11	45.69	35.80	7.40	11.11	46.93	25.92	16.04	11.11
Western	17.24	1.72		72.90	15.25	6.77	5.08	53.14	28.12	9.37	9.37	25.42	61.04	10.16	3.38	28.81	55.95	11.86	3.38	27.11	64.43	5.08	3.38
Bundelkhand	28.16	14.08	5.63	28.16	39.45	23.94	8.45	20.84	62.50	16.66		22.53	38.04	26.76	12.67	28.16	31.01	28.16	12.67	23.94	36.64	19.71	19.71
Grand Total	26.11	5.22	1.86	56.43	23.80	14.28	5.49	48.77	30.57	11.57	9.09	35.53	38.84	16.48	9.15	35.16	39.94	15.75	9.15	33.69	39.58	15.01	11.72

ST – Sometime
R – Rarely
N – Never

Table 42

Women Representatives Require held of Family Members

(Percentage Distribution)

					Attending Officials				*Attending Official Work*		
Regioin	*F*	*O*	*N*	*A*	*F*	*O*	*N*	*A*	*F*	*O*	*N*
Eastern	22.50	25.00	15.83	35.85	21.66	25.83	16.66	36.68	20.83	25.83	16.66
Central	26.71	13.01	8.90	50.00	28.09	13.01	8.90	49.33	26.71	15.06	8.90
Western	28.03	29.90	9.34	29.90	32.73	25.23	12.14	28.03	26.16	33.67	12.14
Bundelkhand	27.64	26.01	14.63	34.98	26.01	26.01	13.00	35.79	26.82	22.76	14.63
Grand Total	26.20	22.78	12.09	38.52	27.01	21.97	12.50	38.32	25.20	23.58	12.90

F – Frequently
O – Occasionally
N – Never

and children of many women representatives feel the political role as fiefdom of their own. They see their future in women's political role, hence less aggrieved or not aggrieve. (Tables- 43, 44, 45)

It is an irony that women, who are placed as home manager are not being given the status of a partner even in many family matters. The analysis reveals that husband is enjoying the privileges linked with the politics as role of his wife (on behalf of his wife) but he is not ready to associate the wife with his decision making power even in family matters. Majority of the women respondents find their husband belonging to old school and want them to confine to their traditional functions and are not prepared to part their powers with wife. More than one-fifth of women representatives feel never consulted by husband in taking any decision. He never asks for her suggestion. (Tables - 46, 47 48)

In connection with their quitting politics under the pressure from husband, responses are quite revealing. Almost all women respondents at all the three tiers find their husband not asking to quit politics. Surprisingly, Varanasi is the only district where significant number of women belonging to all the tiers express the desire of their husbands asking to leave the politics. These may be aberrations because of special family circumstances. (Tables - 49, 50, 51)

CONFLICTS AND ADJUSTMENT IN MANAGING CHILDREN

In Indian rural society the responsibility of bringing up the children lies on the mother, whether she is people's representative or full time housewife. However mothers who have to work outside, face difficult situations both at home and outside at work place. They make various adjustments despite their inconvenience. It is often found that mothers willingly sacrifice or subordinate their interests for the betterment of their children. The so-called male chauvinism still prevents men to participate in household activities. Freedom of women due to other role outside home creates

Table 43
Grievance Level of Family Members
Zila Panchayat

(Percentage Distribution)

				Grievances of Husband				*Grievances of in-laws (Parents)*				*Grivenances of brother/ Sister (in-laws)*				*Grievances of Relations*			
Region	*ST*	*R*	*N*	*A*	*ST*	*R*	*N*	*A*	*ST*	*R*	*N*	*A*	*ST*	*R*	*N*	*A*	*ST*	*R*	*N*
Eastern	16.66	58.34	25.00			50.00	50.00		88.89	11.11			16.66	25.00	58.34		16.66	25.00	58.34
Central	15.00	45.00	30.00		10.00	35.00	55.00		15.38	76.93	7.69		10.00	65.00	25.00		20.00	70.00	10.00
Western	16.67	16.67	61.11		11.76	23.52	64.72		7.14	64.29	28.57			38.89	61.11		11.11	22.22	66.67
Bundelkhand	41.18	23.53	29.41			18.75	81.25		20.00	50.00	30.00		17.64	35.28	47.08	5.88	41.18	23.53	29.41
Grand Total	21.52	37.98	35.44		5.19	33.76	61.05		28.26	54.35	17.39		11.39	40.50	48.11	1.26	21.52	35.44	41.78

ST – Sometime
R – Rarely
N – Never

Table 44
Grievance Level of Family Members
Kshetra Panchayat

(Percentage Distribution)

					Grievances of Husband				*Grievances of in-laws (Parents)*				*Grivenances of brother/ Sister (in-laws)*				*Grievances of Relations*		
Region	*ST*	*R*	*N*	*A*	*ST*	*R*	*N*	*A*	*ST*	*R*	*N*	*A*	*ST*	*R*	*N*	*A*	*ST*	*R*	*N*
Eastern	20.58	17.64	61.78		18.18	27.27	54.55		62.50	37.50			17.64	48.08	35.28		20.58	41.16	38.26
Central	6.66	42.22	48.90	2.22		31.11	66.67		25.92	33.33	40.75	2.22	8.88	42.22	46.68	2.22	17.77	35.55	44.46
Western	3.33	30.00	66.67		3.33	33.33	63.34		18.18	27.27	54.55		6.67	33.33	60.00		13.33	30.00	56.67
Bundelkhand	25.71	22.85	48.59		5.70	17.10	77.20	12.50	50.00	31.25	6.25	17.10	22.85	37.20	22.85	11.42	31.42	34.32	22.84
Grand Total	13.88	29.16	55.57	0.70	6.29	27.27	65.74	3.28	34.43	32.79	29.50	4.86	13.89	40.28	40.97	3.47	20.83	35.42	40.28

ST – Sometime
R – Rarely
N – Never

Table 45
Grievance Level of Family Members
Gram Panchayat

(Percentage Distribution)

				Grievances of Husband				Grievances of in-laws (Parents)				Grivenances of brother/ Sister (in-laws)				Grievances of Relations			
Region	ST	R	N	A	ST	R	N	A	ST	R	N	A	ST	R	N	A	ST	R	N
Eastern	9.67	24.19	66.14		6.55	29.50	63.95		44.45	25.92	29.63		14.51	40.32	45.17		20.96	29.04	50.00
Central	13.58	55.56	29.63	1.28	3.84	43.58	51.30		23.68	42.10	34.22	1.23	18.51	34.56	45.70	1.23	22.22	32.11	44.44
Western	15.25	35.59	49.16		12.07	34.48	53.45		28.12	37.51	34.37	1.69	20.33	42.19	35.59		32.20	37.30	30.50
Bundelkhand	26.76	23.94	49.30		8.45	22.53	69.02		33.33	37.50	29.17	2.81	19.71	29.57	47.91	14.08	18.31	28.16	39.45
Grand Total	16.48	35.89	47.27	0.37	7.46	32.83	59.34		31.40	36.36	32.24	1.46	18.31	36.26	43.97	4.02	23.07	31.50	41.41

ST – Sometime
R – Rarely
N – Never

Table 46
Behaviour of Husband
Zila Panchayat

(Percentage Distribution)

					Ask Suggestion			*Approaches when in Grief*					*Observe Time Punctuality*						
Region	*F*	*S T*	*R*	*N*	*A*	*F*	*S T*	*R*	*N*	*A*	*F*	*S T*	*R*	*N*	*A*	*F*	*S T*	*R*	*N*
Eastern	4.16	54.18	8.33	33.33			50.00	12.50	37.50		25.00	33.33	8.33	33.34		33.33	25.00	8.33	33.34
Central	11.76	47.08	11.76	17.64	10.00	10.00	45.00	15.00	20.00	10.00	35.00	25.00	30.00		10.00	40.00	25.00	25.00	
Western	22.22	27.78	22.22	27.78		23.52	52.96	11.76	11.76	5.55	27.77	33.34	33.34		5.55	11.11	50.00	27.79	5.55
Bundelkhand		43.75	37.50	12.50	6.25	12.50	43.75	31.25	6.25		29.41	52.95	17.64			31.25	37.50	31.25	
Grand Total	9.33	44.00	18.67	24.00	3.89	10.38	48.08	16.88	20.77	3.79	29.11	35.47	21.51	10.12	3.84	29.48	33.36	21.79	11.53

F – Frequently
ST – Some Times
R – Rarely
N – Never

Table 47
Behaviour of Husband
Kshetra Panchayat

(Percentage Distribution)

					Ask Suggestion				Approaches when in Grief					Observe Time Punctuality					
Region	*F*	*S T*	*R*	*N*	*A*	*F*	*S T*	*R*	*N*	*A*	*F*	*S T*	*R*	*N*	*A*	*F*	*S T*	*R*	*N*
Eastern		30.30	21.21	48.49		6.06	18.18	21.21	54.55		11.76	26.47	23.52	38.25		14.70	14.70	32.35	38.25
Central	20.45	15.90	22.72	40.93		24.44	13.33	26.66	35.57	4.44	28.88	33.33	24.44	8.91	4.44	33.33	26.68	24.44	11.11
Western	10.00	33.34	40.00	16.66	3.33	3.33	50.00	30.00	13.34	10.00	16.66	30.00	36.68	6.66	13.33	20.00	16.66	43.35	6.66
Bundelkhand	6.89	31.03	37.95	24.13		6.89	37.95	27.58	37.58	6.45	22.58	32.27	25.80	12.90	6.89	20.68	27.62	24.13	20.68
Grand Total	10.29	26.47	29.41	33.83	0.72	11.67	27.73	26.27	33.61	5.00	20.71	30.73	27.14	16.42	5.79	23.18	21.73	30.46	18.84

F – Frequently
ST– Some Times
R – Rarely
N – Never

Table 48
Behaviour of Husband
Gram Panchayat

(Percentage Distribution)

					Ask Suggestion					*Approaches when in Grief*				*Observe Time Punctuality*					
Region	*F*	*S T*	*R*	*N*	*A*	*F*	*S T*	*R*	*N*	*A*	*F*	*S T*	*R*	*N*	*A*	*F*	*S T*	*R*	*N*
Eastern	1.63	13.11	27.86	55.77	1.63	1.63	9.83	27.86	59.05	4.83	11.29	16.12	35.51	32.25	1.61	9.67	19.35	37.12	32.25
Central		43.60	28.20	28.20		6.41	41.03	32.05	20.51	7.40	32.13	20.98	16.04	23.45	4.93	29.65	27.16	22.22	16.04
Western	6.89	48.29	17.24	25.86	1.72	5.17	43.12	18.96	31.03	10.34	15.51	31.03	34.50	8.62	12.06	22.41	29.33	25.86	10.34
Bundelkhand	1.40	16.90	22.56	56.33	2.81		11.26	22.53	63.40	5.63	15.49	26.76	38.04	14.08	4.22	8.45	22.53	39.45	25.35
Grand Total	2.23	30.59	24.25	41.44	1.49	3.35	26.49	25.74	42.93	6.98	19.48	23.52	30.17	19.85	5.51	18.01	24.63	30.90	20.95

F - Frequently
ST- Some Times
R - Rarely
N - Never

Table 49
Reasons for Husband Asking to Quit Politics
Zila Panchayat

(Percentage Distribution)

			Not attending his Parents			*Not Properly Family Care*			*Family Tensions*			*Not Caring Children*		
Region	*No*	*Sometime*	*Yes*	*No*	*Some time*	*Yes*	*No*	*Some time*	*Yes*	*No*	*Some time*	*Yes*	*No*	*Some time*
Eastern	100.00			75.00	25.00		91.66	8.34		100.00			83.33	16.67
Central	85.00	15.00		81.25	18.75		85.00	15.00		85.00	15.00		85.00	15.00
Western	100.00			100.00			100.00			100.00			100.00	
Bundelkhand	100.00			83.34	16.66		100.00			100.00			100.00	
Grand Total	96.11	3.89		86.05	13.95		93.51	6.49		96.11	3.89		90.91	9.09

Table 50
Reasons for Husband Asking to Quit Politics
Kshetra Panchayat

(Percentage Distribution)

			Not attending his Parents			*Not Properly Family Care*			*Family Tensions*			*Not Caring Children*		
Region	*No*	*Sometime*	*Yes*	*No*	*Some time*	*Yes*	*No*	*Some time*	*Yes*	*No*	*Some time*	*Yes*	*No*	*Some time*
Eastern	93.94	6.06		85.72	14.28		90.91	9.09		90.91	9.09		90.91	9.09
Central	95.56	4.44		96.16	3.84		97.78	2.22		97.78	2.22		93.34	6.66
Western	93.34	6.66		100.00			96.67	3.33		96.67	3.33		96.67	3.33
Bundelkhand	82.87	11.42		86.67	13.33	5.71	88.58	5.71		85.72	14.28	5.71	85.72	8.57
Grand Total	90.22	8.39		93.45	6.55	1.39	93.72	4.89		93.01	6.99	1.39	91.62	6.99

Table 51
Reasons for Husband Asking to Quit Politics
Gram Panchayat

(Percentage Distribution)

			Not attending his Parents			Not Properly Family Care			Family Tensions			Not Caring Children		
Region	No	Sometime	Yes	No	Some time	Yes	No	Some time	Yes	No	Some time	Yes	No	Some time
Eastern	93.45	6.55		78.27	21.73		90.17	9.83		93.45	6.55		95.09	4.91
Central	85.90	1.28	21.05	73.69	5.26	11.53	82.06	6.41	11.53	79.50	8.97	15.38	78.21	6.41
Western	87.94	12.06		96.67	3.33		89.66	10.34		91.38	8.62		89.66	10.34
Bundelkhand	92.96	7.04		100.00			94.37	5.63		97.19	2.81		97.19	2.81
Grand Total	89.56	6.71	6.89	84.49	8.62	3.30	87.51	9.19	3.35	89.94	6.71	4.47	89.56	5.97

tension in the existing authoritarian typical India rural family structure and relationships. While playing the role of a mother by a working woman, various factors play major role in creating tense situations and causing conflict.

The women representatives having large number of children (above 6) and minor ones experience maximum role conflict because they have a major responsibility towards their children and have to devote more time on this count, while women representatives having less and grown-up children experience lesser role conflict.

The analysis depicts that mothers who have proper childcare arrangements while they are out to fulfill their non-traditional functions, are found to be less tensed and experience lesser conflict. It is found that in their absence the responsibility of children is mostly left to in-laws and husband. Those having grown up children do not have any problem, while those women respondents having young kids and living in nuclear family experience maximum conflict as they have to leave their children either with parents or in servants care or have to find some other way for child care. In many cases husbands also take care of children when their wives are away at work. In joint or extended families, case to children is not a great problem as the old ones in family take case of the children. More so, women belonging to lower or poor castes do not face such problems because their older children are many a times saddled with this responsibility.

Table 52
Care of Children
Zila Panchayat

(Percentage Distribution)

Region	*Serv-ants*	*Pare-nts*	*Husb-and*	*In crèches*	*Neigh-bours*	*Sist-ers*	*Rela-tion*
Eastern	33.33	33.33				16.67	16.67
Central		60.00			20.00	10.00	10.00
Western		92.30				7.70	
Bundelkhand		42.86			7.14	21.43	28.57
Gramd Total	6.78	57.63			8.47	13.56	13.56

Table 53
Care of Children
Kshetra Panchayat

(Percentage Distribution)

Region	*Serv-ants*	*Pare-nts*	*Husb-and*	*In crèches*	*Neigh-bours*	*Sist-ers*	*Rela-tion*
Eastern		36.36			9.09	18.19	36.36
Central		54.06			18.91	13.51	13.51
Western		43.34	3.33		16.67	10.00	26.66
Bundelkhand		43.76			3.12	25.00	28.12
Gramd Total		45.46	0.83		12.39	16.53	24.79

Table 54
Care of Children
Gram Panchayat

(Percentage Distribution)

Region	*Serv-ants*	*Pare-nts*	*Husb-and*	*In crèches*	*Neigh-bours*	*Sist-ers*	*Rela-tion*
Eastern		53.35	2.22		4.44	15.55	24.44
Central		50.78			23.08	13.84	12.30
Western	7.40	59.27	3.70		5.57	7.40	16.66
Bundelkhand		34.45	4.91		16.39	14.75	29.50
Gramd Total	1.77	48.90	2.68		13.33	12.88	20.44

Table 55
Child Care
Zila Panchayat

(Percentage Distribution)

Region	*Proper*	*Improper*	*Neglected*	*Total*
Eastern	83.33	16.67		100.00
Central	75.00	25.00		100.00
Western	100.00			100.00
Bundelkhand	64.29	28.57	7.14	100.00
Grand Total	79.67	18.64	1.69	100.00

At this level women were asked as to whether they are satisfied with the present child care arrangement. The analysis reveals that seven out of ten women representatives are found satisfied as their children are getting proper care. But the remaining one-fifth of the respondents are the cause of concern. The women representatives at Kshetra and Gram Panchayats mainly fall in this category. Improper care of children may become one major reason for conflicts among husband and wife.

The husband should take the equal responsibility of child care, if they are responsible partner. Children are the responsibility of both-husband and wife. In no case women should be given this responsibility solely.

Table 56
Child Care
Kshetra Panchayat

(Percentage Distribution)

Region	*Proper*	*Improper*	*Neglected*	*Total*
Eastern	68.19	31.81		100.00
Central	75.69	18.91	5.40	100.00
Western	73.34	26.66		100.00
Bundelkhand	75.00	18.75	6.25	100.00
Grand Total	73.56	23.14	3.30	100.00

Table 57
Child Care
Gram Panchayat

(Percentage Distribution)

Region	*Proper*	*Improper*	*Neglected*	*Total*
Eastern	84.45	15.55		100.00
Central	72.32	24.61	3.07	100.00
Western	75.93	24.07		100.00
Bundelkhand	70.50	24.59	4.91	100.00
Grand Total	75.12	22.66	2.22	100.00

Surprisingly, children (especially young ones) of majority of women representatives do not like their mother's joining politics. They always have grievances and want more time and attention of their mother. The grievances of children become a major reason of conflict for women representatives as they have lesser time due to dual role responsibility. The elected women with grown up children always get support from their children and their children help them in performing their new role. A large number of women respondents feel that they rarely neglect their duties towards children but many a times due to dual responsibility at home and also outside, they get lesser time for children. Many of the women are found satisfied with the time they spare for their children. Those with younger children are however highly dissatisfied. Time factor is found to be a major reason for conflict among such women performing their political role.

CONFLICTS AND ADJUSTMENTS WITH IN-LAWS, RELATIVES AND NEIGHBOURS

Family does not mean only husband, wife and children, it also includes in-laws, parents, brothers, sisters and other relatives. Married women in the society have a major responsibility towards their in-laws. In-laws are expected to show cooperation and sympathetic attitude towards women who work outside home, especially those having active political and social life. It is found that their attitudes differ in terms of varying expectations. Sweet relations become bitter when expectations turn to demands. Women representatives actively involved in Panchayat functions at times find difficult to fulfill the demands and expectations of in-laws which leads to frictions and conflicts in joint family.

Most of the women representatives are found to get support frequently from their in-laws. They also like their joining politics. However, in-laws of many elected women are found to have a lot of grievances against them. The major grievance of in-laws relates to the neglect of duties towards them and little time and care given. The attitude of in-laws towards their daughters-in-law's new role and adjustment problems and grievances are major reasons of tension in family causing oral dual with husbands, which, if held frequently, may lead to role conflict among women representatives.

Likewise, relatives and neighbours also play a very important role in the adjustment pattern of working women. The data analysed earlier show that most of the women representatives get support from relatives and also get their help in discharging official functions. Women respondents feel that their duties towards relatives do not get neglected, most of the time, so they have lesser grievances. Similarly neighbors also provide them support and help. However, there are many instances when relatives and neighbours are found instigating the in-laws against women representatives. In such cases same conflicts crop in.

The women representatives feel that due to their raised status they are now more respected by relatives and neighbors and always get their help and support.

Many a times elected women may get aggrieved due to the grievances from family members and this creates a lot of tension which has an impact on their mental health and also on performance of their roles. The responses illustrate that more than one fourth women representatives of Zila Panchayats and less than one-fifth at other tiers feel aggrieved due to behaviour of husband, children, in-laws and other family members and relatives. But the highest number of women at all levels feel aggrieved sometimes. About one-tenth of women respondents even don't care, and they involve them unhesitatingly in carrying another new responsibility.

Table 58
Feel Aggrieved
Zila Panchayat

(Percentage Distribution)

Region	*Yes*	*No*	*Don't Care*	*Some times*	*Total*
Eastern	33.33	16.66	8.33	41.68	100.00
Central	20.00	–	25.00	55.00	100.00
Western	22.22	11.11	11.11	55.56	100.00
Bundelkhand	41.19	23.52	5.88	29.41	100.00
Grand Total	29.11	12.65	12.65	45.59	100.00

At this level, women representatives were asked to reveal whether they think to quit politics because of the grievances of their family members. The responses reflect the emerging boldness in women and they flatly refuse to leave their new role. Some times, women may feel like that but in general they are found enjoying their new roles and responsibilities. (Tables - 61, 62, 63)

Table 59
Feel Aggrieved
Kshetra Panchayat

(Percentage Distribution)

Region	*Yes*	*No*	*Don't Care*	*Some times*	*Total*
Eastern	20.58	44.13	2.94	32.35	100.00
Central	8.88	26.66	13.33	51.13	100.00
Western	13.33	26.66	23.33	36.68	100.00
Bundelkhand	28.57	20.00	17.14	34.29	100.00
Grand Total	17.36	29.16	13.88	39.60	100.00

Table 60
Feel Aggrieved
Gram Panchayat

(Percentage Distribution)

Region	*Yes*	*No*	*Don't Care*	*Some times*	*Total*
Eastern	19.35	25.80	9.67	45.18	100.00
Central	13.58	20.98	18.51	46.93	100.00
Western	23.72	8.47	22.03	45.78	100.00
Bundelkhand	22.53	22.53	16.90	38.04	100.00
Grand Total	19.41	19.78	16.84	43.97	100.00

Further, the women representatives getting full help from their family members and Panchayat officials in discharging their functions. Satisfactorily a significant number of women don't require any help from their family members. This is a good beginning.(Tables - 64, 65, 66)

It thus suggests that women representatives are found to be satisfied with their family. They feel that most of the time family members understand their problems, appreciate them and try to make adjustments with them. They are feeling empowered because of this new role and they are developing capability to cope with the situation, of course, at slow pace. But in spite of this, there are lot of grievances and conflicting situations within the family, which women representatives have to handle in order to maintain a balance between both the roles.

The family members were further asked to divulge the areas in which they extend help to women representatives in

Table 61
Reasons for Thinking to Quit Politics
Zila Panchayat

(Percentage Distribution)

	For Husband			*For Children*			*In-laws/Parents*			*For Sister/Brother (in-laws)*			*Relations*			*Neighbours*		
	Yes	*Some time*	*Never*	*Yes*	*Some time*	*Never*	*Yes*	*Some time*	*Never*	*Yes*	*Some time*	*Never*	*Yes*	*Some time*	*Never*	*Yes*	*Some time*	*Never*
Eastern	-	16.66	83.34	8.33	25.00	66.67	-	88.89	11.11	-	8.33	91.67	-	-	100.00	-	4.16	95.84
Central	-	25.00	75.00	10.00	25.00	65.00	-	23.08	76.92	-	-	100.00	-	5.00	95.00	-	-	100.00
Western	-	5.88	94.12	-	22.22	77.78	-	14.28	85.72	-	-	100.00	-	-	100.00	-	-	100.00
Bundelkhand	-	18.75	81.25	11.76	47.07	41.17	-	30.00	70.00	-	-	100.00	-	-	100.00	-	-	100.00
Grand Total	-	16.88	83.12	7.59	29.11	63.30	-	34.78	65.22	-	2.53	97.47	-	-	100.00	-	2.16	98.74

Table 62
Reasons for Thinking to Quit Politics
Kshetra Panchayat

(Percentage Distribution)

	For Husband			*For Children*			*In-laws/Parents*			*For Sister/Brother*		*(in-laws)*	*Relations*			*Neighbours*		
	Yes	*Some time*	*Never*	*Yes*	*Some time*	*Never*	*Yes*	*Some time*	*Never*	*Yes*	*Some time*	*Never*	*Yes*	*Some time*	*Never*	*Yes*	*Some time*	*Never*
Eastern	3.03	24.24	72.73	8.82	35.29	55.89	-	37.50	62.50	2.94	14.70	82.36	2.94	17.64	79.42	-	5.88	96.12
Central	6.66	22.22	71.12	15.55	20.00	64.45	-	18.51	81.49	2.22	6.66	91.12	-	4.44	95.56	-	2.22	97.78
Western	6.66	20.00	73.34	10.00	36.66	53.34	-	54.55	45.45	3.33	3.33	93.34	3.33	3.33	93.34	10.00	16.66	73.34
Bundelkhand	8.57	14.28	77.15	11.42	28.58	60.00	13.33	26.67	60.00	-	-	100.00	-	2.85	97.15	-	-	100.00
Grand Total	6.29	20.27	73.44	11.80	29.16	59.04	3.27	29.50	67.23	2.08	6.25	91.67	1.38	6.94	91.68	2.08	5.55	92.37

Table 63
Reasons for Thinking to Quit Politics
Gram Panchayat

(Percentage Distribution)

	For Husband			For Children			In-laws/Parents		For Sister/Brother			(in-laws)	Relations			Neighbours		
	Yes	Some time	Never	Yes	Some time	Never	Yes	Some time	Never	Yes	Some time	Never	Yes	Some time	Never	Yes	Some time	Never
Eastern	11.47	31.14	57.39	14.51	33.87	51.62	3.70	62.97	33.33	1.61	16.12	82.27	1.61	17.74	80.65	-	12.90	87.10
Central	19.23	19.23	61.54	14.81	30.86	54.33	10.52	15.78	73.70	4.93	4.93	90.14	1.23	6.17	92.60	1.23	3.70	95.07
Western	3.44	24.13	72.43	5.08	35.59	59.33	-	25.00	75.00	3.38	3.38	93.24	3.38	3.38	93.24	1.69	3.38	94.93
Bundelkhand	7.04	21.12	71.84	8.45	32.39	59.16	4.16	45.84	50.00	2.81	7.04	90.15	1.40	2.81	95.79	-	1.40	98.60
Grand Total	10.82	23.50	65.68	10.98	32.96	56.06	4.95	34.71	60.34	3.29	7.69	89.02	1.83	7.32	90.85	0.73	5.12	94.15

carrying out their political role without any hurdle. Surprisingly, more than one-fourth of family respondents do not help them in discharging their day-to-day chores, against the remaining ones who always help in the matter. Further, barring a few cases, family members are found there to help her in attending the meetings and discharging other official responsibilities. Despite depicting the proxy representation, there is a ray of hope. Gradually, with proper orientation and exposure women may act independently or be able to refuse any help from husband or other family members. (Table-67)

Further, family members were requested to rate the women representatives in their new role. Pleasantly, about one third of family member find them as learners in politics, while a significant number (every seventh) feel them disinterested. A few cuddos her for bearing the family flag high. This shows the near true assessment of women representatives as they are really in learning process. A proper learning arrangement and enabling environment should be created for developing their mental penalty.

At this stage the family members were further asked as to whether they would like their women to develop in politics. Enthusiastically, seven out of ten members favour her developing a political career, as against one fourth who feel other wise. This is a welcome situation that women are getting full developmental environment in their family. This is a good trend. It is the family which shapes the personality of a girl (woman). The number of such families may be less, but they are the path breakers.

Seeing the interest of family members in the prospective career of women representatives in politics, it was thought pertinent to know whether the family has any political background. Interestingly, majority of the women representatives do not have political family background, but their family members want them to develop a political career. This indicates the positive impact of affirmative action of bringing women to the political front.

Table 64
Help in Discharging Official Funtions
Zila Panchayat

(Percentage Distribution)

	Parents / In- laws					Husband					Children					Brother					Officials					Relatives				
Region	F	A	ST	N	DR	F	A	ST	N	DR	F	A	ST	N	DR	F	A	ST	N	DR	F	A	ST	N	DR	F	A	ST	N	DR
Eastern			44.44	11.12	44.44	79.17	20.83				25.00	16.66	33.34		25.00	25.00		50.00	25.00			41.67	33.33	25.00			25.00	50.00	25.00	
Central	30.76	23.07	38.48		7.69	90.00	10.00				60.00	20.00	15.00		5.00	35.00	10.00	40.00	10.00	5.00	25.00	15.00	55.00	5.00		35.00	10.00	35.00	15.00	5.00
Western	21.42	37.73	28.57		14.28	94.12	5.88				33.35	27.77	11.11	5.55	22.22	44.46	16.66	22.22	5.55	11.11	22.22	27.77	44.46	5.55		16.66	33.34	50.00		
Bundel-khand	10.00	40.00	10.00		40.00	93.75	6.25				23.52	17.67	17.64		41.17	23.52	35.30	35.30	5.88		5.88	11.76	64.72	17.64		11.76	23.52	58.84	5.88	
Grand Total	17.39	26.08	30.45	2.17	23.91	88.32	11.68				35.46	20.25	20.25	1.26	22.78	31.64	13.92	38.00	12.65	3.79	12.65	25.31	40.12	13.92		15.18	22.78	48.13	12.65	1.26

F = Fully
A = Always
S = Some Time
N = Never
DR = Don't Require

Table 65
Help In Discharging Official funtions
Kshetra Panchayat

(Percentage Distribution)

	Parents / In- laws					*Husband*					*Children*					*Brother*					*Officials*					*Relatives*				
Region	*F*	*A*	*ST*	*N*	*DR*	*F*	*A*	*ST*	*N*	*DR*	*F*	*A*	*ST*	*N*	*DR*	*F*	*A*	*ST*	*N*	*DR*	*F*	*A*	*ST*	*N*	*DR*	*F*	*A*	*ST*	*N*	*DR*
Eastern		33.33	33.33	11.11	22.23	93.94	6.06				50.00	17.65	14.70		17.65	26.47	14.7	52.9	5.88		2.94	8.82	35.29	52.95		8.82	32.35	44.13	11.76	2.94
Central	3.70	7.40	48.17	22.22	18.51	77.79	13.33	8.88			20.00	22.23	31.11	6.66	20.00	13.33	4.44	66.69	8.88	6.66	4.44		48.90	46.66		6.66	17.77	53.36	13.33	8.88
Western	9.09	27.27	36.37		27.27	100.00					46.67	13.33	30.00		10.00	16.66	13.33	53.35	10.00	6.66	3.33	3.33	43.34	50.00		16.67	30.00	50.00	3.33	
Bundel-khand	13.34	13.34	40.00	26.66	6.66	82.87	14.28	2.85			25.71	14.28	28.58	2.85	28.58	11.42	28.57	37.16	22.85		5.71		25.71	68.58		17.14	17.14	45.73	17.14	2.85
Grand Total	6.45	16.12	41.95	17.74	17.74	87.42	9.09	3.49			34.05	17.36	26.38	2.77	19.44	16.66	14.6	53.5	11.80	3.47	3.47	3.47	38..88	54.18		11.80	23.61	48.63	11.80	4.16

F = Fully
A = Always
S = Some Time
N = Never
DR = Don't Require

Table 66
Help In Discharging Official funtions
Gram Panchayat

(Percentage Distribution)

	Parents / In- laws					Husband					Children					Brother					Officials					Relatives				
Region	F	A	ST	N	DR	F	A	ST	N	DR	F	A	ST	N	DR	F	A	ST	N	DR	F	A	ST	N	DR	F	A	ST	N	DR
Eastern	7.69	23.07	34.63	7.69	26.92	90.18	3.27	6.55			32.28	19.35	24.9	1.61	20.96	24.2	6.45	50.00	11.3	8.06	1.61	4.83	46.8	43.5	3.22	9.67	24.19	42	3.22	21
Central	5.26	26.31	55.28	5.26	7.89	79.49	19.23	1.28			32.11	25.92	24.69		17.28	16.04	20.98	49.41	6.17	7.40	3.70	8.64	39.50	43.2	4.93	9.87	20.98	45.70	19.75	3.70
Western	28.13	25.00	37.50	9.37		81.05	13.79	3.44	1.72		37.31	28.81	27.11	1.69	5.08	13.55	18.64	57.7	10.2		1.69	5.06	42.4	50.9		13.55	27.11	47.48	11.86	
Bundel-khand	25.00	16.66	41.68	12.50	4.16	80.29	15.49	4.22			25.37	21.12	22.53	7.04	23.94	14.08	32.39	32.39	19.74	1.40	2.81	4.22	31	62		14.08	22.53	42.27	12.67	8.45
Grand Total	15.32	25.80	41.95	8.06	8.87	82.46	13.43	3.73	0.37		31.53	23.80	24.90	2.56	17.21	16.84	20.14	46.91	11.72	4.4	2.6	5.9	40	50	2.2	11.72	23.44	44.34	12.45	8.05

F = Fully
A = Always
S = Some Time
N = Never
DR = Don't Require

Table 67
Family Member Extend Help

(Percentage Distribution)

Region	In Discharging Day-to-day Problems				In Attending Meetings				By Reliving from Works at Home				By Accompanying her to Panchayat with Officials				By Accompanying her to Panchayat Meetings				By Encouraging her				By Supporting her Morally			
	A	F	O	N	A	F	O	N	A	F	O	N	A	F	O	N	A	F	O	N	A	F	O	N	A	F	O	N
Eastern	19.16	16.66	25.83	38.35	38.35	24.16	18.33	19.16	20.00	18.33	24.17	37.50	44.18	20.83	15.83	19.16	42.50	21.67	18.33	17.50	25.83	40.44	17.50	15.83	27.50	37.50	18.34	16.66
Central	30.15	23.28	25.34	21.23	46.59	28.76	10.27	14.38	30.84	21.23	30.13	17.80	47.97	27.39	12.32	12.32	47.97	27.39	12.32	12.32	41.80	27.39	19.17	11.64	43.17	26.71	17.80	12.32
Western	21.49	17.75	28.97	31.79	37.40	26.16	19.62	16.82	21.49	20.56	25.23	32.72	32.73	26.16	23.36	17.75	31.79	25.23	26.16	16.82	28.05	26.16	25.23	20.56	28.03	29.92	23.36	18.69
Bundel-khand	16.26	18.69	27.64	37.41	29.29	26.01	26.01	18.69	17.88	19.51	22.76	39.85	31.73	29.26	20.32	18.69	30.90	30.90	19.51	18.69	29.29	37.39	17.88	15.44	32.53	33.33	19.51	14.63
Grand Total	22.17	19.35	26.81	31.67	38.32	26.41	18.14	17.13	22.98	19.75	25.80	31.27	39.73	26.00	17.54	16.73	38.93	26.41	18.54	16.12	31.87	32.86	19.75	15.52	33.48	31.65	19.55	15.32

A = Always
F = Frequently
O = Occasionally
N = Never

Table 68
Family Members Rating Women Representatives

(Percentage Distribution)

Region	*District*	*Excellent*	*Highly Successful*	*Successful*	*In Learning Process*	*Disinterested*	*Bearing Family Banner*	*Total*
Eastern	Varanasi	13.79	6.89	37.96	34.48	3.44	3.44	100.00
	Gorakhpur		4.16	41.68	25.00	16.66	12.50	100.00
	Ballia		2.32	18.60	44.20	20.93	13.95	100.00
Total		3.33	4.16	32.50	34.18	15.00	10.83	100.00
Central	Lucknow	3.33	16.66	23.33	31.69	16.66	8.33	100.00
	Balrampur	8.33	5.55	22.22	27.80	22.22	13.88	100.00
	Sitapur		20.00	44.00	24.00	8.00	4.00	100.00
Total		3.42	15.06	30.17	28.08	15.06	8.21	100.00
Western	Bagpat	2.94	5.88	32.35	38.25	14.70	5.88	100.00
	Mathura	6.45	16.12	38.73	29.03	9.67		100.00
	Moradabad	2.38	9.52	33.33	33.33	14.30	7.14	100.00
Total		3.73	10.28	34.58	33.64	13.08	4.67	100.00
Bundelkhand	Banda	2.27	11.36	38.65	34.09	13.63		100.00
	Hamirpur		8.10	21.62	37.86	18.91	13.51	100.00
	Jhansi	2.38	2.38	45.26	23.80	21.42	4.76	100.00
Total		1.62	7.31	35.80	31.70	17.88	5.69	100.00
Grand Total		3.02	9.47	33.09	31.65	15.32	7.45	100.00

Table 69
Family Members Like Her to Develop in Politics

(Percentage Distribution)

Region	*District*	*Yes*	*No*	*Total*
Eastern	Varanasi	65.52	34.48	100.00
	Gorakhpur	64.59	35.41	100.00
	Ballia	62.80	37.20	100.00
Total		64.17	35.83	100.00
Central	Lucknow	23.34	26.66	100.00
	Balrampur	63.89	36.11	100.00
	Sitapur	80.00	20.00	100.00
Total		73.29	26.71	100.00
Western	Bagpat	82.36	17.64	100.00
	Mathura	83.88	16.12	100.00
	Moradabad	85.72	14.28	100.00
Total		84.12	15.88	100.00
Bundelkhand	Banda	79.55	20.45	100.00
	Hamirpur	62.17	37.83	100.00
	Jhansi	66.67	33.33	100.00
Total		69.92	30.08	100.00
Grand Total		72.59	27.41	100.00

Table 70
Family is Politically Active

(Percentage Distribution)

Region	*District*	*Yes*	*No*	*Total*
Eastern	Varanasi	55.18	44.82	100.00
	Gorakhpur	29.16	70.84	100.00
	Ballia	13.95	86.15	100.00
Total		30.00	70.00	100.00
Central	Lucknow	36.66	63.34	100.00
	Balrampur	38.88	61.12	100.00
	Sitapur	8.00	92.00	100.00
Total		27.39	72.61	100.00
Western	Bagpat	29.41	70.59	100.00
	Mathura	6.45	93.55	100.00
	Moradabad	26.19	73.81	100.00
Total		21.49	78.51	100.00
Bundelkhand	Banda	25.00	75.00	100.00
	Hamirpur	18.91	81.11	100.00
	Jhansi	9.52	90.48	100.00
Total		17.88	82.12	100.00
Grand Total		24.39	75.61	100.00

This is a welcome scenario emerging in local governance in the most populous state of the country. Despite having been victim of old social traditions this low literate and caste-ridden state has started showing a good sign of women empowerment. Women in specific pockets are getting proper enabling family environment and outside support in playing their destined roles.

5

CONFLICTS AND ADJUSTMENTS IN SOCIETY & SELF

WOMEN IN SOCIETY

Women representatives have major responsibilities not only towards family and Panchayat but towards themselves and society as well. Within the household unit the relationship between husband and wife is characterized by dominance and dependence. Thus despite the new roles provided by the educational and occupational opportunities to the women their social position in the family remains largely unchanged because the system of arranged marriage reasserts the authority of caste norms and the obligation of conformity to the traditional image of women as wife or mother, with low ritual status.

In spite of facing multifaceted problems in dual role of family and decision-making, they are found to be more sensitive towards the needs of people and society. It is observed that women representatives of Zila Panchayats are more active and concerned about the welfare of the people in any comparison to their counterparts at other levels. It is found that more than one-tenth women representatives in Zila Panchayats are member of some social organization. Lucknow tops the list with two-fifths women representatives are member of some social organisation. Varanasi, Gorakhpur, Sitapur and Hamirpur are the districts where such women are in significant member. In Kshetra Panchayats, Balrampur tops the list by recording about one-third women joining some social forum, followed by Gorakhpur. The analysis of Gram Panchayats reveals that Balrampur, Varanasi and Gorakhpur districts have women interested in social works. It seems that interest of women representatives in society is either area specific or their personal choice.

Table 1
Member of Social Orgainsation
Zila Panchayat

(Percentage Distribution)

Region	*Yes*	*No*	*Total*
Eastern	16.67	83.33	100.00
Central	10.00	90.00	100.00
Western		100.00	100.00
Bundelkhand	5.88	94.12	100.00
Grand Total	12.65	87.35	100.00

Table 2
Member of Social Orgainsation
Kshetra Panchayat

(Percentage Distribution)

Region	*Yes*	*No*	*Total*
Eastern	8.82	91.12	100.00
Central	8.88	91.12	100.00
Western		100.00	100.00
Bundelkhand		100.00	100.00
Grand Total	4.86	95.14	100.00

Table 3
Member of Social Orgainsation
Gram Panchayat

(Percentage Distribution)

Region	*Yes*	*No*	*Total*
Eastern	4.83	95.17	100.00
Central	3.70	96.30	100.00
Western		100.00	100.00
Bundelkhand		100.00	100.00
Grand Total	2.19	97.81	100.00

Women representatives were further asked as to whether they are member of any association specifically dealing with

Table 4
Member of Women Association
Zila Panchayat

(Percentage Distribution)

Region	*Yes*	*No*	*Total*	*If Yes as*					
				President	*Secretary*	*Treasury*	*Committee Member*	*Ordinary Member*	*Total*
Eastern	8.33	91.67	100.00				50.00	50.00	100.00
Central	20.00	80.00	100.00					100.00	100.00
Western	5.55	94.45	100.00					100.00	100.00
Bundelkhand	11.76	88.24	100.00					100.00	100.00
Grand Total	11.39	88.61	100.00				22.22	77.78	100.00

Table 5
Member of Women Association
Kshetra Panchayat

(Percentage Distribution)

Region	*Yes*	*No*	*Total*	*If Yes as*					
				President	*Secretary*	*Treasury*	*Committee Member*	*Ordinary Member*	*Total*
Eastern		100.00	100.00						–
Central	4.44	95.56	100.00					100.00	100.00
Western		100.00	100.00						–
Bundelkhand		100.00	100.00						–
Grand Total	1.34	98.62	100.00					100.00	100.00

Table 6
Member of Women Association
Gram Panchayat

(Percentage Distribution)

Region	*Yes*	*No*	*Total*	*If Yes as*					
				President	*Secretary*	*Treasury*	*Committee Member*	*Ordinary Member*	*Total*
Eastern	1.61	98.39	100.00					100.00	100.00
Central	3.70	96.30	100.00				25.00	75.00	100.00
Western		100.00	100.00						–
Bundelkhand		100.00	100.00						–
Grand Total	1.46	98.54	100.00				20.00	80.00	100.00

women affairs. The responses are not encouraging. We find some women representatives at Zila Panchayats who are member of such associations, but not at other levels. The responses in this regard are also area specific. Varanasi, Lucknow, Sitapur, Bagpat, Hamirpur, Balrampur and Gorakhpur are the districts, where women representatives are interested in women issue and thus they have joined such fora.

In real sense, there is derth of associations dealing exclusively the women affairs. If there is any, the women belonging to influential class are the role occupants and there is generally no place for common women or they do not have knowledge, time and resources to be thereat.

As this juncture, women representatives were asked that despite their not joining any formal association whether they participate in social works. The responses are quite interesting. A little less than half of the women in Zila Panchayats do participate in social works, but women at Kshetra Panchayats level are not so interested and less than one-fifth of them participate in social works. But scenario at Gram Panchayats level is quite different, where a little less than one-fourth of women are socially active.

Table 7
Participation in Social Work
Zila Panchayat

(Percentage Distribution)

Region	*Yes*	*No*	*Total*
Eastern	58.34	41.66	100.00
Central	40.00	60.00	100.00
Western	27.77	72.23	100.00
Bundelkhand	58.83	41.17	100.00
Grand Total	46.83	53.17	100.00

Surprisingly, Eastern and Bundelkhand regions show that more than half of women in their Zila Panchayats are interested in social activities and participate in such works. These districts top in respect of Kshetra Panchayats as well with about one-third and one-fifth of women respectively participating in social activities. Amongst Gram Panchayats it is the Central region, which reports one-third of women representatives socially active.

Table 8
Participation in Social Work
Kshetra Panchayat

(Percentage Distribution)

Region	*Yes*	*No*	*Total*
Eastern	32.35	67.65	100.00
Central	4.44	95.56	100.00
Western	16.67	83.33	100.00
Bundelkhand	22.85	77.15	100.00
Grand Total	18.05	81.95	100.00

The respondents were further asked as to whether they visit their areas to have first hand knowledge of the problems. Responses are on similar lines. Two-fifths of women representatives of Zila Panchayats do visit their areas, while their number is reduced to one-fourth in Kshetra Panchayats and more than that in the Gram Panchayats. Here also, Eastern, Central and Bundelkhand regions record the most women visiting the areas in connection with social works.

Table 9
Participation in Social Work
Gram Panchayat

(Percentage Distribution)

Region	*Yes*	*No*	*Total*
Eastern	20.96	79.04	100.00
Central	34.36	65.64	100.00
Western	11.86	88.14	100.00
Bundelkhand	22.53	77.47	100.00
Grand Total	23.44	76.56	100.00

It seems that women at Kshetra Panchayats and Gram Panchayats are less interested in visiting the villages for developing contacts with community. It may be because they are not interested in politics. They are there not because on their own but due to compulsion and hence do not like feel to visiting villages. The needy citizens themselves may be contacting the members.

Further, in villages there is no need by women representatives to visit the areas as village being small they all live together and meet their own. The members of Kshetra Panchayats are also not required because they come from some village only–a small unit. However, the members of Zila Panchayats are required to visit areas.

Table10
Visit Villages
Zila Panchayat

(Percentage Distribution)

Region	*District*	*Yes*	*No*	*Total*
Eastern	Varanasi	50.00	50.00	100.00
	Gorakhpur	50.00	50.00	100.00
	Ballia	50.00	50.00	100.00
Total		50.00	50.00	100.00
Central	Lucknow	42.85	57.15	100.00
	Balrampur		100.00	100.00
	Sitapur	50.00	50.00	100.00
Total		35.00	65.00	100.00
Western	Bagpat	16.67	83.33	100.00
	Mathura	100.00		100.00
	Moradabad	25.00	75.00	100.00
Total		38.88	61.12	100.00
Bundel-khand	Banda		100.00	100.00
	Hamirpur	60.00	40.00	100.00
	Jhansi	66.67	33.33	100.00
Total		41.17	58.83	100.00
Grand Total		41.77	58.23	100.00

It was further probed whether during their visit or otherwise do they spend some time with common people, who have elected them to the units of local governance. The responses are quite encouraging. A little less than half at Zila Panchayats level and more than one-third at Kshetra Panchayats and two-fifths in Gram Panchayats do spend some time for their clientele. Bundelkhand is the only region where more than half of the women representatives at all the three tiers spend time with community, followed by Eastern region (in Zila Panchayats) and Western region (in other two tiers) following the suits. This warrants the proper training to women representatives focusing on their roles and responsibilities towards village people.

Table 11
Visit Villages
Kshetra Panchayat

(Percentage Distribution)

Region	*District*	*Yes*	*No*	*Total*
Eastern	Varanasi	50.00	50.00	100.00
	Gorakhpur		100.00	100.00
	Ballia	9.09	90.91	100.00
Total		14.70	85.30	100.00
Central	Lucknow	5.55	94.45	100.00
	Balrampur	15.38	84.62	100.00
	Sitapur		100.00	100.00
Total		6.66	93.34	100.00
Western	Bagpat		100.00	100.00
	Mathura		100.00	100.00
	Moradabad		100.00	100.00
Total			100.00	100.00
Bundel-khand	Banda	25.00	75.00	100.00
	Hamirpur	40.00	60.00	100.00
	Jhansi	15.38	84.62	100.00
Total		25.71	74.29	100.00
Grand Total		11.80	88.20	100.00

Table 12
Visit Villages
Gram Panchayat

(Percentage Distribution)

Region	*District*	*Yes*	*No*	*Total*
Eastern	Varanasi	23.52	76.48	100.00
	Gorakhpur	14.28	85.72	100.00
	Ballia		100.00	100.00
Total		11.29	88.71	100.00
Central	Lucknow	28.57	71.43	100.00
	Balrampur	33.33	66.67	100.00
	Sitapur	39.28	60.72	100.00
Total	33.33	66.67	100.00	
Western	Bagpat	5.55	94.45	100.00
	Mathura	15.78	84.22	100.00
	Moradabad		100.00	100.00
Total	6.77	93.23	100.00	
Bundel-khand	Banda	11.53	88.47	100.00
	Hamirpur		100.00	100.00
	Jhansi	26.08	73.92	100.00
Total		12.67	87.33	100.00
Grand Total		17.21	82.79	100.00

Pleasantly, all the members of Jhansi and Mathura districts spend time with common man, contrary to Balrampur Zila Panchayat where none spends time. Likewise, members of Kshetra Panchayats in Jhansi and Moradabad districts score highest in meeting the community, whereas in Bagpat and Sitapur districts none spares time. The responses at Gram Panchayats level are quite distributive.

Table 13
Spending Time with Common Man
Zila Panchayat

(Percentage Distribution)

Region	*Yes*	*No*	*Total*
Eastern	58.34	41.66	100.00
Central	35.00	65.00	100.00
Western	38.88	61.12	100.00
Bundelkhand	58.83	41.17	100.00
Grand Total	48.10	51.90	100.00

As regards their initiating the development plan, the women representatives prove themselves as real development agent at local level. More than half of the women representatives in Zila Panchayats have taken up development plan of some kind. Here Western region tops with two-thirds women who (followed by Bundelkhand and Central regions) go for development activities. Mathura, Varanasi and Jhansi are the Zila Panchayats where all representatives have launched development works within their respective areas. Bagpat is at the bottom.

Table 14
Spending Time with Common Man
Kshetra Panchayat

(Percentage Distribution)

Region	*Yes*	*No*	*Total*
Region	Yes	No	Total
Eastern	38.23	61.77	100.00
Central	8.88	91.12	100.00
Western	53.34	46.66	100.00
Bundelkhand	57.15	42.85	100.00
Grand Total	36.80	63.20	100.00

Table 15
Spending Time with Common Man
Gram Panchayat

(Percentage Distribution)

Region	*Yes*	*No*	*Total*
Region	Yes	No	Total
Eastern	30.64	69.36	100.00
Central	38.27	61.73	100.00
Western	49.15	50.85	100.00
Bundelkhand	59.16	40.84	100.00
Grand Total	44.32	55.68	100.00

In case of Kshetra Panchayats and Gram Panchayats, more than one-third women have gone for development works. At Kshetra Panchayats level Central and Western regions are at the lowest side, while Bundelkhand is at the top.

Astonishingly, women representatives in Bundelkhand region are more development oriented, while women from Western region seem least interested. It shows the apathy of women representatives in Western region, a comparatively prosperous region in the state. It may be that there is no need of any development in villages falling in Western region. Bundelkhand being hilly terrain require more development. Surprisingly members of Moradabad Zila Panchayat initially refuse to initiate any development work in these areas. Likewise, Sitapur, Bagpat and Mathura are the districts wherein not a single member of Kshetra Panchayats has opted for development activities. At the Gram Panchayat level responses are skewed.

Table 16
Development Plan Taken Up
Zila Panchayat

(Percentage Distribution)

Region	*Yes*	*No*	*Total*
Eastern	66.67	33.33	100.00
Central	50.00	50.00	100.00
Western	27.77	72.23	100.00
Bundelkhand	58.83	41.17	100.00
Grand Total	51.90	48.10	100.00

Table 17
Development Plan Taken Up
Kshetra Panchayat

(Percentage Distribution)

Region	*Yes*	*No*	*Total*
Eastern	52.95	47.05	100.00
Central	20.00	80.00	100.00
Western	26.66	73.34	100.00
Bundelkhand	57.15	42.85	100.00
Grand Total	38.19	61.81	100.00

Table 18
Development Plan Taken Up
Gram Panchayat

(Percentage Distribution)

Region	*Yes*	*No*	*Total*
Region	Yes	No	Total
Eastern	32.25	67.75	100.00
Central	37.03	62.97	100.00
Western	15.25	84.75	100.00
Bundelkhand	53.53	46.47	100.00
Grand Total	35.53	64.47	100.00

After having assessed their interests in social activities and development, women representatives were asked to give their opinion on common social issues. Their attention was drawn towards other social problems like dowry, inter-caste marriage, inter-religion marriage, child marriage, widow marriage, divorce, family welfare programmes etc. Their responses are appreciative and praise worthy. It reflects the perceptions, consciousness and concern of women respondents about social problems. (Tables - 19, 20, 21)

It is heartening that women representatives are found quite aware and concerned about social issues and problems. Majority of the women respondents at all the levels do not favour dowry system. About half of them advocate inter-caste marriage but they all forcefully condemn contractual marriage. A good number of them favour love marriage, while majority of the women representatives support widow marriage. An absolute number of women oppose child marriage, while all

Table 19
Approval of Social Issues
Zila Panchayat

(Percenatage Distribution)

Region	Dowry System			Inter-caste Marriage			Inter-religion Marriage			Contractual Marriage			Love Marriage			Widow Marriage			Child Marriage			Divorce			Compulsory Family Planning			Job Reservation for Women			Punishing Wicked Husband		
	A	ST	N	A	ST	N	A	ST	N	A	ST	N	A	ST	N	A	ST	N	A	ST	N	A	ST	N	A	ST	N	A	ST	N	A	ST	N
Eastern		25.00	75.00	8.33	66.67	25.00		16.67	83.33		8.33	91.67		66.67	33.33	33.33	66.67				100.00	8.33	75.00	16.67	75.00	25.00		83.33	16.67		75.00		25.00
Central	20.00		80.00	10.00	45.00	45.00		15.00	85.00			100.00		50.00	50.00	35.00	35.00	30.00			100.00		60.00	40.00	60.00	20.00	20.00	75.00	25.00		35.00	20.00	45.00
Western	11.11	27.77	61.12	5.55	50.00	44.45		5.55	94.45	11.11		88.89		50.00	50.00	38.90	33.33	27.77		5.55	94.45	5.55	50.00	44.45	33.33	61.12	5.55	72.23	22.22	5.55	16.66	38.88	44.46
Bundelkhand		5.88	94.12		67.71	32.29		11.76	88.24			100.00		58.83	41.17	29.41	41.18	29.41		11.76	88.24		35.29	64.71	76.48	23.52		82.36	17.64		29.41	47.07	23.52
Grand Total	7.59	15.18	77.23	6.32	56.98	36.70		12.65	87.35		2.53	94.94		56.97	43.03	34.17	45.58	20.25		3.79	96.21	3.79	56.97	39.24	62.04	31.64	6.32	78.49	20.25	1.26	41.78	24.05	34.17

A – Always
ST – Some Time
N – Never

Table 20
Approval of Social Issues
Kshetra Panchayat

(Percenatage Distribution)

Region	Dowry System			Inter-caste Marriage			Inter-religion Marriage			Contractual Marriage			Love Marriage			Widow Marriage			Child Marriage			Divorce			Compulsory Family Planning			Job Reservation for Women			Punishing Wicked Husband		
	A	ST	N	A	ST	N	A	ST	N	A	ST	N	A	ST	N	A	ST	N	A	ST	N	A	ST	N	A	ST	N	A	ST	N	A	ST	N
Eastern	2.94	32.35	64.71	17.64	47.07	35.29	5.88	5.88	88.24			100.00	5.88	32.35	61.77	32.35	38.23	29.42		17.64	82.36	2.94	50.00	47.06	50.00	35.30	14.70	38.24	38.24	23.52	35.29	20.58	44.13
Central	11.11	15.55	73.34	2.22	28.88	68.90		8.88	91.12			100.00	2.22	24.44	73.34	26.66	35.55	37.79		11.11	88.89		20.00	80.00	31.11	35.56	33.33	35.55	44.45	20.00	13.33	31.11	55.56
Western	10.00	30.00	60.00	3.33	13.33	83.34		7.14	92.86			100.00	3.33	23.33	73.34	60.00	16.67	23.33		3.33	96.67		46.66	53.34	23.33	56.67	20.00	50.00	46.67	3.33	16.66	46.68	36.66
Bundelkhand	5.71	11.42	82.87	11.42	40.00	48.58		14.28	85.72			100.00	11.42	42.85	45.73	62.86	28.57	8.57		11.42	88.58	5.71	28.57	65.72	65.73	22.85	11.42	80.00	14.29	5.71	37.15	28.57	34.28
Grand Total	7.63	21.52	70.85	8.33	32.63	59.04	1.38	9.02	89.60			100.00	5.55	30.55	63.90	43.76	30.55	25.69		11.11	82.89	2.08	34.72	63.20	42.36	36.81	20.83	50.00	36.12	13.88	25.00	31.25	43.75

A – Always
ST – Some Time
N – Never

Table 21
Approval of Social Issues
Gram Panchayat

(Percenatage Distribution)

Region	*Dowry System*			*Inter-caste Marriage*			*Inter-religion Marriage*			*Contractual Marriage*			*Love Marriage*			*Widow Marriage*			*Child Marriage*			*Divorce*			*Compulsory Family Planning*			*Job Reservation for Women*			*Punishing Wicked Husband*		
	A	*ST*	*N*	*A*	*ST*	*N*	*A*	*ST*	*N*	*A*	*ST*	*N*	*A*	*ST*	*N*	*A*	*ST*	*N*	*A*	*ST*	*N*	*A*	*ST*	*N*	*A*	*ST*	*N*	*A*	*ST*	*N*	*A*	*ST*	*N*
Eastern	16.12	29.03	54.85	8.06	50.00	41.94		11.29	88.71			100.00		38.70	61.30	16.12	66.12	17.76		9.67	90.33		61.29	38.71	35.48	37.11	27.41	59.69	24.19	16.12	46.79	16.12	37.09
Central	2.46	28.39	69.15		37.03	62.97		2.46	97.54			100.00		25.92	74.08	7.40	56.80	35.80		19.75	80.25	7.40	23.45	69.15	38.27	45.69	16.04	59.25	35.82	4.93	18.51	25.92	55.57
Western	3.38	18.64	77.98		16.94	83.06		5.08	94.92			100.00		15.25	84.75	25.42	22.03	52.55	1.69	1.69	96.62		35.59	64.41	32.20	45.77	22.03	44.06	47.47	8.47	27.11	40.69	32.20
Bundelkhand	7.04	16.90	76.06	5.63	42.25	52.12		4.22	95.78			100.00	1.40	32.39	66.21	52.12	30.98	16.90		12.67	87.33		30.98	69.02	53.54	36.61	9.85	74.66	21.12	4.22	32.41	29.57	38.02
Grand Total	6.95	23.44	69.61	3.29	36.99	59.72		5.49	94.51			100.00	0.36	28.20	71.44	24.90	44.70	30.40	0.36	11.72	87.92	2.19	36.63	61.18	40.29	41.40	18.31	60.09	31.86	8.05	30.40	27.83	41.77

A – Always
ST – Some Time
N – Never

support compulsory family planning. They support job reservation for women. About half of the women representatives want wicked husbands to be punished. This perception of women representatives about civil society is quite clear and encouraging. If given a chance they would contribute tremendously in creating a society of their dream.

After knowing their views on various social issues, women representatives were requested to give their opinion on women's freedom. The responses are quite interesting and balanced. Every sixth woman representative each of Zila Panchayats and Kshetra Panchayats and one-fourth at Gram Panchayats want women to be confined to house management as their first preference. Three out of ten women representatives of Zila Panchayats favour full freedom, while such women are about one-fourth at other two levels. 'Home first, freedom later' is the first priority for one third of women representatives of Zila Panchayats, whereas their numbers reach to about one-half in lower tiers. The number is meagre in respect of women preferring 'freedom first, home later'. A significant number of women at all the levels want a balancing mix between tradition and freedom. This middle path reflects the development extent of rural Indian women, who want to enjoy the fruits of freedom and modernization but do not venture to come out of traditions. Thus, women representatives in Panchayati Raj Institutions in Uttar Pradesh prefer to lead a balanced life-a blend of happy home and a responsible and responsive people's representative. (Tables- 22, 23, 24).

PERSONAL LIFE

Time for rest and recreation is necessary for every person. Under the new dispensation women representatives are burdened with many responsibilities. Their day schedule is tight and they often suffer from tension, fatigue etc. It was therefore thought imperative to know as to how they spend their leisure time. Due to dual role responsibilities women representatives hardly get time for themselves. Whenever they get time they like spending their leisure time playing with children and watching television. They spend some time on

Table 22
Views on Women's Freedom
Zila Panchayat

(Percentage Distribution)

Region	Limited to Home Management					Give Full Freedom					Home First, Freedom Later					Freedom First, Home Later					Balancing Mix to Tradition and Freedom				
	1	2	3	4	5	1	2	3	4	5	1	2	3	4	5	1	2	3	4	5	1	2	3	4	5
Eastern		50.00	41.67	8.33		50.00			41.67	8.33	25.00	25.00	8.33	16.67	25.00			41.67	8.33	50.00	25.00	25.00	16.67	16.67	16.66
Central	30.00	20.00	25.00	20.00	5.00	20.00	10.00	20.00	50.00		20.00	30.00	5.00	5.00	40.00	10.00	10.00	15.00	10.00	55.00	20.00	30.00	25.00	25.00	
Western	11.11	27.77	27.79	22.22	11.11	22.22	5.55	22.22	44.46	5.55	55.57	5.55	5.55		33.33			44.44	11.12	44.44	11.11	61.12		22.22	5.55
Bundel-khand	35.29	23.52	41.19			23.52		11.76	52.96	11.76	41.19	29.41	5.88		23.52				35.29	64.71		47.07	41.17	11.76	
Grand Total	17.72	31.67	34.17	12.65	3.79	30.37	3.79	12.65	46.87	6.32	34.21	22.78	6.32	6.32	30.37	2.53	2.53	26.56	15.18	53.20	15.18	39.27	20.25	18.98	6.32

Table 23
Views on Women's Freedom
Kshetra Panchayat

(Percentage Distribution)

Region	*Limited to Home Management*					*Give Full Freedom*					*Home First, Freedom Later*					*Freedom First, Home Later*					*Balancing Mix to Tradition and Freedom*				
	1	2	3	4	5	1	2	3	4	5	1	2	3	4	5	1	2	3	4	5	1	2	3	4	5
Eastern	14.70	11.76	41.20	11.76	20.58	5.88		20.58	50.00	23.54	55.89	38.23		5.88				17.64	29.41	52.95	23.54	50.00	20.58		5.88
Central	8.88	8.88	71.14	8.88	2.22	20.00		4.44	35.56	40.00	46.68	26.66	2.22	2.22	22.22	4.44	4.44	20.00	35.56	35.56	26.66	42.24	17.77	11.11	2.22
Western	13.33	16.67	63.33	6.67		26.66	6.66	6.66	56.69	3.33	63.34	3.33	3.33		30.00		20.00	13.33	3.33	63.34		56.68	13.33	26.66	3.33
Bundel-khand	28.57	11.42	42.88	11.42	5.71	5.71	14.28	5.71	45.73	28.57	25.73	40.00	11.42	14.28	8.57	2.85	5.71	22.85	28.59	40.00	37.16	28.57	17.14	5.71	11.42
Grand Total	15.97	11.8	56.57	9.72	6.94	14.58	4.86	9.02	45.83	25.71	47.25	27.77	4.16	5.55	15.27	2.08	6.94	18.75	25.69	46.54	22.93	43.75	17.36	10.41	5.55

Table 24
Views on Women's Freedom
Gram Panchayat

(Percentage Distribution)

Region	Limited to Home Management					Give Full Freedom					Home First, Freedom Later					Freedom First, Home Later					Balancing Mix to Tradition and Freedom				
	1	2	3	4	5	1	2	3	4	5	1	2	3	4	5	1	2	3	4	5	1	2	3	4	5
Eastern	11.29	16.12	38.73	24.19	9.67	8.06	4.83	22.58	41.95	22.58	67.77	20.96	3.22	4.83	3.22	1.61		12.90	25.80	59.69	14.51	64.53	17.74		3.22
Central	19.75	19.75	40.76	9.87	9.87	17.28	11.11	7.40	30.88	33.33	50.65	18.51	4.93	16.04	9.87		12.34	30.86	20.98	35.82	12.34	38.29	18.51	17.28	13.58
Western	37.32	11.86	33.89	13.55	3.38	28.81	20.33	5.08	35.62	10.16	22.03	13.55	20.33		44.09		33.92	23.72	22.03	20.33	11.86	23.72	13.55	28.84	22.03
Bundel-khand	36.61	9.85	42.28	8.45	2.81	5.63	16.90	11.26	59.17	7.04	46.50	25.35	9.85	5.63	12.67		1.40	14.08	16.90	67.62	9.85	46.50	23.94	12.67	7.04
Grand Total	26	14.65	39.21	13.55	6.59	14.65	13.18	11.35	41.78	19.04	47.27	19.78	9.15	7.32	16.48	0.36	11.35	20.87	21.24	46.18	12.08	43.24	18.68	14.65	11.35

shopping and visiting friends and relatives also. Interestingly, one-fifth of women representatives spend some of their time in playing with their children, while a significant number attend household responsibilities. Ironically, such women representatives like their fellow women have no clear concept of leisure time or devoting sometime exclusively for themselves.

Table 25
Spending Leisure Time
Zila Panchayat

(Percentage Distribution)

Region	*Sleeping*	*Watching TV*	*Shopping*	*Visiting Relations/ Friends*	*Playing with Children*	*Attending House holds*	*Gossiping/ Talking*	*Total*
Eastern	16.66				33.33	8.33	41.68	100.00
Central	15.00	10.00		10.00	15.00	25.00	25.00	100.00
Western	11.11	22.23	5.55		22.23	27.77	11.11	100.00
Bundelkhand	11.76	11.76	11.76	17.64	23.56	17.64	5.88	100.00
Grand Total	13.92	10.12	3.79	6.32	24.09	18.98	22.78	100.00

Table 26
Spending Leisure Time
Kahetra Panchayat

(Percentage Distribution)

Region	*Sleeping*	*Watching TV*	*Shopping*	*Visiting Relations/ Friends*	*Playing with Children*	*Attending House holds*	*Gossiping/ Talking*	*Total*
Eastern	26.47			8.82	8.82	20.58	35.31	100.00
Central	15.55	2.22		8.88	20.00	35.58	17.77	100.00
Western	6.66			13.33	33.33	36.68	10.00	100.00
Bundelkhand	5.71		5.71	14.28	31.42	37.17	5.71	100.00
Grand Total	13.88	0.69	1.38	11.11	22.91	32.67	17.36	100.00

As regards getting support from family members, to cope with the burden of dual role, the women representatives are having full support from their husband, children, parents, in-laws, sister/brother (in-laws) and relations. A meagre number feels not getting support. (Tables- 28, 29,30)

Table 27
Spending Leisure Time
Gram Panchayat

(Percentage Distribution)

Region	*Sleeping*	*Watching TV*	*Shopping*	*Visiting Relations/ Friends*	*Playing with Children*	*Attending Households*	*Gossiping/ Talking*	*Total*
Eastern	11.29	1.61	4.83	17.74	19.35	19.35	25.83	100.00
Central	13.58		3.70	9.87	17.28	27.16	28.41	100.00
Western	11.86		8.47	15.25	10.16	35.62	18.64	100.00
Bundelkhand	11.26		4.22	8.45	35.23	32.39	8.45	100.00
Grand Total	12.08	0.36	5.12	12.45	20.87	28.61	20.51	100.00

In all, the women entering into the new role and performing outside their home, feel satisfied with their family life. A few aberrations are there, but may be because of peculiar specific familial reasons. This depicts that women having a satisfactory and happy family life can perform in a better way in their new role. They would be able to devote more time and energy to their political role.

Keeping their happy family life and successful political role in mind, the respondents were further asked to reveal their human behavioural attitudes. Pleasantly, a good number of women at all the levels do not feel shy. Majority of them are never submissive, but a significant number feel neglected, but not depressed. Sometimes women representatives do become nervous, but their number is negligible. A good number of women suffer from anxiety and many feel moral guilt. This mixed psychological behaviour indicates the transition in their life. An attitudinal churning seems to be taking place in their psyche, which through proper training and enabling cooperative environment may lead to their empowerment. (Tables - 34, 35, 36)

At last, the women representatives were asked to rank their different roles. Surprisingly, majority of the women representatives at all the levels treat 'house manager' as their first role, closely followed by 'mother' role and 'wife' role. Their new role (political) comes next for women representatives. It seems that despite enjoying their new role under certain constraints, women feel their traditional role as the prime one. (Tables - 37, 38, 39)

Table 28
Extent of Getting Support
Zila Panchayat

(Percenatage Distribution)

Region	Husband						Children						Parnets/in-laws						Sister/Brother (in-laws)						Relations					
	F	G	S	L	N	I	F	G	S	L	N	I	F	G	S	L	N	I	F	G	S	L	N	I	F	G	S	L	N	I
Eastern	83.33	16.67					50.00	16.66	16.67	16.67				11.11	66.67	22.22			25.00	33.33	41.67				25.00	8.33	66.67			
Central	90.00	10.00					65.00	20.00	10.00	5.00			53.86	30.76	7.69	7.69			40.00	40.00	5.00	5.00	10.00		40.00	40.00	5.00	5.00	15.00	
Western	100.00						50.00	44.45		5.55			50.00	35.72	14.28				22.23	33.33	33.33	11.11			22.22	33.33	38.90	5.55		
Bundel-khand	100.00						35.29	41.19	17.64			5.88	40.00	50.00	10.00				17.64	35.32	23.52	23.52			23.52	35.32	17.64	23.52		
Grand Total	92.21	7.79					50.65	29.11	11.39	7.59		1.26	39.15	32.6	21.73	6.52			26.58	35.45	26.58	8.86	2.53		27.84	27.84	32.94	7.59	3.79	

F – Full
G – Great
S – Some
L – Little
N – Never
I – Indifferent

Table 29
Extent of Getting Support
Kshetra Panchayat

(Percenatage Distribution)

Region	Husband						Children						Parnets/in-laws						Sister/Brother (in-laws)						Relations					
	F	G	S	L	N	I	F	G	S	L	N	I	F	G	S	L	N	I	F	G	S	L	N	I	F	G	S	L	N	I
Eastern	93.94		6.06				73.54	2.94	14.70	8.82			37.50	25.00	25.00	12.50			17.64	47.07	26.47	5.88	2.94		20.58	35.31	29.41	11.76	2.94	
Central	86.67	13.33					46.67	20.00	11.11	20.00	2.22		37.06	22.22	25.92	7.40	7.40		35.58	15.55	24.44	20.00	2.22	2.22	37.80	20.00	17.77	17.77	4.44	2.22
Western	80.00	20.00					63.34	23.33	10.00		3.33		36.36	54.55	9.09				3.33	16.66	46.68	13.33	20.00		6.66	20.00	43.34	10.00	20.00	
Bundel-khand	91.44	2.85	5.71				28.60	25.71	25.71	14.28	2.85	2.85	26.68	13.33	46.66		13.33		20.00	28.60	25.71	11.42	11.42	2.85	14.28	31.46	22.85	11.42	14.28	5.71
Grand Total	88.12	9.09	2.79				52.11	18.05	15.27	11.8	2.08	0.69	34.46	26.22	27.86	4.91	6.55		20.83	26.38	29.89	13.19	8.33	1.38	21.52	26.38	27.11	13.19	9.72	2.08

F - Full
G - Great
S - Some
L - Little
N - Never
I - Indifferent

Table 30
Extent of Getting Support
Gram Panchayat

(Percenatage Distribution)

Region	Husband						Children						Parnets/in-laws						Sister/Brother (in-laws)						Relations					
	F	G	S	L	N	I	F	G	S	L	N	I	F	G	S	L	N	I	F	G	S	L	N	I	F	G	S	L	N	I
Eastern	95.10	2.27	1.63				67.76	12.90	14.51	3.22	1.61		29.64	29.64	18.51	14.81		7.40	30.67	27.41	24.19	16.12		1.61	32.27	30.64	11.29	22.58	1.61	1.61
Central	88.47	11.53					67.92	16.04	6.17	6.17	3.70		44.76	28.94	13.15	5.26	7.89		20.98	33.36	24.69	14.81	4.93	1.23	24.69	32.13	18.51	16.04	7.40	1.23
Western	87.94	12.06					61.04	30.50	1.69	5.08	1.69		43.76	40.62	9.37	6.25			6.77	10.16	47.50	27.11	6.77	1.69	8.47	16.94	40.71	22.03	10.16	1.69
Bundel-khand	80.30	7.04	9.85	2.81			45.10	18.30	28.16	2.81	5.63		41.67	25.00	33.33				15.49	21.12	25.38	21.12	14.08	2.81	15.49	25.35	32.41	16.90	7.04	2.81
Grand Total	87.70	7.83	3.73	0.74			60.46	19.04	12.82	4.39	3.29		40.52	31.4	17.35	6.61	2.47	1.65	18.68	23.8	29.69	19.41	6.59	1.83	20.51	26.76	25.27	19.04	6.59	1.83

F – Full
G – Great
S – Some
L – Little
N – Never
I – Indifferent

Table 31
Feeling with Family
Zila Panchayat

(Percentage Distribution)

Region	*Fully Satisfied*	*Satis-fied*	*Indif-ferent*	*Burd-ened*	*Very happy*	*Not happy*	*Total*
Eastern	50.00	25.00			25.00		100.00
Central	45.00	20.00	5.00	5.00	25.00		100.00
Western	22.22	38.89			38.89		100.00
Bundelkhand	47.07	29.41			23.52		100.00
Grand Total	41.80	27.84	1.26	1.26	27.84		100.00

Table 32
Feeling with Family
Kshetra Panchayat

(Percentage Distribution)

Region	*Fully Satisfied*	*Satis-fied*	*Indif-ferent*	*Burd-ened*	*Very happy*	*Not happy*	*Total*
Eastern	38.24	38.24	2.94		20.58		100.00
Central	24.44	44.46	4.44		22.22	4.44	100.00
Western	10.00	53.34			33.33	3.33	100.00
Bundelkhand	31.42	34.31		5.71	22.85	5.71	100.00
Grand Total	26.38	42.39	2.08	1.38	24.30	3.47	100.00

Table 33
Feeling with Family
Gram Panchayat

(Percentage Distribution)

Region	*Fully Satisfied*	*Satis-fied*	*Indif-ferent*	*Burd-ened*	*Very happy*	*Not happy*	*Total*
Eastern	12.90	43.56		9.67	33.87		100.00
Central	24.69	33.34	7.40		33.34	1.23	100.00
Western	16.95	40.68			40.68	1.69	100.00
Bundelkhand	14.08	60.58	4.22		21.12		100.00
Grand Total	17.58	44.35	3.29	2.19	31.86	0.73	100.00

Thus, it seems that women representatives are facing lots of problems while performing their role at home and outside. However, tradition oriented family where the typical pattern of husband-wife relationship has been 'male dominance and female dependence' is gradually changing. With the assumption of the additional role of women representatives out side the home, her task is enlarged. The new role on one hand brings the women out of the limited spheres of home

Table 34
General Human Feelings
Zila Panchayat(

(Percenatage Distribution)

Region	Shyness					Submissiveness					Neglected					Depressed					Nervousness					Anxiety					Moral guilty				
	A	F	ST	R	N	A	F	ST	R	N	A	F	ST	R	N	A	F	ST	R	N	A	F	ST	R	N	A	F	ST	R	N	A	F	ST	R	N
Eastern			33.33	50.00	16.67				50.00	50.00			16.66	66.68	16.66			8.33	33.33	58.34				75.00	25.00				83.33	16.67				66.67	33.33
Central	5.00	15.00	20.00	25.00	35.00			10.00	40.00	50.00			30.00	45.00	25.00			5.00	45.00	50.00		5.00	60.00	25.00	10.00			50.00	45.00	5.00			25.00	50.00	25.00
Western	5.55	5.55	11.11	27.79	50.00			5.55	27.77	66.68			16.66	22.22	61.12				38.88	61.12			11.11	27.77	61.12		11.11	33.33	27.78	27.78		16.66	38.91	27.77	16.66
Bundel-khand	5.88	29.41	35.30	29.41				23.52	76.48			17.64	35.29	47.07				29.41	70.59			29.41	11.76	58.83			52.95	29.41	17.64			29.41		52.95	17.64
Grand Total	2.53	6.32	24.05	35.46	31.64			3.79	36.70	59.51			20.25	44.30	35.45			3.79	36.70	59.51		1.26	24.05	37.99	36.70		2.53	31.64	49.38	16.45		3.79	21.51	50.65	24.05

A – Always
F – Frequently
ST– Some Time
R – Rarely
N – Never

Table 35
General Human Feelings
Ksherra Panchayat(

(Percenatage Distribution)

Region	Shyness					Submissiveness					Neglected					Depressed					Nervousness					Anxiety					Moral guilty				
	A	F	ST	R	N	A	F	ST	R	N	A	F	ST	R	N	A	F	ST	R	N	A	F	ST	R	N	A	F	ST	R	N	A	F	ST	R	N
Eastern		2.94	14.70	11.76	70.60			2.94	11.76	85.30			44.13	14.70	41.17			2.94	8.82	88.24			8.82	35.29	55.89		5.88	32.35	26.47	35.30			11.76	32.35	55.89
Central	4.44		20.00	15.56	60.00		2.22	4.44	26.66	66.68	6.66	2.22	22.22	20.00	48.90		2.22	4.44	15.55	77.79	6.66	2.22	15.55	15.55	60.02	4.44	2.22	31.11	15.55	46.68	2.22	2.22	20.00	17.77	57.79
Western	6.66	3.33	56.68	23.33	10.00			6.66	36.66	56.68		3.33	46.67	33.33	16.67			3.33	26.67	70.00			13.33	33.33	53.34		10.00	16.67	43.33	30.00	6.66	16.66	6.66	36.69	33.33
Bundel-khand	2.85	34.29	31.43	31.43			2.85	25.71	71.44			17.14	34.28	48.58		2.85	5.71	25.71	65.73	5.71	2.85	11.42	31.42	48.60	11.42	8.57	20.00	34.30	25.71		11.42	31.42	22.85	34.31	
Grand Total	2.77	2.08	29.86	20.13	45.16		0.69	4.16	25.00	70.15	2.08	1.38	31.25	25.00	40.29		1.38	4.16	18.75	75.71	3.47	1.38	12.50	27.77	54.88	4.16	6.25	25.69	28.47	35.43	2.08	6.94	18.05	26.38	46.55

A – Always
F – Frequently
ST – Some Time
R – Rarely
N – Never

Table 36
General Human Feelings
Gram Panchayat(

(Percenatage Distribution)

Region	*Shyness*					*Submissiveness*					*Neglected*					*Depressed*					*Nervousness*					*Anxiety*					*Moral guilty*				
	A	F	ST	R	N	A	F	ST	R	N	A	F	ST	R	N	A	F	ST	R	N	A	F	ST	R	N	A	F	ST	R	N	A	F	ST	R	N
Eastern	3.22	16.12	17.74	19.35	43.57			6.45	14.51	79.04		4.83	43.56	22.58	29.03			4.83	12.90	82.27			24.19	35.48	40.33		1.61	27.41	38.73	32.25			6.45	25.80	67.75
Central	8.64	6.17	30.86	9.87	44.46		1.23	6.17	18.51	74.09	3.70	6.17	13.58	22.22	54.33		1.23	3.70	23.45	71.62	2.46	4.93	23.45	17.28	51.88	7.40	7.40	29.64	25.92	29.64	8.64	8.64	25.92	16.04	40.76
Western		1.69	35.61	33.89	28.81			8.47	44.06	47.47		8.47	25.42	35.61	30.50			15.25	38.99	45.76			16.94	42.39	40.67		5.08	25.42	47.47	22.03		3.38	23.72	39.01	33.89
Bundel-khand	2.81	9.85	14.08	23.94	49.32		1.40	12.67	12.67	73.26		1.40	21.12	19.71	57.74		2.81	5.63	21.12	70.44		2.81	18.30	25.35	53.54	4.22	2.81	22.53	32.39	38.05		5.63	12.67	38.02	43.68
Grand Total	4.02	8.42	24.54	20.87	42.15		0.73	8.42	21.61	69.24	1.09	5.12	24.90	24.54	44.35		0.73	6.98	23.89	68.40	0.73	2.19	20.87	28.93	47.28	3.29	4.39	26.37	35.19	30.76	2.56	4.76	17.58	28.93	46.17

A - Always
F - Frequently
ST- Some Time
R - Rarely
N - Never

Table 37
Ranking the Roles
Zila Panchayat

(Percentage Distribution)

Region	Political Role					As House Manager					As Mother					As Wife					As Daughter-in-law				
	1	2	3	4	5	1	2	3	4	5	1	2	3	4	5	1	2	3	4	5	1	2	3	4	5
Eastern	16.66	8.33	16.66	41.69	16.66	83.34	8.33		8.33		8.33	58.34	8.33	25.00			16.66	58.35	16.66	8.33			55.56	22.22	22.22
Central	20.00	20.00	5.00	30.00	25.00	80.00	10.00	10.00				65.00	30.00	5.00			5.00	45.00	40.00	10.00		15.38	7.69	46.15	30.78
Western	5.55	33.33	11.12		50.00	94.45	5.55					44.44	55.56				5.88	23.52	52.96	17.64		8.33	25.00	66.67	
Bundel-khand	5.88	29.41	29.42	29.41	5.88	82.36	11.76	5.88			11.76	52.96	23.52	11.76			6.25	31.25	25.00	37.50				50.00	50.00
Grand Total	12.65	21.51	15.18	26.61	24.05	84.82	8.86	3.79	2.53		5.06	55.71	27.84	11.39			9.09	41.55	32.48	16.88		6.81	20.45	47.74	25.00

Table 38
Ranking the Roles
Kshetra Panchayat

(Percentage Distribution)

Region	Political Role					As House Manager					As Mother					As Wife					As Daughter-in-law				
	1	2	3	4	5	1	2	3	4	5	1	2	3	4	5	1	2	3	4	5	1	2	3	4	5
Eastern	5.88	17.64	17.64	52.96	5.88	85.30	8.82	5.88			20.58	29.41	32.37	17.64		3.03	48.49	27.27	21.21					42.85	57.15
Central	6.66	4.44	6.66	22.24	60.00	91.12	2.22	6.66				75.57	17.77	2.22	4.44	2.50	7.50	40.00	47.50	2.50		8.00	44.00	48.00	
Western		6.66		66.68	26.66	86.67		13.33			13.33	63.34	23.33				26.66	43.34	30.00			7.69	46.17	15.38	30.76
Bundel-khand	17.14	22.85	20.00	31.44	8.57	74.29	17.14	8.57			8.57	42.85	45.73	2.85			17.14	22.85	42.87	17.14			5.26	42.10	52.64
Grand Total	7.63	12.50	11.11	40.99	27.77	84.73	6.94	8.33			9.72	54.16	29.19	5.55	1.38	0.72	24.08	33.57	36.53	5.10		7.57	27.27	37.89	27.27

Table 39
Ranking the Roles
Gram Panchayat

(Percentage Distribution)

Region	*Political Role*					*As House Manager*					*As Mother*					*As Wife*					*As Daughter-in-law*				
	1	*2*	*3*	*4*	*5*	*1*	*2*	*3*	*4*	*5*	*1*	*2*	*3*	*4*	*5*	*1*	*2*	*3*	*4*	*5*	*1*	*2*	*3*	*4*	*5*
Eastern	6.45	8.06	14.51	40.34	30.64	82.27	6.45	6.45	4.83		4.83	58.09	20.96	16.12		6.55	31.14	41.00	21.31				28.57	61.91	9.52
Central	2.46	2.46	9.87	34.56	50.65	71.62	14.81	7.40	6.17		1.23	64.22	32.09	2.46		1.38	22.22	65.30	6.94	4.16		2.77	13.88	52.80	30.55
Western	6.77		5.08	38.98	49.17	69.85	17.46	12.69			11.86	67.81	15.25	5.08			25.39	26.98	44.46	3.17		12.90	74.20	12.90	
Bundel-khand	12.67	15.49	7.04	47.90	16.90	83.35	6.94	5.55	4.16		2.81	62.05	30.98	4.16			15.49	46.49	26.76	11.26			29.16	54.18	16.66
Grand Total	6.95	6.59	9.15	40.32	36.99	76.63	11.51	7.91	3.95		4.76	63.00	25.65	6.59		1.87	23.22	45.71	24.34	4.86		4.46	36.60	43.77	15.17

and on the other makes continuous demands on her time and energy. In doing so some of the expectations of other members of the family may be left unfulfilled, thereby creating conflicting situations. In order to make life happy and harmonious, most of the women representatives try to strike a balance and make adjustments through different means in every sphere of life. It seems that a good beginning in right direction has taken place. Period of a decade is not sufficient to change the societal mind set towards women. The seed has been sown, germination is taking place and within a couple of decades healthy society may emerge where women would have equal status and role.

6

EPILOGUE

Problems of a woman working beyond their familial role, mainly due to her dual roles, are not new. A house wife gets more time and energy to devote to the fulfillment of the demands of her family members. While a working/ professional woman with the additional role set she has to handle, if the members of the family continue to have similar expectations from her like that of the house-wife, her chances of being getting frustrated are indeed great. Lack of sympathetic appreciation of the new situation, the new set of demands on her new status and the unpreparedness to modify the expectations and demand structure are the major causes which lead to disharmonious functioning of the family structure. Lack of adequate articulation of roles in role-sets and of the role expectations and demands among the members of the role-set etc. are no less important causes to disturb the family harmony. Marital harmony is normal facilitated where care is taken to forestall the above mentioned problems.

The problems of women representatives of Panchayati Raj Institutions are all the more pronounced. They have multidimensional roles to perform. As a house wife, she holds the traditional status of a mother, wife, sister, daughter-in-law and, as people's representative, she has to perform for the fulfillment of people's aspirations and expectations. Therefore as compared to their other counterparts in society, these women representatives have to perform two sets of roles i.e. traditional or prescribed, as a woman in a male dominated

Indian society and; an achieved or ascribed, by acquiring political status. Her role is now divided into two sets of role for family and, for society. This leads to role conflict.

The present work is an humble attempt to study the role conflict and problems of adjustment of women representatives in Panchayati Raj Institutions in Uttar Pradesh. This most populars state contains about one-sixth of national population but about four percent of country's geographical area. Uttar Pradesh, in pursuance to the 73rd Amendment to the Constitution, restructured its Panchayati Raj system and, presently, there are 70 Zila (District) Panchayats, 820 Kshetra (Block) Panchayats and 52,000 Gram (Village) Panchayats. The numbers of elected representatives (as per last elections held in 2005) are as under:

Table 1

Unit	*Category*	*No.*	*Women Percentage*
Gram Panchayat	Pradhan	52,000	50
	Members	6,54,637	38
Kshetra Panchayat	Pramukh	820	51
	Members	65,04	37
Zila Panchayat	Adhyaksha	70	74
	Members	2631	40

Out of this, 12 Zila Panchayats, 36 Kshetra Panchayats and 108 Gram Panchayats were selected for in depth study. These consist one third of units headed by male chairpersons. In all, 1003 women representatives from all the three tiers were personally interviewed on the basis of a structured questionnaire. In addition, the views of officials and family members of selected women representatives were also fetched for supplementing the views of women respondents. Analysis done on the basis of the responses received through personal interviews, discussions and personal observations.

The findings of the study reveal that elected women representatives in Panchayati Raj Institutions face maximum conflicting situations and adjustment problems at home. Women representatives having large number of smaller/minor children and those who do not have satisfactory child-care facilities at home, while they are out for panchayat functions, face more role related problems. Time constraint and grievances of children are major areas of concern creating stressful situations for women having both the roles. But such is the case in respect of a few women representatives who are politically active or want to assert themselves in their new role. Tragically, majority of the women are there under constitutional compulsion. The local male leaders whose fiefdom had been the local government leadership, dominate the scene and put female of their family or relatives or their acquaintance, in case seat having been reserved for women. At the primary stage they make an attempt to influence decisions and try to get the reservation of their choice. Hence such women just represent on paper to fulfill the constitutional obligations and the functions associated with the role are discharged by male family members. These women representatives never face any role conflict, because they are only bestowed with role and are not performing the role.

The study further highlights that those women representatives whose husbands do not help them in household chores and do not have favorable attitude towards their political role face maximum stressful situations and role conflict. It is observed that major grievance of husband is less time given by their wives towards home, children and in-laws. Though most of the husbands support their wives' political career, they still carry a traditional mindset of women's role and want them to give priority to home responsibilities. These problems are also more faced by those women representatives who want to be active in their political role and have serious involvement in panchayat affairs. They are constrained to devote sufficient time towards husband and family and face adjustment problems in managing both roles effectively.

Attitude of family members is very important in the performance of both roles. It is observed that in-laws of women representatives, though are supportive, do not cooperate much in both household and official functions. Women representatives face conflicting situations when their role as daughter-in-law gets neglected due to other role.

Relations and friends though appreciate women's new role but in most cases are not all that cooperative and supportive. Women representatives face criticism when they are unable to fulfill any social and family obligation. Many times relations and friends, especially aged ones, instigate the in-laws against the women representatives. The in-laws in turn put pressure on husband (their son) to keep the wife (their daughter-in-law) i.e. women representative, under control that she does not go beyond established traditions.

Results also point out that type of family, number of modern kitchen aids and having or not having economic obligations towards the family are other factors which have a direct bearing on role conflict among women representatives. In a nuclear family woman representatives experience low degree of role conflict. Contrarily, those living in joint families do get help from other family members but are more prone to role conflicts. In nuclear family, husband plays all the role in the name of woman representative (wife), whereas in joint family, any body of dominating nature in family represents the woman representative hence, no conflict. In nuclear family adjustment among husband, wife and children is easier in comparison to joint or extended family, wherein a number of sectors are involved.

With regard to their political role, it is found that most of the women representatives are new to this field and do not have prior knowledge, orientation and experience of this field, hence they are not very much clear about their role as representative. Since entry of women in such a large number in politics at local level is a decade old phenomenon, there is no set pattern of behaviors, so adaptability in role will take some time.

It is observed that majority of women representatives were brought into this new role by their husband and male family members. Some were brought under pressure because of their seats were reserved for women. Such women representatives only work as rubber stamps for their husband and male family members. These women representatives are found to be totally dependent on their husband. They do not take independent decisions and all official functions are performed by their husbands. They are found to have no special interest in their new role and hence lack initiatives or they are not given any chance to take initiative. Male family members (husband, children, in-laws) just treat them as show piece and their political mascot. Had there been no mandatory provision of reserving seats to the tune of one-third for women, there would have been only negligible number of women, moreso those who have political background. Such women do not face problem of role conflict, as they seldom perform their ascribed role.

But those women representatives who are active in politics and have come in this role on their own for making a career in politics are found to be very active and independent in their role as representative. They take all decisions independently and take active part in panchayat affairs and village development. Such women are found confident and are able to display good leadership qualities, but more prone to role conflict. Their number is too less but they are the real torch bearer in the process of women empowerment in the country.

Women representatives who have been in local politics for quite sometime have been able to develop a good rapport among the local people and are found to be performing much better than those who are new to the job. The new ones lack confidence as well, because they are not fully conversant with their roles and responsibilities.

In respect of relationship between male and female members, it is observed that though male members speak positive about women representatives, in practice their attitude towards women counterpart is not encouraging all the time. They generally are given second class treatment in the official functioning such as planning, decision making and implementation of the development programmes. Such a neglect of women representatives by male ones, many a times, leads to creation of disinterest among newly elected women representatives. They instead prefer to enjoy their non-involvement, hence no conflict, but the state of affairs in respect of active women is otherwise. Majority of the active women, despite their meagre number, are able to turn the table and they make their male colleagues pay full respect to their opinions.

Observations reveal that where there is male chairperson, women representatives feel not much comfortable and hesitate in putting forth their views. If they dare to give opinion contrary to their male counterparts, role conflicts appear unfailingly. Whereas where the chairperson is a woman, the women members are found to be very comfortable and they actively participate in planning, decision-making and implementation of the development programmes. In this situation less scope for role conflict, because all sail in the same boat. In many cases women chairpersons are guided by their political leanings. So is the case with women representatives. In this scenario group (political) interests overshadow individual roles. So no scope for role conflict for any body.

It is further observed that though women representatives wish to participate actively in panchayat affairs and devote more time towards problems and issues, the household responsibilities and pressure from husbands, children and relatives deter them to work in their full capacity. The social norms and social taboos associated with the women folk in society adversely affect the participation of women in the affairs of rural local governance. The demands of familial role most of the time overburdens them and inability to perform political role effectively dissatisfies them and create conflicting situations. The women therefore prefer to confine themselves to their traditional familial roles and they even forget their new role.

The study further highlights that a major factor behind the low performance of women representatives in Panchayati Raj Institutions, is their low educational status and lack of proper knowledge about the panchayat affairs and prior experience in dealing with multidimensional village development issues and its complexities. Due to these reasons women representatives are found to be dependent on their husband

and other family members. The women dependent on their male family members face little or no conflict, because real performers are their husband and other family members and, she is treated as a show piece, for the sake of constitutional provisions.

In addition, role of money power, muscle power, backroom dealings, communalization and criminalization of politics also prevent women in making active participation in local governance. Many a times these evils deter women performers and they keep away from any ugly situation and prefer not to take any initiative. Otherwise, they have to face the created artificial conflicting situations. A good number of women representatives, especially chairpersons, ignore these factors and go ahead boldly with their determination, they are made victim of character assassination and social discard. The male chauvinism fails, generally, to tolerate the women performers.

In spite of these problems and conflicts, a good number of women representatives are making sincere efforts towards gaining high political efficacy. They are aware and sensitive towards the needs, problems and issues of rural community and their level of participation is also rising. This new role has given them a new status, a new image, a new position, a new hope and this in turn shape their personality and perceptions and helps them to discover a new person in them.

In sum, for better appreciation of their problems faced by women members, two pronged strategy needs to be followed. On one hand they should be oriented towards their new roles and responsibilities through vigorous training and development activities and, on the other, the societal mind set needs to be changed. The women, specially belonging to vulnerable classes of the society, need to be empowered educationally, economically, mentally, psychologically and socially.

Although 73rd Amendment to the Indian Constitution is a turning point and land mark in the history of rural local government in the country, the community should be empowered to bear the fruits of democratic decentralization. Government of India is concerned about the political empowerment of women, especially from lower strata of the society but the state governments have to show sufficient administrative and political willingness to help achieve the desired results. The governmental interventions would not accomplish the objectives unless and until social transformation takes place. Hence, the male dominated Indian rural society needs to change its mind set in tune to the change of time and circumstances. A class of women is also responsible for their own harassment. The elites in women representatives enjoy sufficient power and they never encourage the common women to come forward.

The new enactment is a good beginning and the time is not far off when women will be able to occupy their due status in all fields of society, politics and economy. The male chauvinism and domination are reducing, of course , on a snail's pace and, the women are getting empowered and conflict areas reducing in a slow but steady and sustainable manner. The grass root administration in the country is breaking the path and the women are heading in the desired direction of empowerment and development. The sudden change in perception may lead to aggravating the conflicting extent as the community, in general, and women, in particular, are not made ready–mentally, socially, economically, psychologically and aesthetically, to practice the political role imposed overnight as a result of democratic decentralization. Had the decentralization process succeeded the societal preparedness, the situation would have been quite different. However, the ray of hope is emerging and the move is in right direction. The period of a decade or so is not sufficient to bring the social transformation, but a good beginning has been initiated. The male dominated political society is providing, per force and miserably, the scope for women to play their ascribed role of decision maker.

MAJOR RECOMMENDATIONS

Following are the policy inputs in this regard to empowerment of women, which is the step to reduce role conflicts:

Central Government

1. The Government of India and the State Governments should prepare a comprehensive empowerment action plan for developing the capacity of women representatives. The action plan should aim to achieve social empowerment, economic empowerment, knowledge building etc.
2. There are three Ministries at the Union level dealing with rural affairs. The Ministry of Rural Development is responsible for implementation of different Central Sector Schemes. The Ministry of Social Justice & Empowerment implements various programmes, which encompass welfare, development and protective measures for SCs & STs. The Ministry of Panchayati Raj is responsible for functioning of PRIs. In addition, there are other Ministries of Environment & Forest, Health, Agriculture-as well, which have development programmes for women.

   The Panchayati Raj Institutions should be made responsible for identification, formulation and implementation of all the development programmes (irrespective of the Ministry). Like their counterparts in urban areas, PRIs should be made role machanism for village development.
3. The social mind set is the sine qua non for women empowerment. It is proportionally linked to educational level. If society in general and women in particular are educated, the scope for women empowerment is more. Hence attempts should be made to increase literacy level, especially in women.

State Government

4. An effective mechanism for training and development to women representatives (rather all representatives) should be developed. The existing training arrangements are adhoc, and insufficient.
5. The training facilities should not be only for elected representatives but also for officials involved in panchayati raj system and rural development.

6. Training and development of women representatives (elected representatives) should be a joint venture. The state training institutes are not quite sufficient to cover all the representatives in a fixed time frame because of limited infrastructure, finance and faculty. Hence NGOs/VOs should also be networked for the purpose.
7. A series of training workshops should be organized for all women representatives to make them aware about their roles and responsibilities, duties and powers, knowledge of Acts, rules and regulations etc.
8. The action plan should be formulated to empower women economically, as economic independence may help boost their mental caliber.
9. There is an imperative need to build up rural bureaucracy. Manning the Panchayati Raj Institutions from officials belonging to other departments can never strengthen these institutions of local governance.
10. The presence of members of upper legislatures in Panchayati Raj Institutions sometimes creates problems. The local leaders having link with them rule the roost. It does also provide scope for proxy representation. Hence the MLAs and MPs in no case (even without voting rights) should be formally associated with Panchayati Raj Institutions.
11. The democratic decentralisation as enunciated by the Constitution has decentralized the politics as well. The local governments have become good place for political parties to play politics, the politics of votes and winning elections, rather than development of political instincts among the uneducated or less educated rural community. The elections to Panchayati Raj Institutions should be made non-partisan.
12. The Acts and rules should be modified to dislodge the chairpersons found guilty of encouraging or practicing proxy representation.
13. The U.P. Panchayati Raj Adhiniyam, 1947 should be amended to empower Gram Sabha not only to articulate

the needs and aspirations of the community but also to check against abuse of powers by Gram Panchayats. Gram Sabhas are supposed to act as watchdog to protect community interest and common property and resources.

14. The Kshetra Panchayat as well as State Government should depute an official to attend the Gram Sabha meeting, to record Gram Sabha's views and report to the state government to take remedial measures. The Gram Sabha should be used as nursery for prospective representatives, besides having a check on proxy representation.

Local Government

15. The Panchayati Raj Institutions should be made responsible for village (rural) development. All the rural development programmes should be formulated, planned, implemented and monitored by Panchayati Raj Institutions. The dual parallel system of Panchayati Raj and Rural Development should be done away.
16. There are instances of officials at different levels hobnobbing with local politicians or influentials. Some mechanism to initiate punitive actions against erring officials is the need of the day.
17. The facilities of educating girls (literacy programmes for elderly women) should be developed.
18. The women chairpersons should be given proper orientation for not allowing the male family members to represent the women representatives. At first meeting only they should make clear to all the members. Actually, it is the chairperson who can turn the table.
19. The women chairpersons should act as role model and then can take any bold steps to stop proxy representation. The laxity on part of women chairpersons is bound to result in encouraging the other women representatives.
20. The meetings of Gram Sabha (Village Assembly) should be held regularly and periodically to make all the adult villages aware of the various rural development

programmes, their management and the roles and responsibilities of Gram Panchayat and its members and officials.

Women Commission

21. The Commission for Women should play an pro-active role. It should treat proxy representation also an important issue related to women.

BIBLIOGRAPHY

Acharya, Itishree Padhi (1998), Working Mothers: Role Conflict and Adjustments, Reliance Publishing House, New Delhi,

Agarwal, S.P. (2001), Women's Education in India, Vol. 3, Concept, Delhi.

Arora, K.K., Bhattacharya and other (1963), Women and Career, A Group Project Report, Submitted to the Tata Institute of Social Sciences, Bombay.

Bailyn, L. (1970), Career and Family Orientation of Husband and Wives in Relation to Marital Happiness, Human Relation, 23(2), 97-113.

Bakshi, S.R. (2002), Empowerment of Women and Politics of Reservation, Mittal, Delhi.

Bhatty & Bhatty (1971), "Demographic Portrait of Professional Women Employed in India" in Educated Women in Indian Society Today, Bombay: Tata Mc Graw Hill.

Blood, R.O. Jr., (1963), The Husband - Wife Relationship, in I.F. Nye and L.W. Hoffman (eds.). The Employed Mother in America, Chicago: Rand Mc Nally and Company.

Blood & Hamblin, (1958), The Effect of the Wife's Employment on the Family Power Structure, Social Forces, 36, 347-352.

Burchard, W.E. (1954), Role Conflict of Military Chaplins, American Sociological Review, 19, 528-535.

Chakraborty, K., (1977), Conflicting Worlds of Working Mother, Calcutta Progressive Publishers.

Desai, A.S. (1963), Women and Part Time Employment, Social Welfare, 10(7) 40-44.

Dohlstrom, E. (1967), The Changing Roles of Men and Women, London, Gerald Dickworth.

Dhingra, O.P. (1972), Women in Employment (unpublished Report), Shri Ram Centre for Industrial Relations and Human Resources, New Delhi, 197-236.

D'Souza, A.A. (1968), Should Wives Work, Social Action, 18 (1), 15-24.

Forbes, G. (1996), Women in India, The New Cambirdge History of India, Vol.2, Cambridge University Press, Cambridge.

Gupta, Anjula (1994), Modernizing Working Women, Delhi.

Goode, G.T., (1960), "A Theory of Role Strain" American Sociological Review 25: 483-496.

—(1988), Government of India , Perspective Plan on Women.

Hall, D.T. Garden, F.E. (1974), Self-image Stereotype of Family: Their Relationship to Women's Role Conflict and Coping, Journal of Applied Psychology, 59(2), 243-243.

Hemlatha, K. and Suryanarayana, R. (1983), Gender and Household Domain in Asia, Allied Publications, Bombay.

Hoffman, L.W., (1963), "Parental Power Relations and the Division of Household Tasks" in Nye and Hoffman (eds) Employed mother in America, Chicago, Rand Mc Nally and Company.

Holahan, C.K. and Gilbert, L.A. (1979), Inter-role Conflict for Working Women: Careers Versus Jobs, Journal of Applied Psychology, 64(1), 86-90.

Jena, S.K. (1993), Working Women and Modernization, Ashish, New Delhi.

Kahn, R.L. (1964), Organisational Stress: Studies in Role Conflict and Ambiquity, New York: Wiley.

Kala Rani, (1976), Role Conflict in Working Women, New Delhi, Chetan Publications.

Kapur, P. (1940), The Changing Status of Working Women in India, Vikas, New Delhi.

Kapur, P. (1974), Changing Status of Working Women in India, Delhi: Vikas Publishing House Pvt. Ltd.

Kapur, R. (1969), Role Conflict Among Employed Housewives, Indian Journal of Industrial Relations, 5(1).

Kundu, S.K. (1999), Role Conflict Among Employed Women: A Case Study of Bhubaneshwar City, Ph.D. Thesis R.M.L. Awadh University, Faizabad (unpublished).

Lashmiswaramma, M. (1991), Working Women and Infant Care, Delhi.

Mahajan, A., (1966), Women's Two Roles: A Study of Role Conflict", Indian Journal of Social Work, 25 (4), 377-80.

Menon, R., (1964), "Indian Working Woman–She Stands Alone", Social Welfare, 11 (5), 3-4.

Mishra, A.D. (1994), Problems and Prospects of Working Women in Urban India, Concept, Delhi.

Mishra, P. and Mahapatra, U. (2003), Women Administrators and Professionals - A Global Perspective, Kalinga, Delhi.

Narsimhan, S. (1999), Expowering Women, Sage, Delhi.

Nichol, K. (1975), Economically Independent.... Emotionally Crushed, "Social Welfare", XXII (6-7), 37-40.

Orden, S.R. and Bradburn, N.M. (1968), Working Wives and Marriage Happiness, American Journal of Sociology.

Pandey, G.S. (2001), Political Participation of Women in India, New Royal Book Co., Lucknow.

Phadka, M. and Kulkarni, A.V. (1977), Field–Dependence–Independence and Employed–not employed as Factor in the Adjustment of House Wife, Indian Journal of Psychology, 52(1), 85-89.

—(2001), Planning Commission, Govt. of India, Report of Task Force on Panchayati Raj Institutions.

Powell, K.S., (1963), "Family Variables" in I.F. Nye and L.W. Hoffman's (eds) The Employed Mother in America, Chicago, Rand Mc Nally and Company.

Purushothamam, S. (1996), The Empowerment of Women in India, Sage, New Delhi.

Raja, Gopalan, (1963), Social Change: An Analysis of Role Conflict and Deviation," Indian Journal of Social Work, 16(4), 219-223.

Rana, Kranti (1998), Modern Working Women and the Development Debate, Delhi.

Rapoport, R. and Rapoport, R.N., (1969), "The Dual Career Family", Human Relations 22(1), 3-30.

Reddy, C.R. (1986), Changing Status of Educated Working Women, Asia Pub., Delhi.

Report of Second Administrative Reforms Commission, Unlocking Human Capital, 2006

Sams, S. (ed) (1991), Women, Law and Social Change, APH, Delhi.

Seth, Meera (2002), Women and Development, Sage, Delhi.

Shah, Beena (2002), Women, Higher Education and Empowerment (Challenges & Prospects), Delhi.

Sharma, Anita (1990), Modernisation and Status of Working Women in India, Delhi.

Singh, K.P., (1972), Career and Family - Women's two Roles Conflict Questionnaire for Women: Some Preliminary Findings, Journal of Consulting and Clinical Psychology, 42(5), 743-749).

Singh, S. and Srivastava, S.P. (eds) (2002), Gender Equality through Women's Empowerment, Bharat Book Co., Lucknow.

Singh, U.B. (2006), Role Conflict Among Elected Women Representatives in Urban Local Government, in U.B. Singh (ed), Leaders in Making, Kalpaz, New Delhi

Singh, U.B. (ed), (2006) Empowerment of Women in Urban Administration, Serials, New Delhi

Singhal, Tara (2003), Working Women and Family, APH, Delhi.

Sinha, Pushpa (1982), Role Conflict Among the Working Women, Janki Prakashan for Anmol, Delhi.

Srivastava, Abhilasha (2001), Role Multiplicity of Lower Middle Class Working Women with Special Reference to the Primary and Higher Secondary Women Teachers of Lucknow City, Ph.D. Thesis, Lucknow University, unpublished.

Styanand, K. (1973), The Status of Working Women in India, 'Eves Weekly', 5, 15.

Suchdev, J. (1974), Working Mothers: An Interview, Social Welfare, 21(2) 10-27.

Sullerst, E. (1971), Women, Society and Change, London: World University Library.

Tapan, Neeta, (2002), Need for Women Empowerment, Rawat, Jaipur

Tripathi, H. (1967), Changing Attitude of Woman in Post Independent India, Journal of Gujarat Research Society, XIXX(2/114)92-97.

Vasantha Kumar, K. (1964), Her Emotional Problems, Social Welfare, Q95) 12-13.

Wardwell, (1952), The Reduction of Strain in a Marginal Social Role, American Journal of Sociology 61, 16-24.

Weller, R.M. (1968), The Employment of Wives Dominance and Fertility, Journal of Marriage & Family, 30, 437-442.

Website

—Sarkaritel.com

—Lok Sabha

—India.com

INDEX